THE KEW BOOK OF
Drawing Flora & Fauna

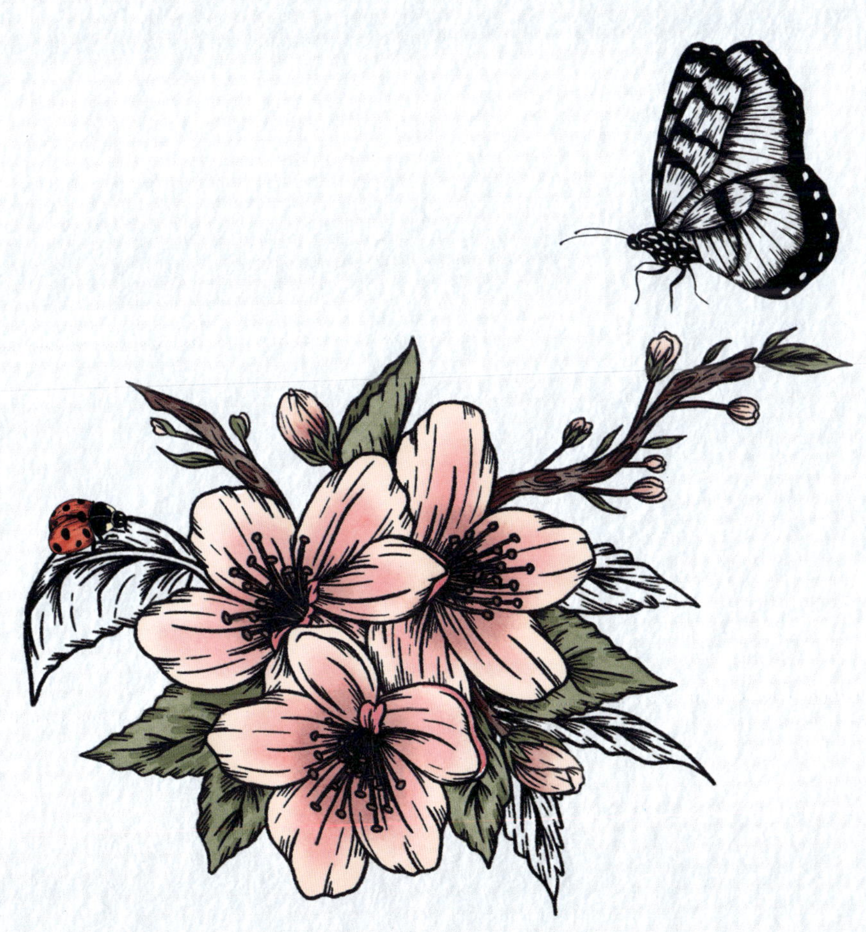

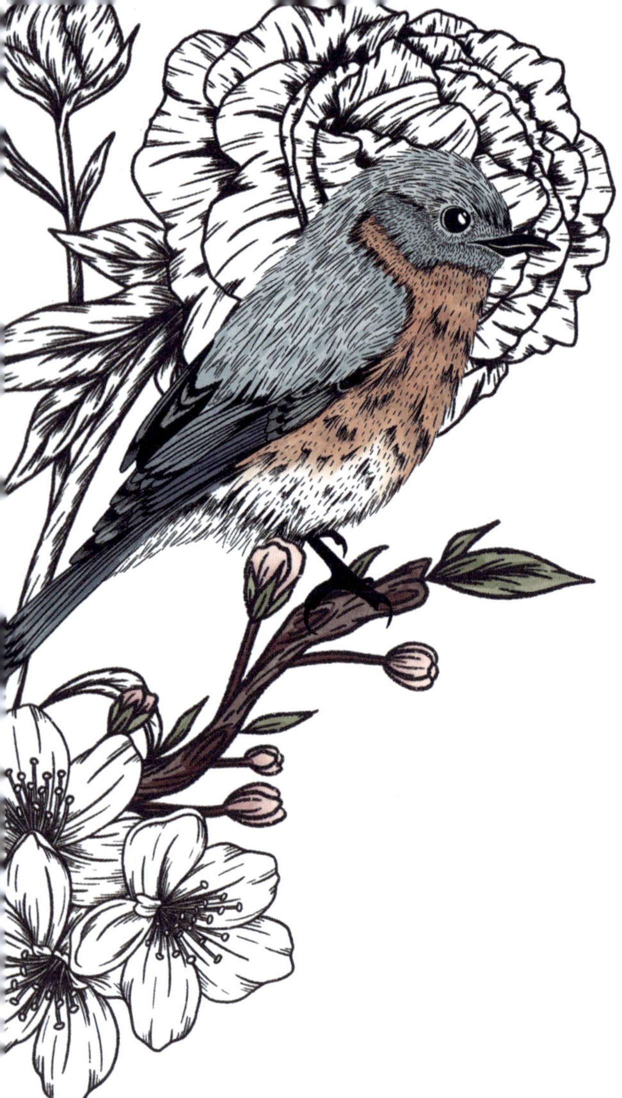

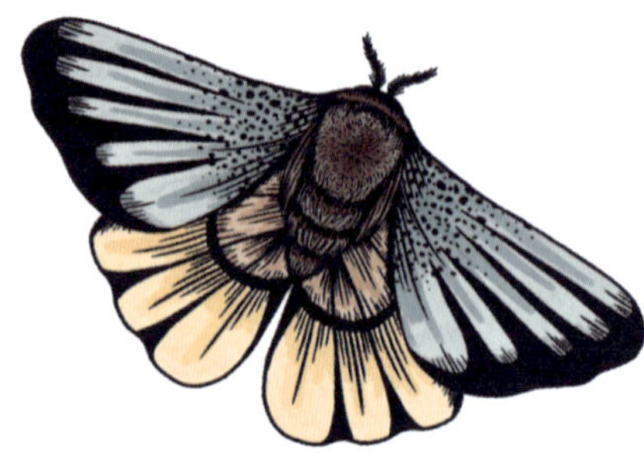

First published in 2025

Search Press Limited
Wellwood, North Farm Road,
Tunbridge Wells, Kent TN2 3DR

2 3 4 5 6 7 8 9 10

Photographs by Joy-Louise Robinson
Text and photographs copyright © Joy-Louise Robinson, 2025
Design copyright © Search Press Ltd, 2025

ISBN: 978-1-80092-234-1
ebook ISBN: 978-1-80093-214-2

Bookmarked Hub
For further ideas and inspiration, and to join our free online community, visit www.bookmarkedhub.com

Publishers' notes
The Publishers, the Royal Botanic Gardens, Kew, and author can accept no responsibility for any consequences arising from the information, advice or instructions given in this publication.

For errata, please visit our website (www.searchpress.com) or the Bookmarked Hub (www.bookmarkedhub.com).

See more from the author at www.felicityandink.com and @felicityandink on Instagram and YouTube.

GPSR information can be found at www.searchpress.com
Printed in China, RRD012026

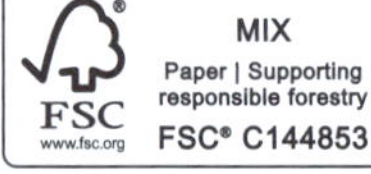

Joy-Louise Robinson

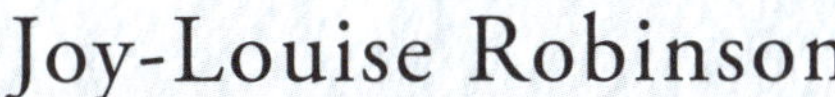

THE KEW BOOK OF

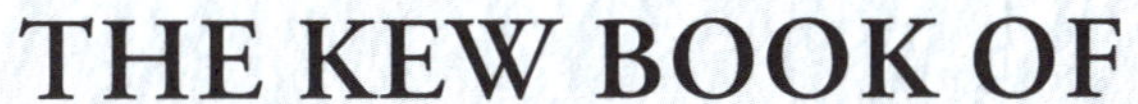

Drawing Flora & Fauna

20 stunning step-by-step tutorials

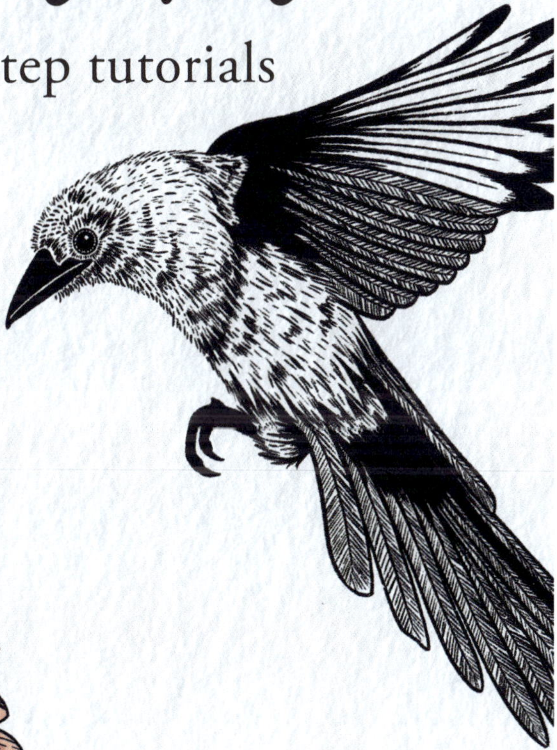

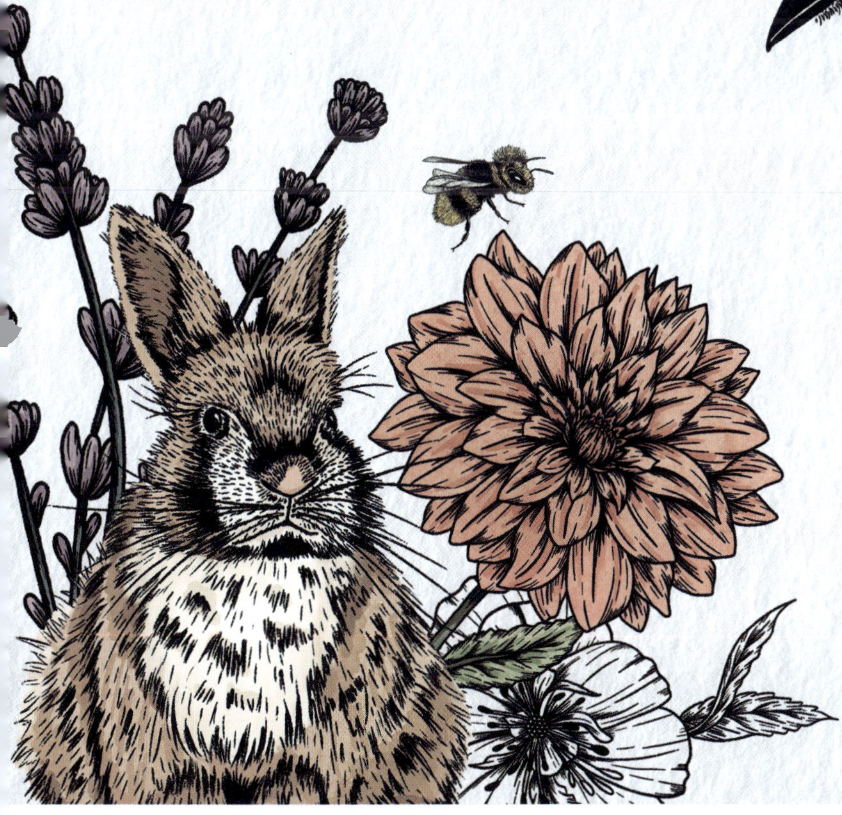

SEARCH PRESS

Contents

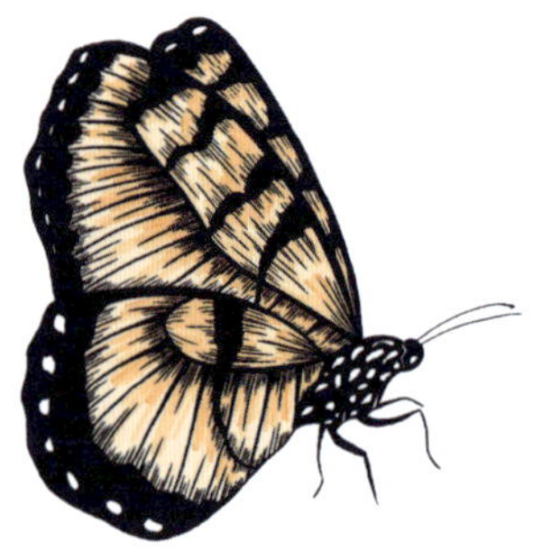

Introduction

Hi, I'm Joy! I'm an artist, designer and illustrator based in Newcastle upon Tyne in the UK and, as clichéd as it sounds, I've been drawing or trying to draw for as long as I can remember. I am mostly self-taught, and remember plenty of times when I was advised to pursue a different path. I absolutely loved drawing, though, and found it was a great way to unwind, so I carried on practising and haven't stopped since.

For more than seven years I've been sharing my art online under the alias *Felicity & Ink*, which led me to create how-to-draw tutorials after receiving so many questions about my techniques. I truly believe that anyone who wants to learn how to draw can, and I love sharing my techniques with everyone who is trying to learn or develop their drawing skills. It doesn't have to be a technical skill to learn and it should be fun and relaxing. I firmly believe that as long as you're willing to dedicate time to practise, you can learn how to draw too.

Flora and fauna is the subject I draw the most. It's an endless source of inspiration for me, so I'm excited to be sharing in this book 20 easy-to-follow, step-by-step projects that include some of my favourite subjects, along with a whole range of my techniques, tips and tricks to help you practise drawing from your own references.

Throughout the projects you'll learn to draw a range of flowers, insects, birds and animals, suitable for anyone to follow. The way each project is broken down is the exact method I would use to draw these subjects myself. The drawings progressively get more advanced as you go through the book, so if you're just starting out I'd recommend working your way through in order. Feel free to experiment with drawing each of the projects in your own style and adapt them in any way you'd like. Remember, have fun – and there truly is no right or wrong way to draw.

I always love to see what you've drawn following my tutorials, so feel free to tag me on Instagram @felicityandink and I can't wait to see what you create!

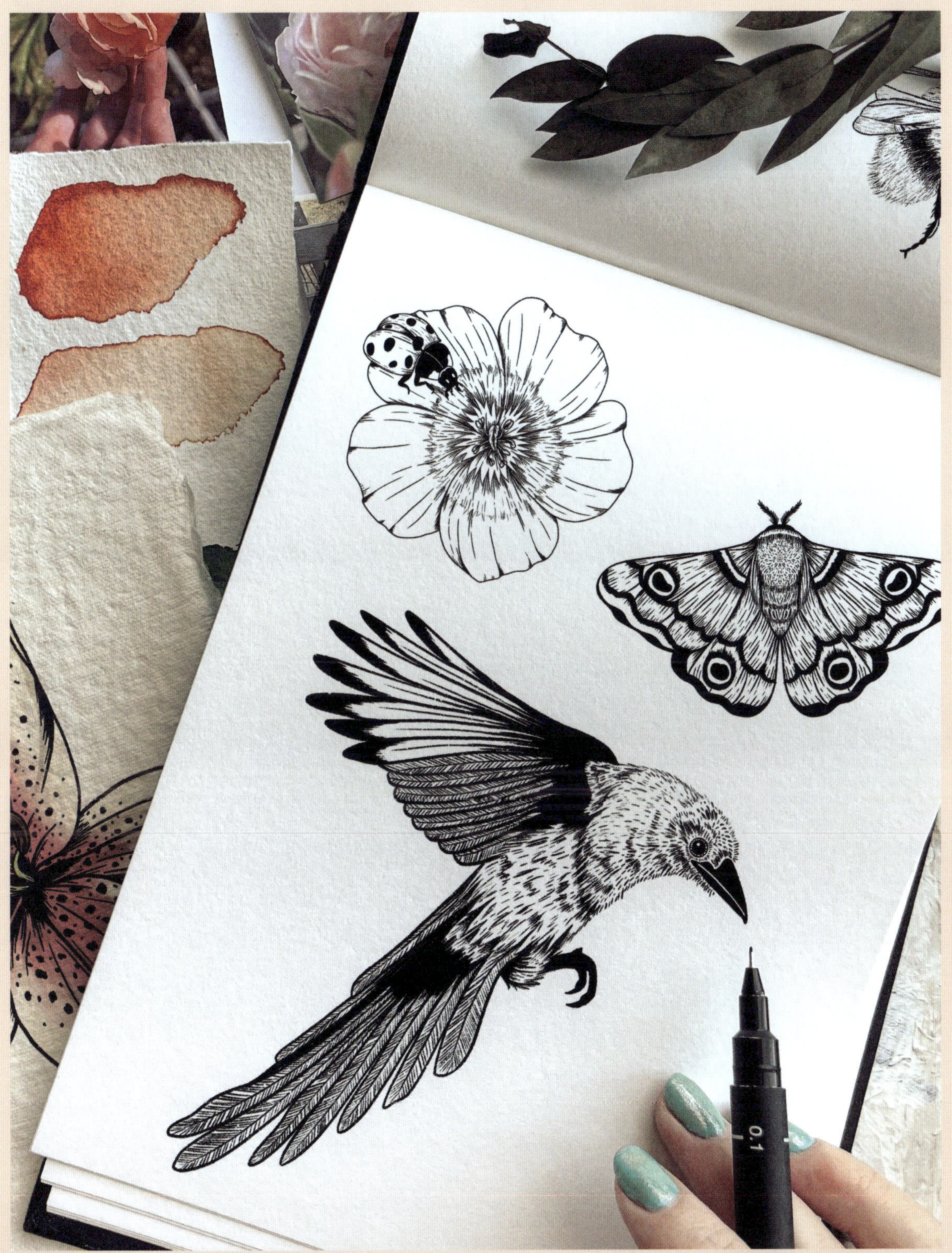

Drawing equipment

One of the great things about drawing is that minimal equipment is needed.
I'd recommend drawing with any pen and paper that you already have – the
main thing to focus on is practice. When I started drawing I'd doodle with
any biro or fineliner pen I could find!

If you'd like to buy some new equipment, a sketchbook with slightly thicker
paper and a 0.1 size fineliner pen is a great place to start. I've compiled a list
of my tried and trusted equipment below.

Sketchbooks and paper

My most-used sketchbooks are Moleskine watercolour
sketchbooks. The paper is thick enough for fineliner
ink and water-based paints to not bleed through, and
they also have a slight hammered texture, which I love!
If I plan on drawing or colouring with pencil I'll opt
for a sketchbook with a smoother paper surface,
such as Talens Art Creation sketchbooks. If I'm not
drawing in my sketchbook I'll usually grab any paper
I have around. I also love to use handmade papers,
I usually search through Etsy for sheets to try.

Pens and pencils

My favourite drawing tool by far is a black fineliner
pen. I have two brands that I use most often: Uni-Pin
and Pigma Micron. I use three different sizes, and
alongside these I sometimes use pencil for outlines
before drawing in ink, which is great for practice.
I use any standard pencil, usually an HB.

0.1 fineliner pen My main fineliner for outlines and
initial shading lines.

0.2 fineliner pen Great for outlines that need to be
a bit thicker, and for blocking in darker areas.

0.05 fineliner pen Always the last pen I use when
drawing, and my forever favourite. The super-fine nib
is perfect for shading tiny details and fine lines. It really
helps to blend shading strokes together.

If you're going to add watercolours on top of your ink
drawings, be sure to use waterproof fineliner pens.

Paints

I sometimes like to add a light wash of watercolour
paint over the top of my drawings. If you'd like to
add some colour to your artwork after drawing, you'll
find some colour-palette suggestions at the start of
each project. The swatches and names of the colours
refer to Winsor & Newton Cotman watercolour paints.
Some of the colour swatches suggest a mix of paints
to achieve the shown colour; always mix these on a
palette before adding to your drawing. My most-used
palette is a handmade ceramic palette by a small
business I found on Etsy called Heath and Sea.

Colouring pencils

As an alternative to paint, I also like to use Prismacolor
pencils to add colour. They're lovely and soft, making
them quite nice to try some blending.

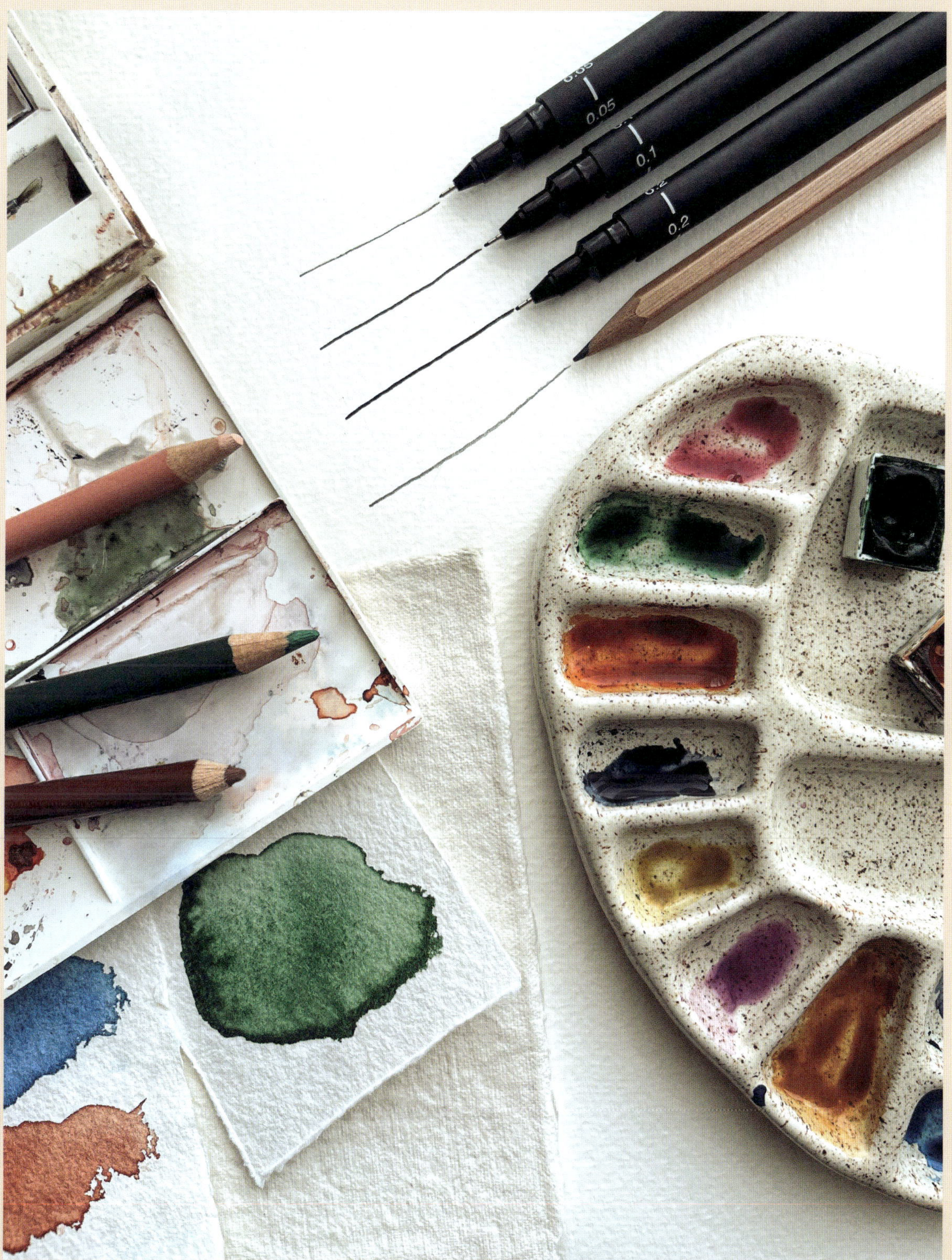

Drawing warm-up

Practising quick drawing motions is a great place to start to get used to your chosen drawing equipment and the pen strokes needed throughout the projects. Simply work your way through the six exercises below, which also have the benefit of loosening up your hand before drawing.

1. Place your pen firmly on the paper and draw as straight a line as you can.

2. Using a quick motion swipe your pen in a line, keeping it as straight as possible. Apply more pressure at first and lighten it as you move, to create a tapered end.

3. Using the same, quick tapered technique, try some shorter angled, vertical lines starting from both the left and right.

4. Now we're warmed up with straight lines, let's get used to curving them. Draw one wavy line that doesn't break. Curve and wave this line in any way you fancy.

5. Revisiting the technique from step 3, this time try the short tapered lines with a slight curve in them. Again, angle from both the left and the right.

6. Lastly, let your hand and pen run free. This is a great way to get used to the pen and its ink flow.

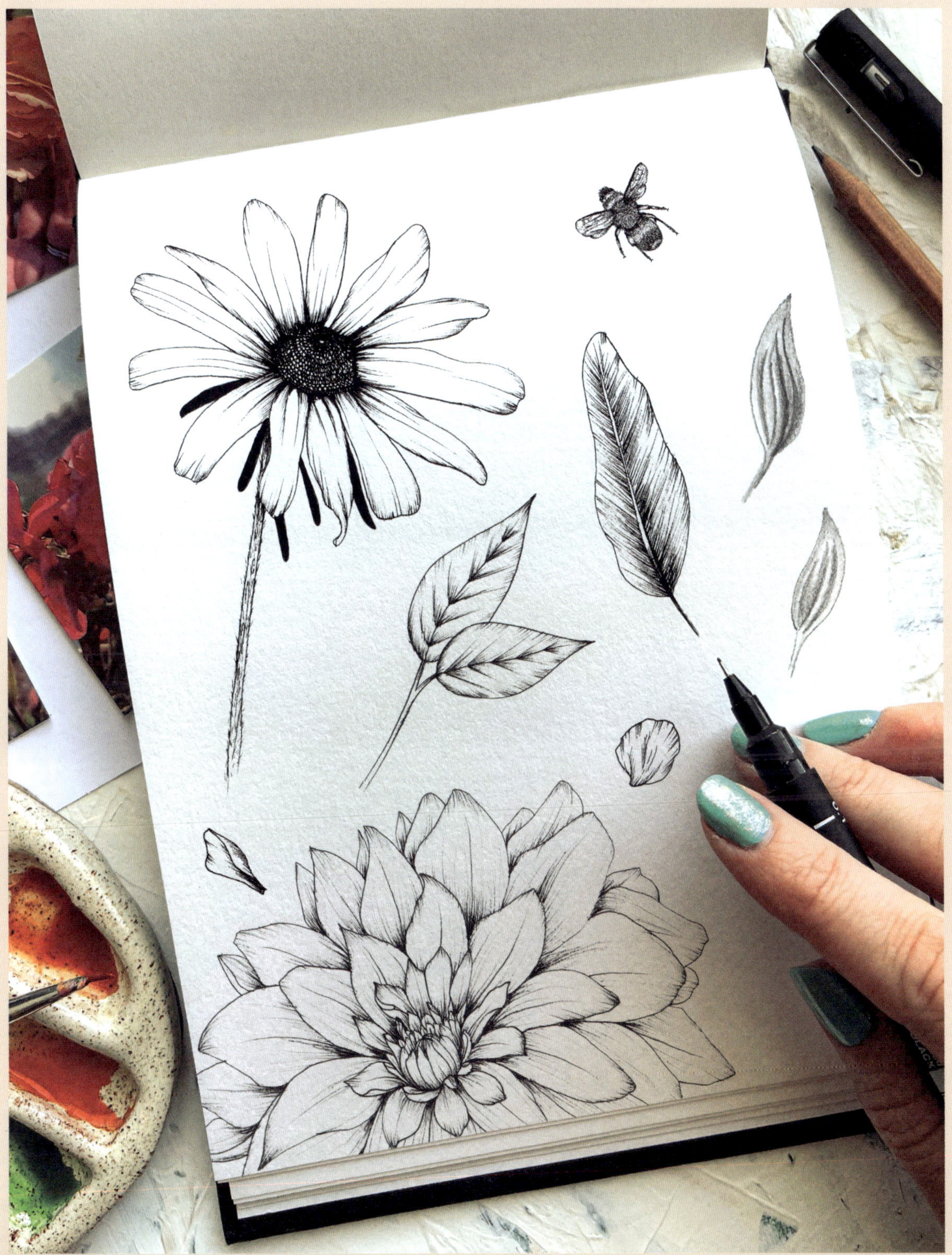

Projects

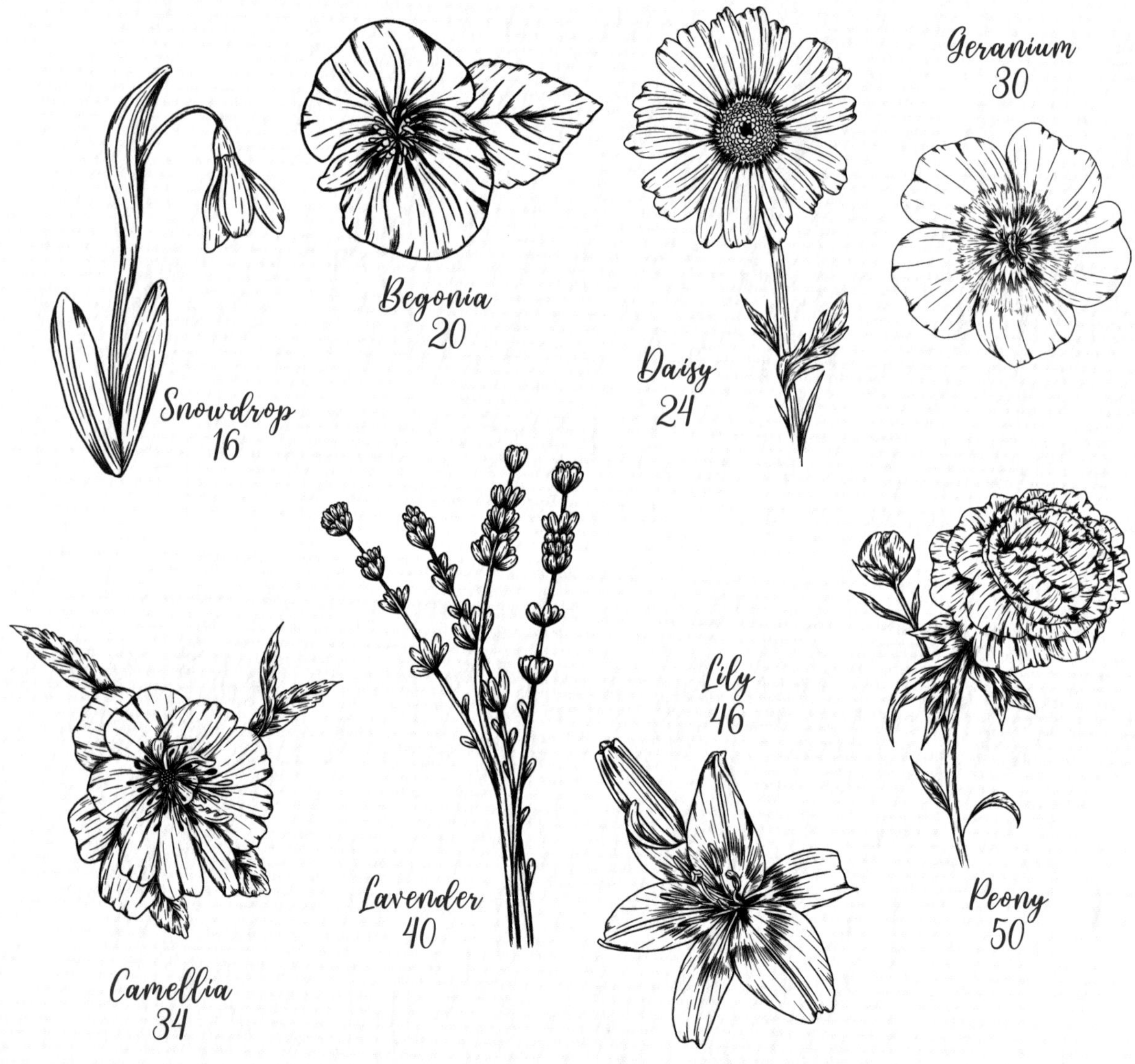

Snowdrop
16
Begonia
20
Daisy
24
Geranium
30
Camellia
34
Lavender
40
Lily
46
Peony
50

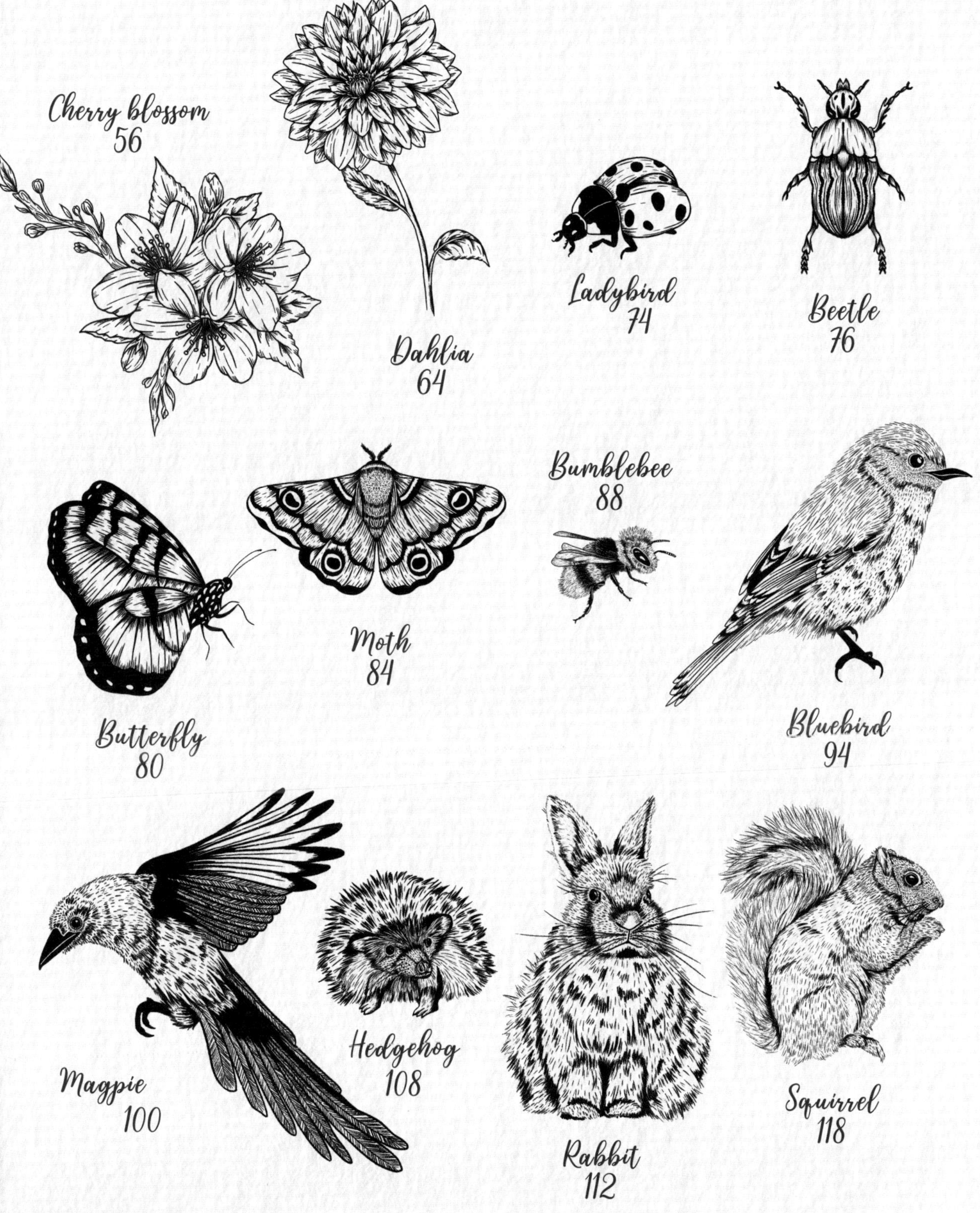

Cherry blossom
56
Dahlia
64
Ladybird
74
Beetle
76
Butterfly
80
Moth
84
Bumblebee
88
Bluebird
94
Magpie
100
Hedgehog
108
Rabbit
112
Squirrel
118

Flowers

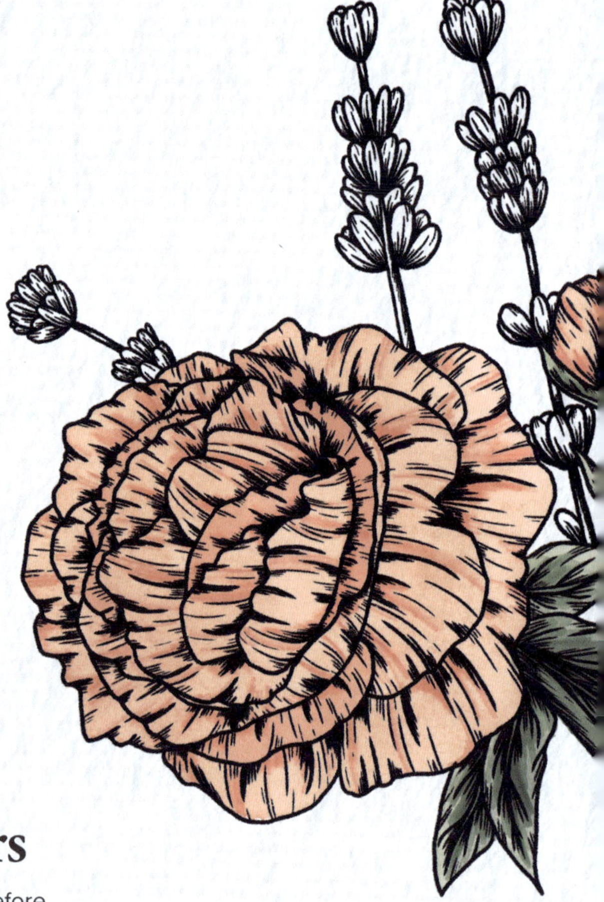

Flowers are always my go-to when I'm looking for something fun and relaxing to draw. The great thing about drawing flowers is, because of their organic nature, you don't have to be too precise. They're all so unique, making them a more forgiving starting point.

You'll learn shading techniques in this section, which will also be beneficial for developing into drawing insects, birds and animals later on in the book.

Top tips for drawing flowers

◆ Focus on getting comfortable drawing the flower heads before moving on to adding stems, leaves or buds.

◆ No two petals are the same, and I'd advise loosening up your hand before drawing them, as looser, wavier lines work well to capture the organic shapes of each petal.

◆ Don't worry about being too precise when drawing the outlines of individual petals, the key is to capture the general shape of the flower.

◆ The same can be said for drawing leaves; have fun with drawing unique outlines for each of them.

◆ When drawing flowers from your own reference images (see page 124), the centre is usually the best place to start, but let your eye guide you to the area that feels most prominent and start there.

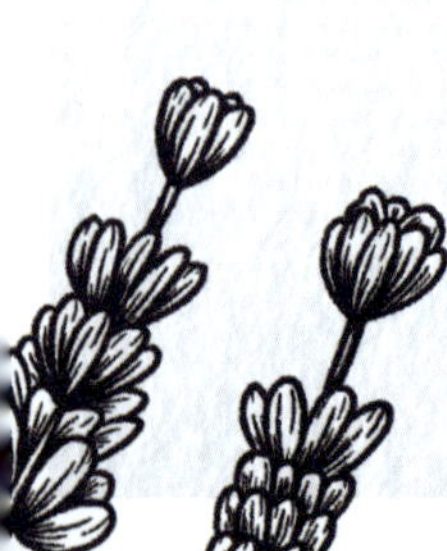

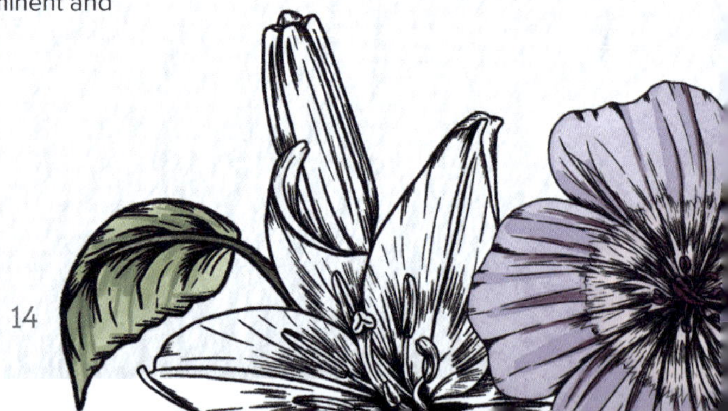

Flower drawing techniques

Petal edge shading

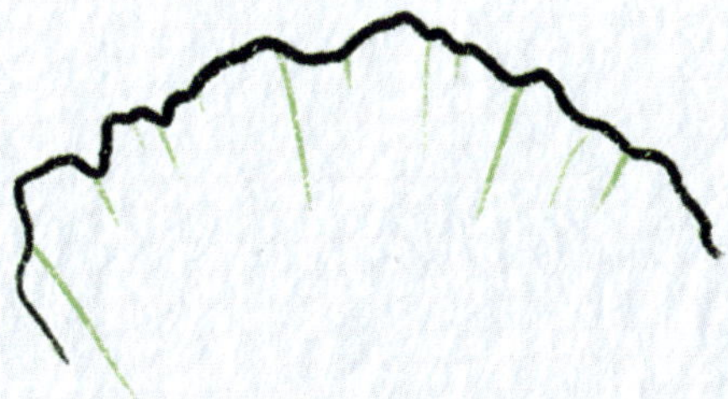 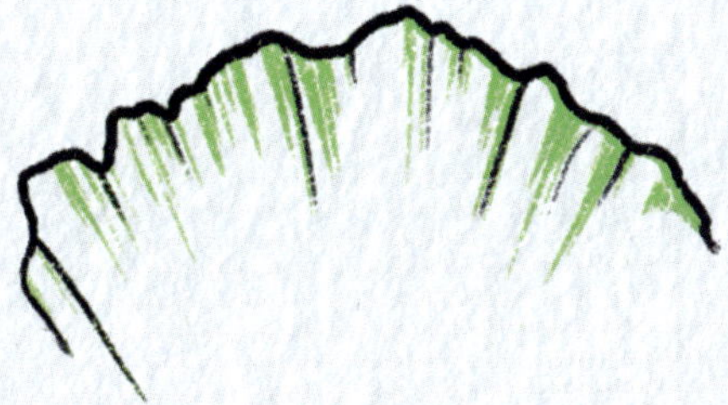

1. Once you've drawn the outline of your petal edge, use quick, tapered pen strokes to start to add some detail to each petal and define the areas to add shading to. Add the initial tapered lines in some areas where the petal outline dips.

2. Use quicker tapered strokes to add some shading. Use a variety of length in your strokes and make sure they follow the curvature of the petal. Make sure to leave enough of a gap in between these shaded areas, so you don't end up with a block of shadow along the whole edge.

Think about where to shade a flower head overall

Once you have drawn the outline of your flower head, add the tapered lines to the dips in the outer petals, as shown in step 1 above.

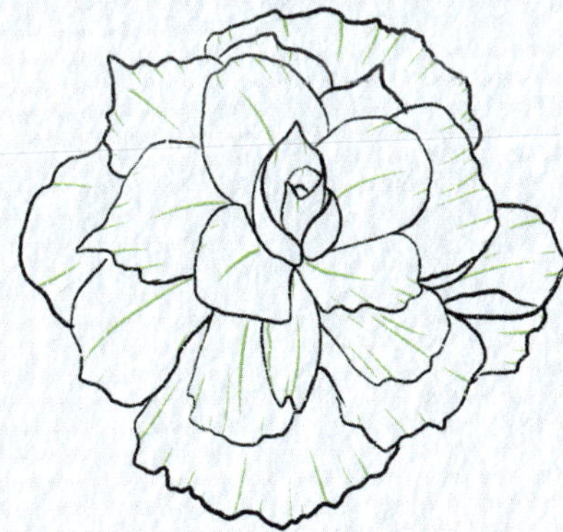 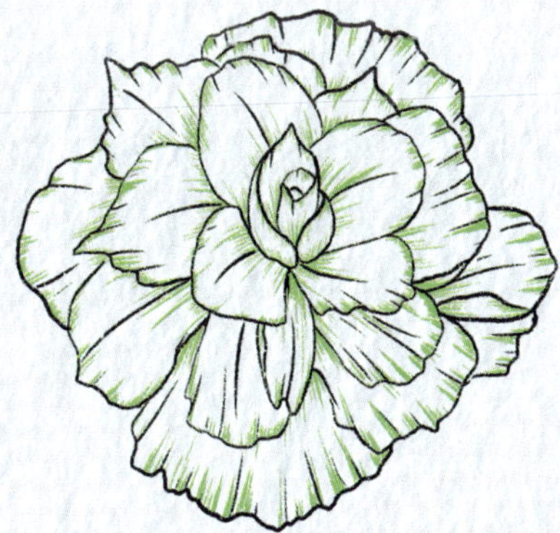

1. Use similar lines that have more of a curve to them to define the centre of the petal from the opposite direction. Draw your lines away from the flower's centre, using a quick motion to create a tapered end to each line.

2. Add lines anywhere you think a shadow would be, generally where the petals overlap or join at the centre. Add shading lines next to these initial lines. Remember to follow the curve of each petal and to leave enough space for the light areas to breathe.

Snowdrop

Let's ease into drawing flowers with a snowdrop, which looks like it might be a bit tricky because of the structure, but it actually takes just eight steps!

We will start with the bottom left leaf and work our way up to drawing the stem with its overlapping leaves and finally add the flower head.

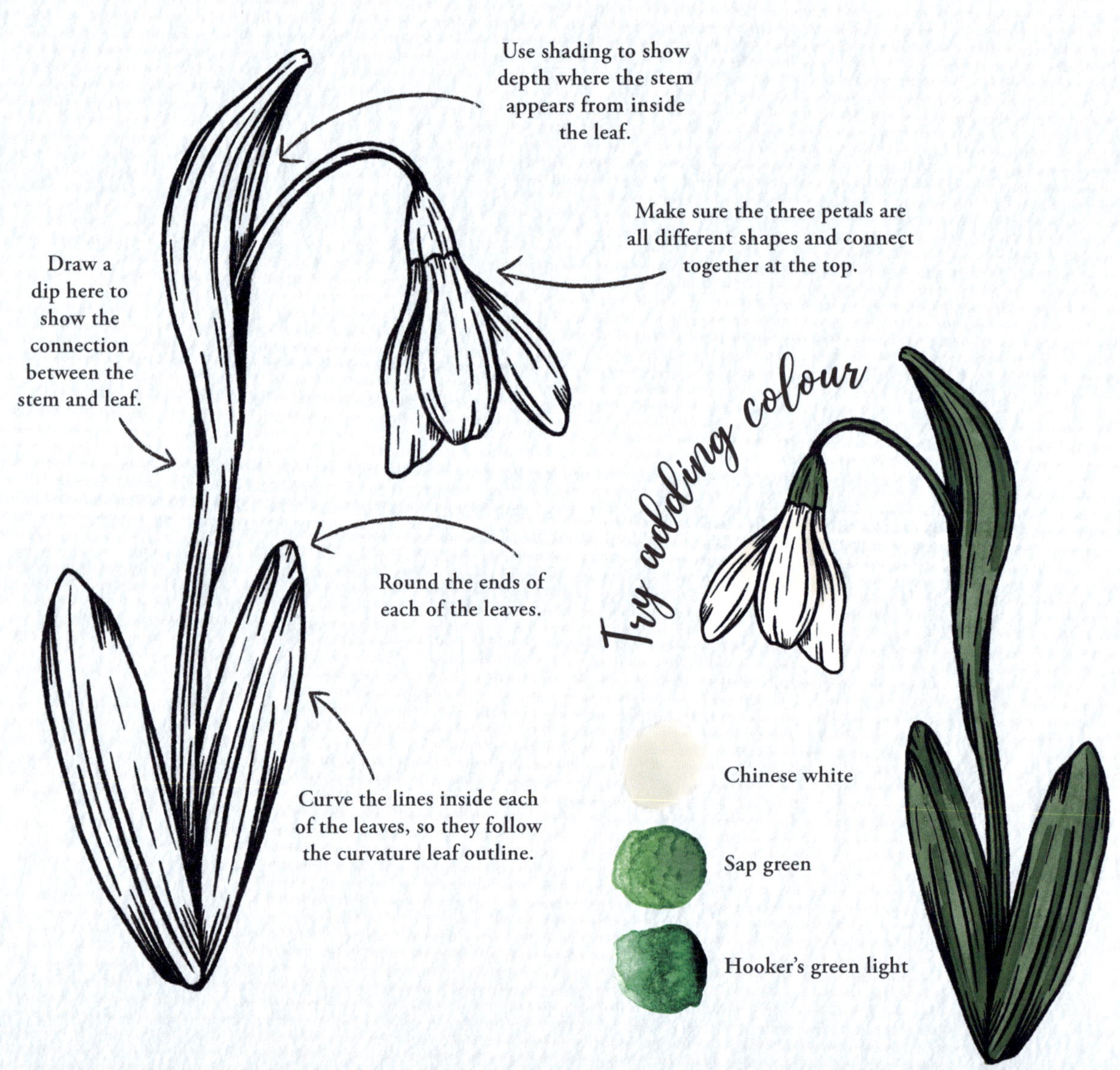

FLOWER OUTLINE

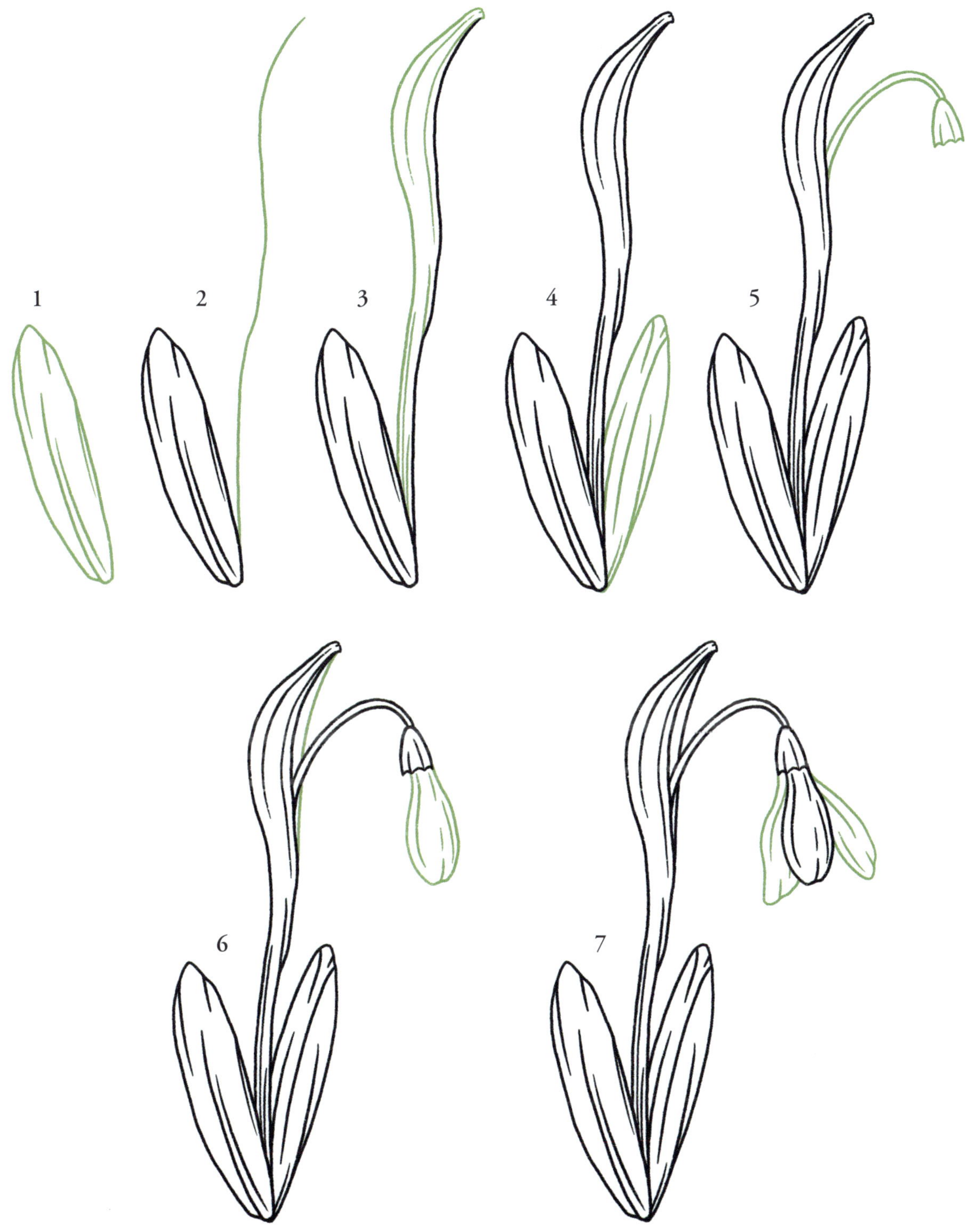

SHADING

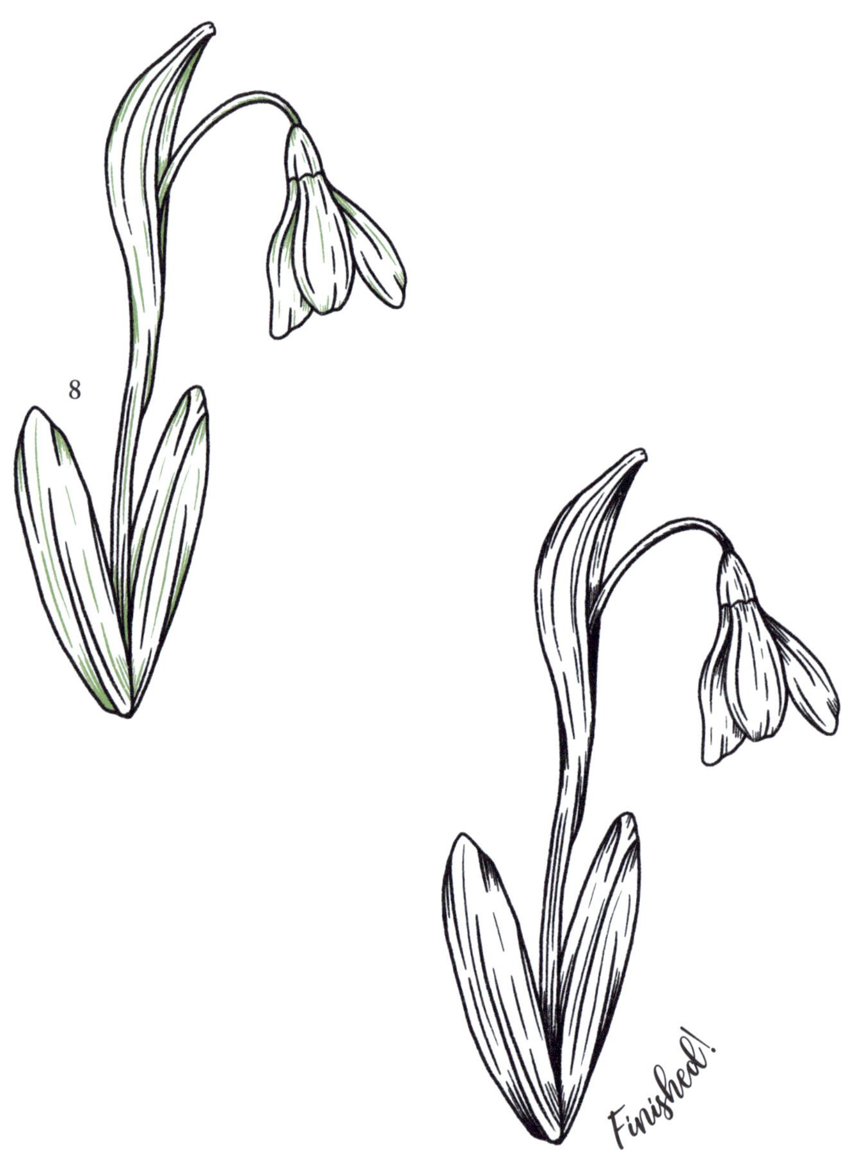

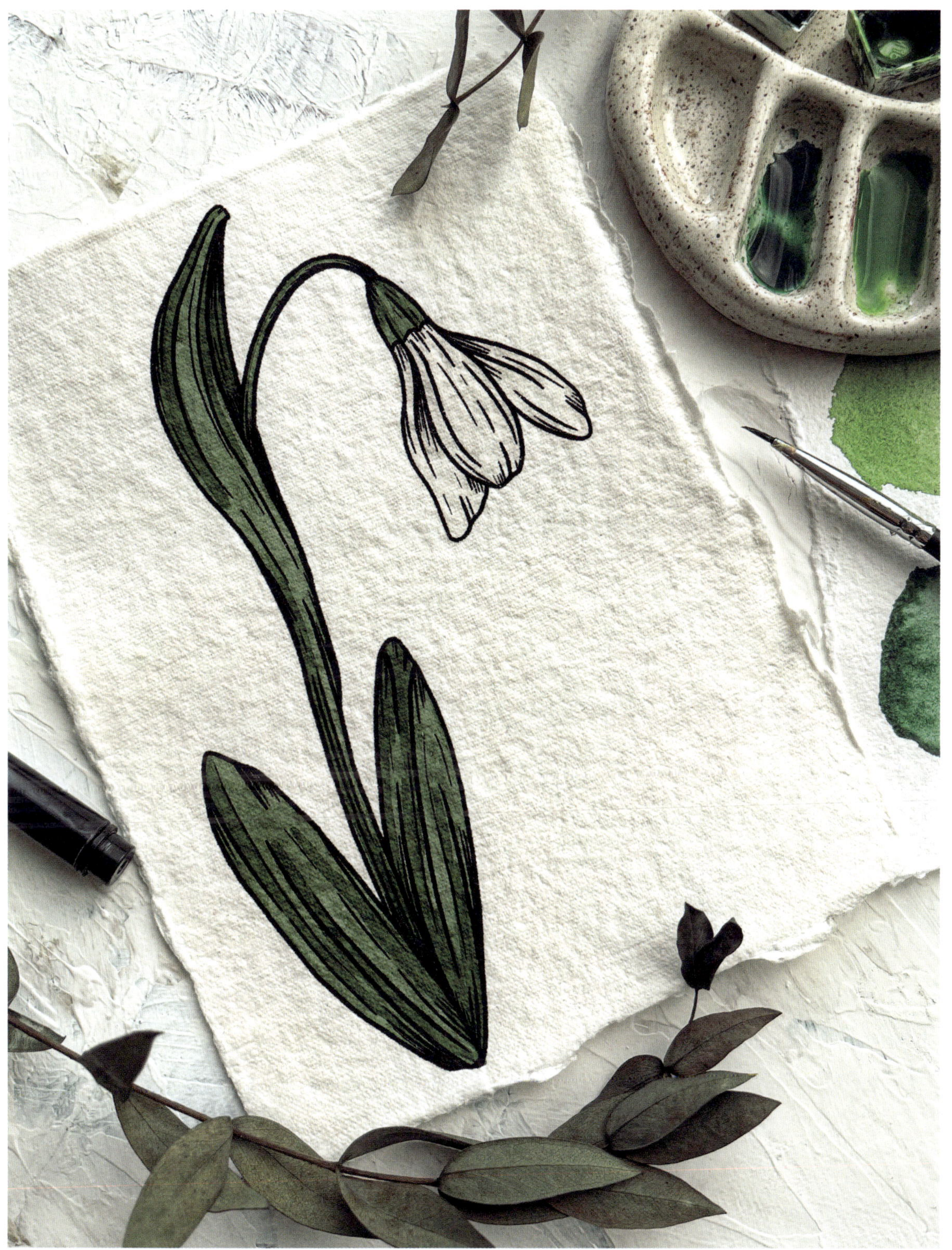

Begonia

Now we've made a start on flowers, let's progress to a simple, wide-open begonia with four visible petals.

For a head-on a flower head like this one, I find it best to start in the middle and work my way out.

We will draw the flower head by itself first, and then you have the option to add a leaf.

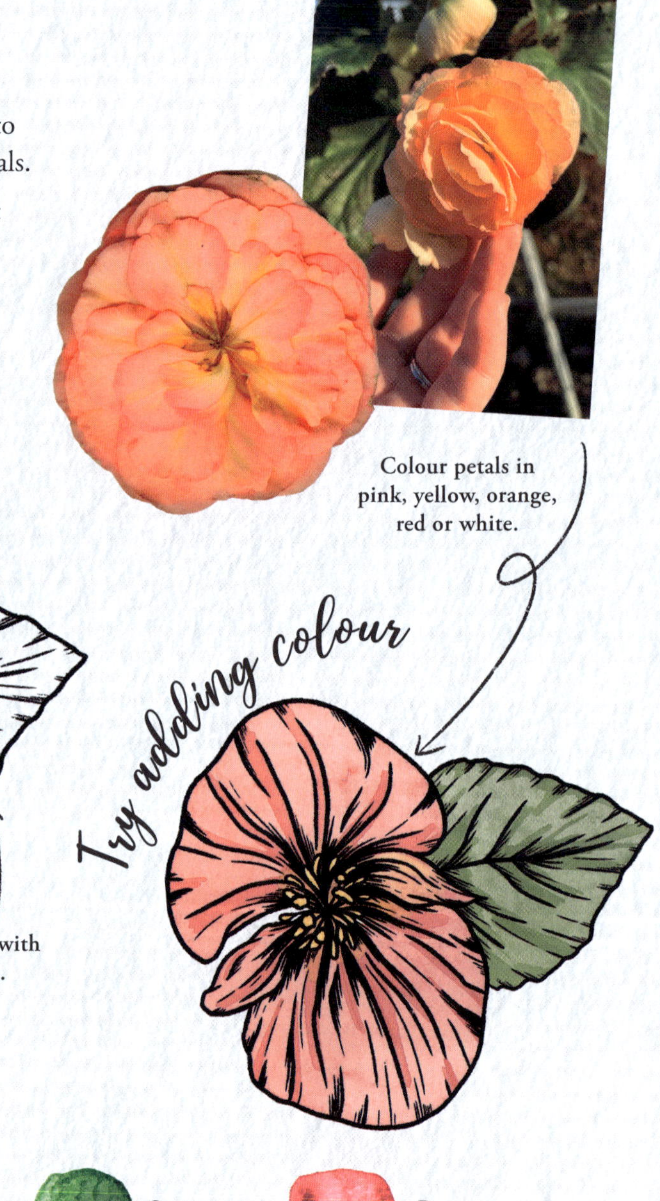

Colour petals in pink, yellow, orange, red or white.

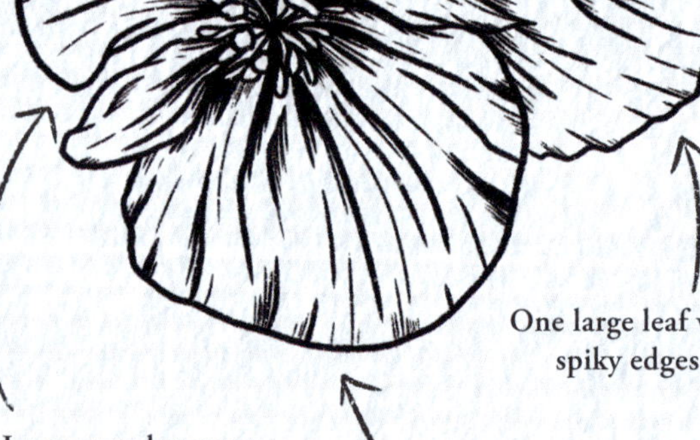

One large leaf with spiky edges.

Leave gaps between all petals.

Draw a slight wave in the petal edges, so they're more organic.

Try adding colour

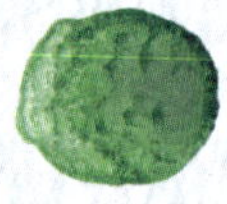
Sap green

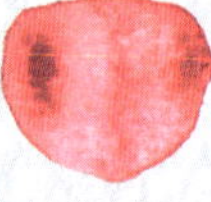
Permanent rose

Cadmium yellow

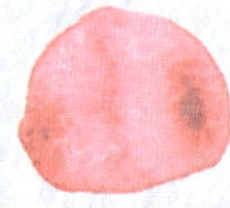
Permanent rose + Chinese white

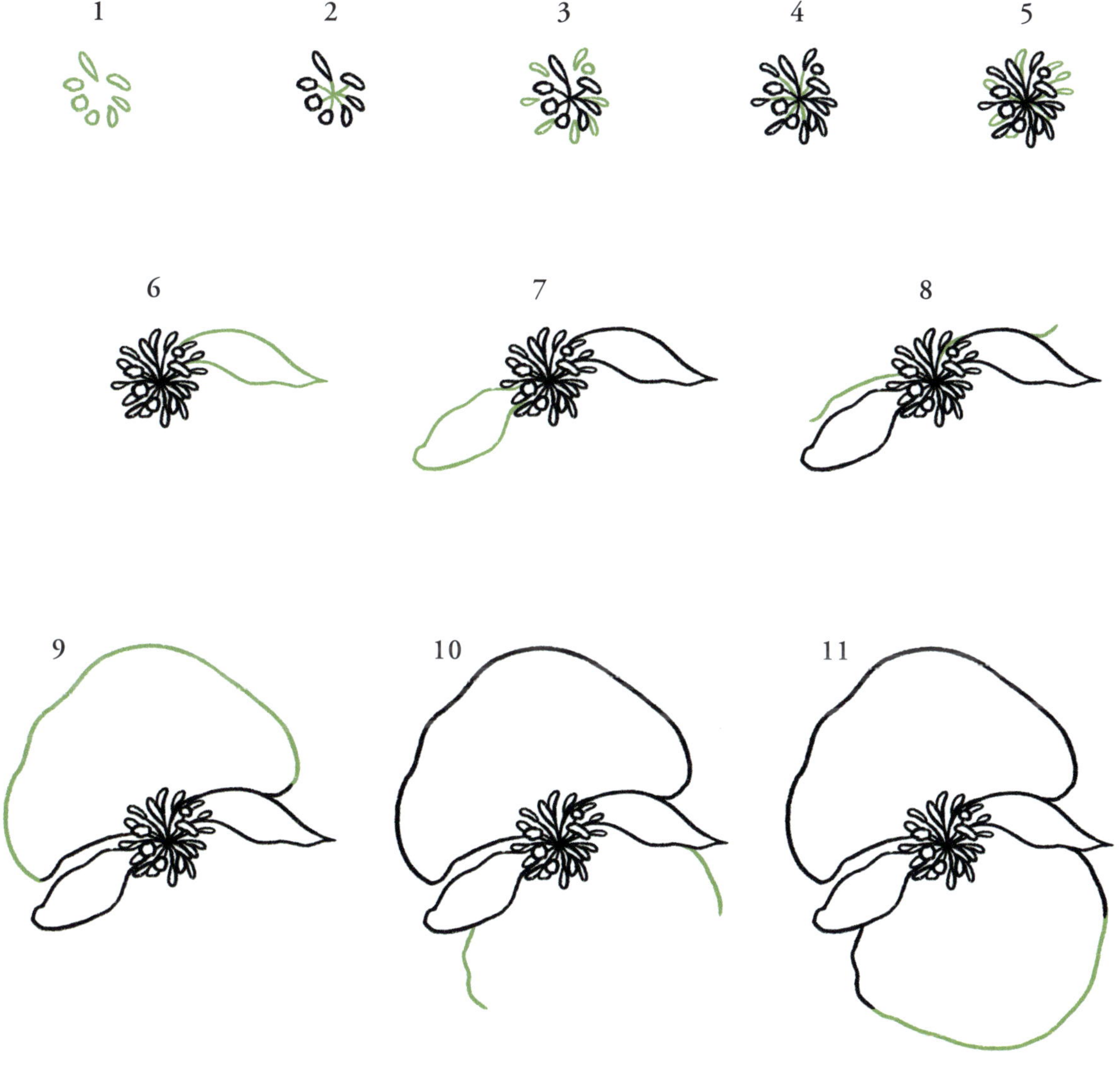

FLOWER DETAILS AND SHADING

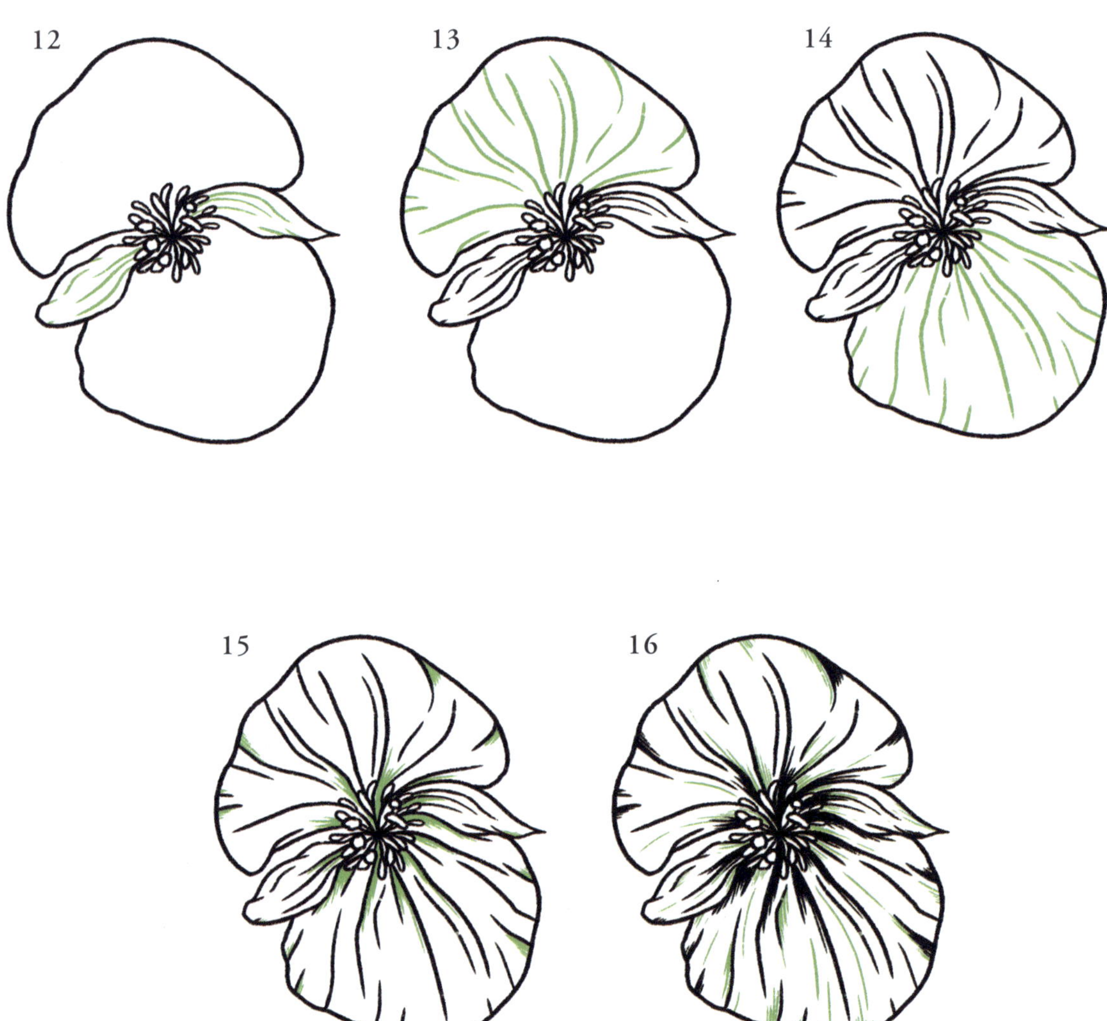

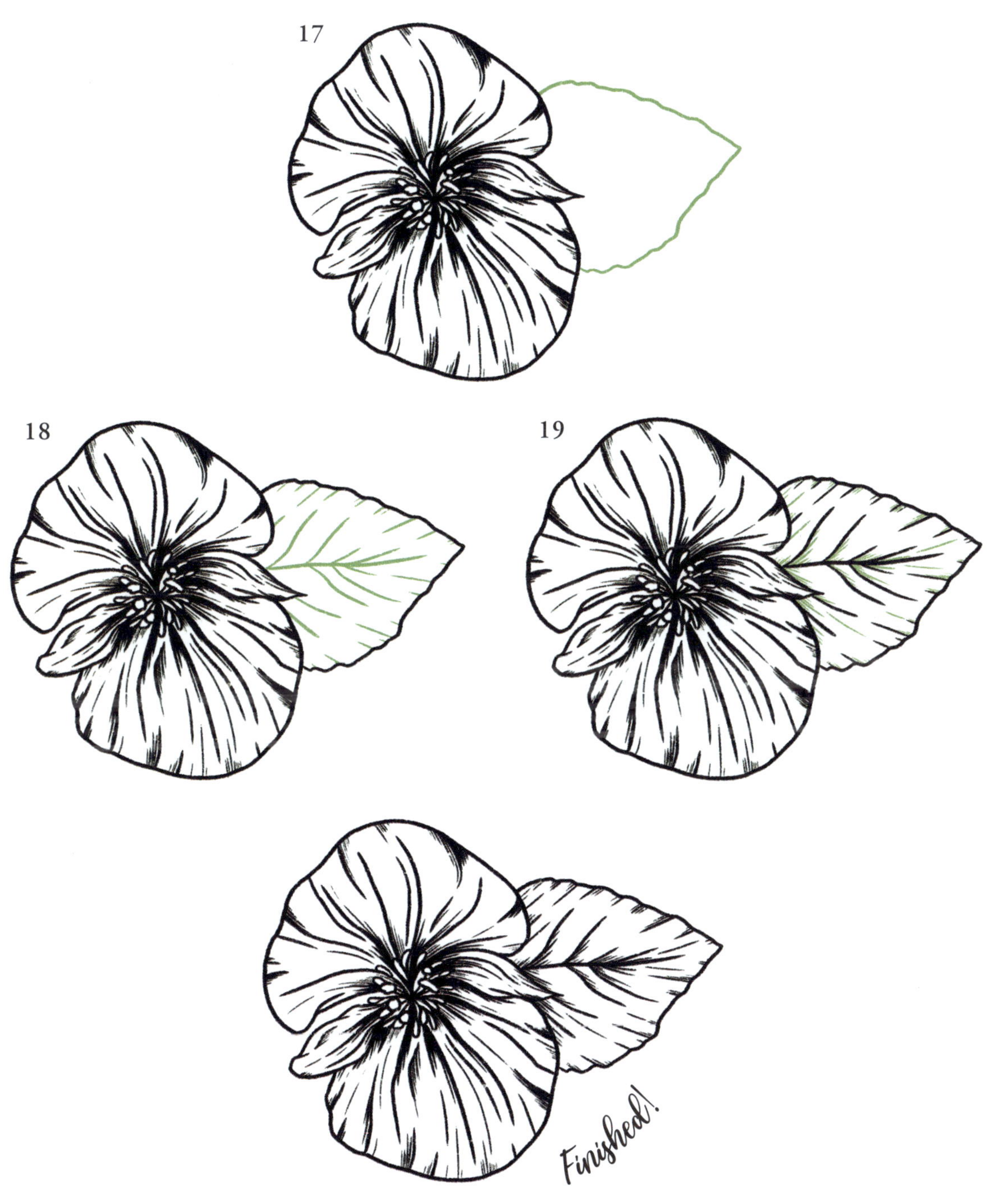

17
18
19
Finished!

Daisy

There are so many types of daisies but for this tutorial we are going to stick to a more common oxeye daisy. This will be our first attempt at a flower with a denser head of petals. Feel free to reduce or add to the amount of petals in your own experiments.

Draw the flower head first, you then have the option to add a simple stem afterwards.

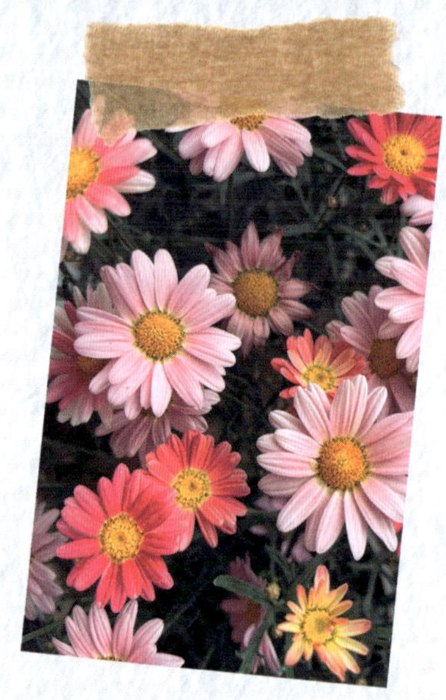

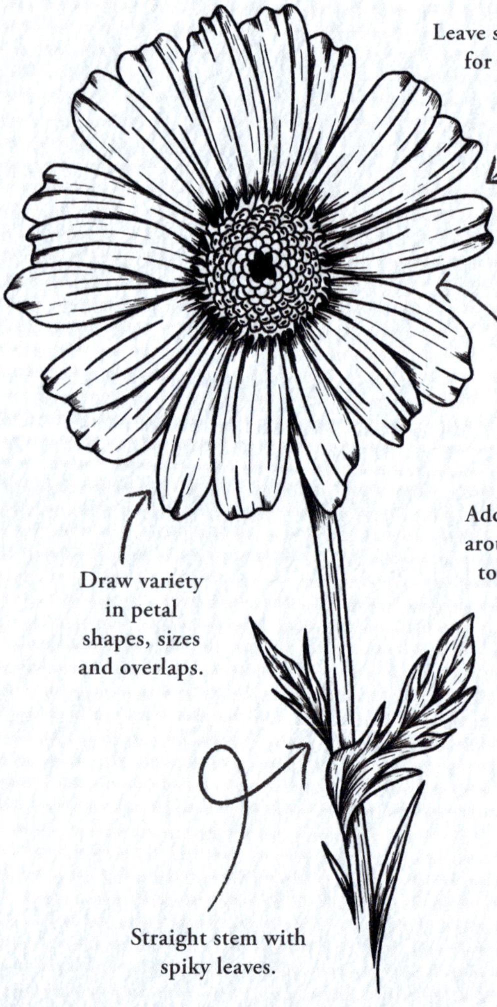

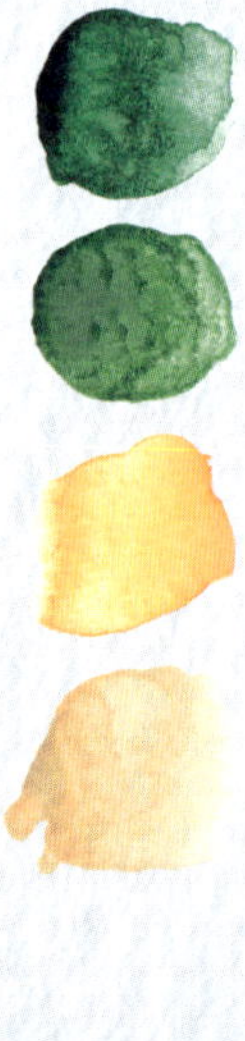

Colour petals in white, yellow, orange, red or pink.

Leave some gaps between petals for a more natural shape.

Try adding colour

Add more shading around centre disc to create depth.

Draw variety in petal shapes, sizes and overlaps.

Straight stem with spiky leaves.

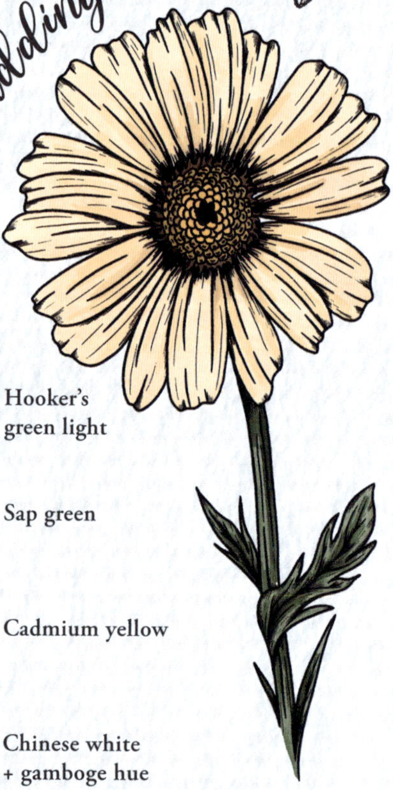

Hooker's green light

Sap green

Cadmium yellow

Chinese white + gamboge hue

FLOWER HEAD OUTLINE

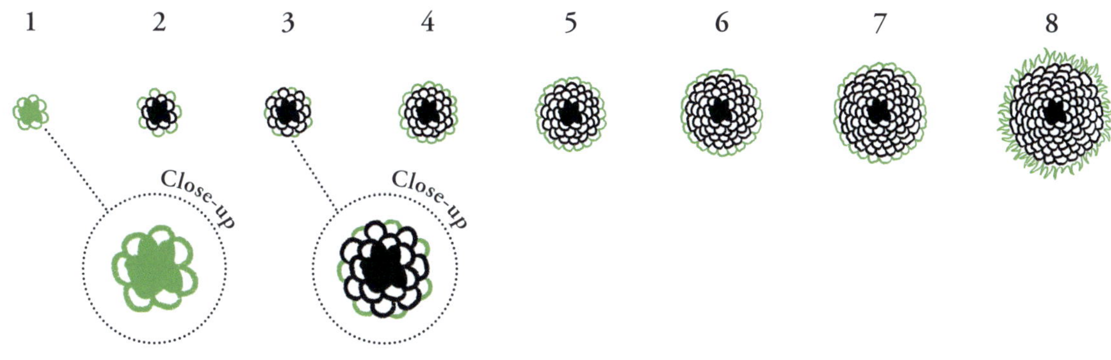

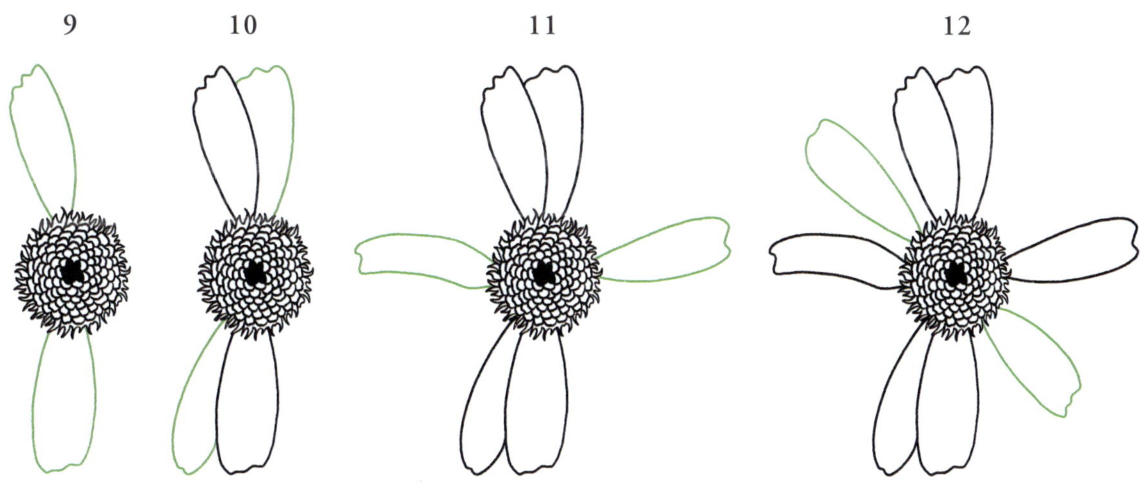

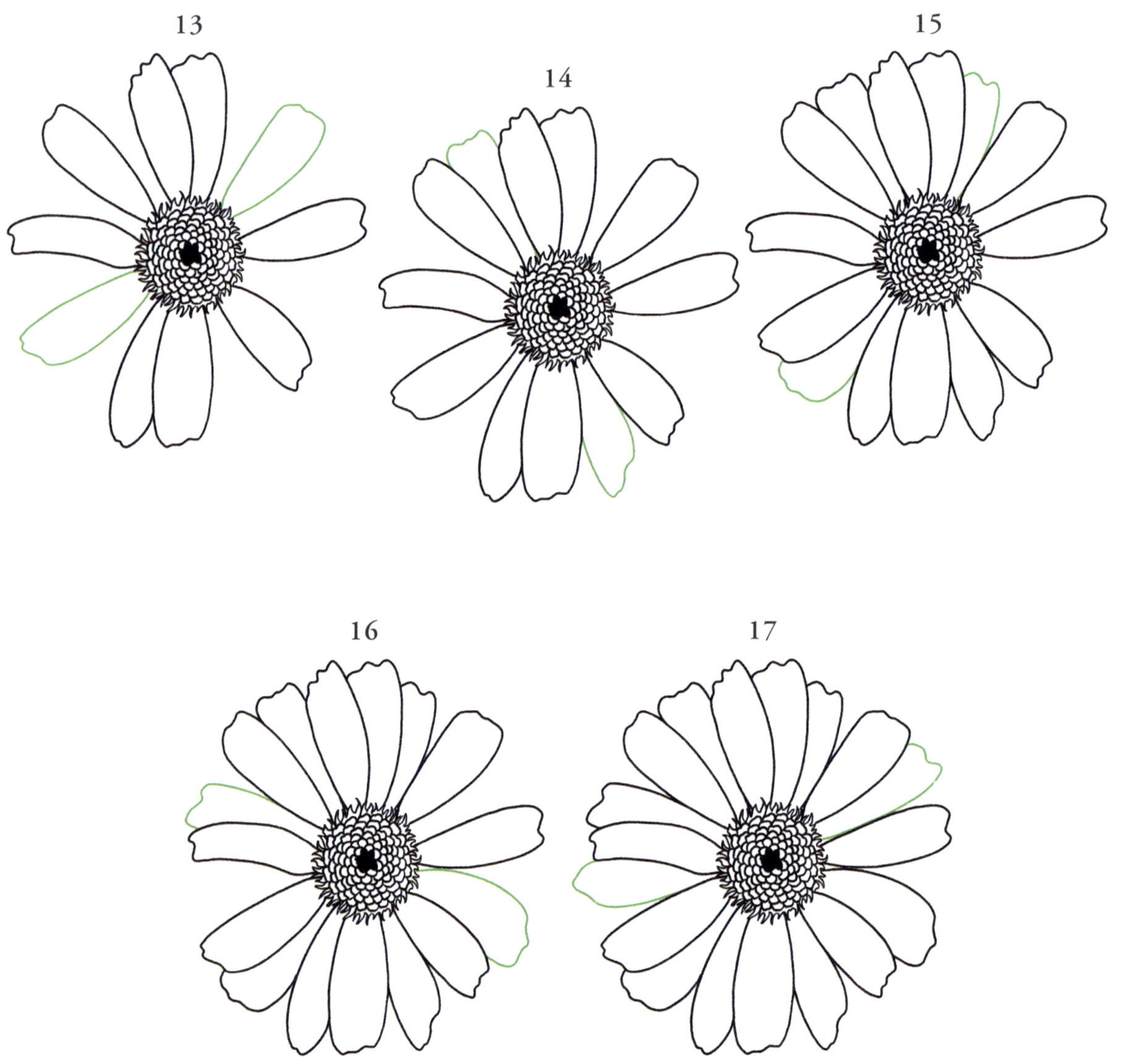

13
14
15
16
17

FLOWER HEAD DETAIL

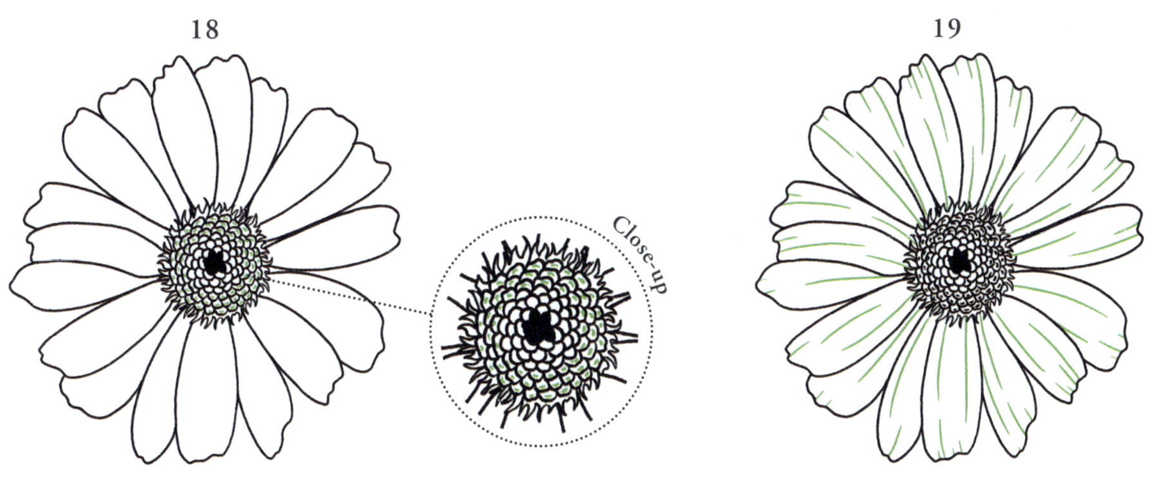

FLOWER HEAD SHADING

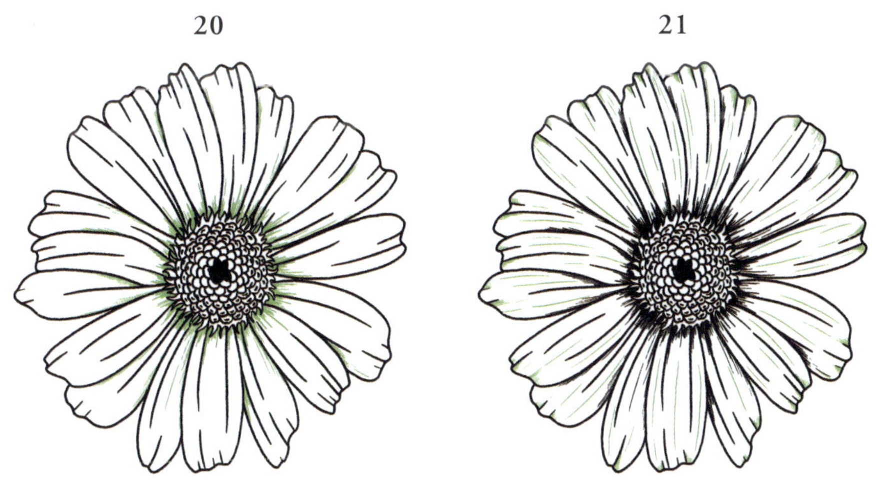

STEM OUTLINE

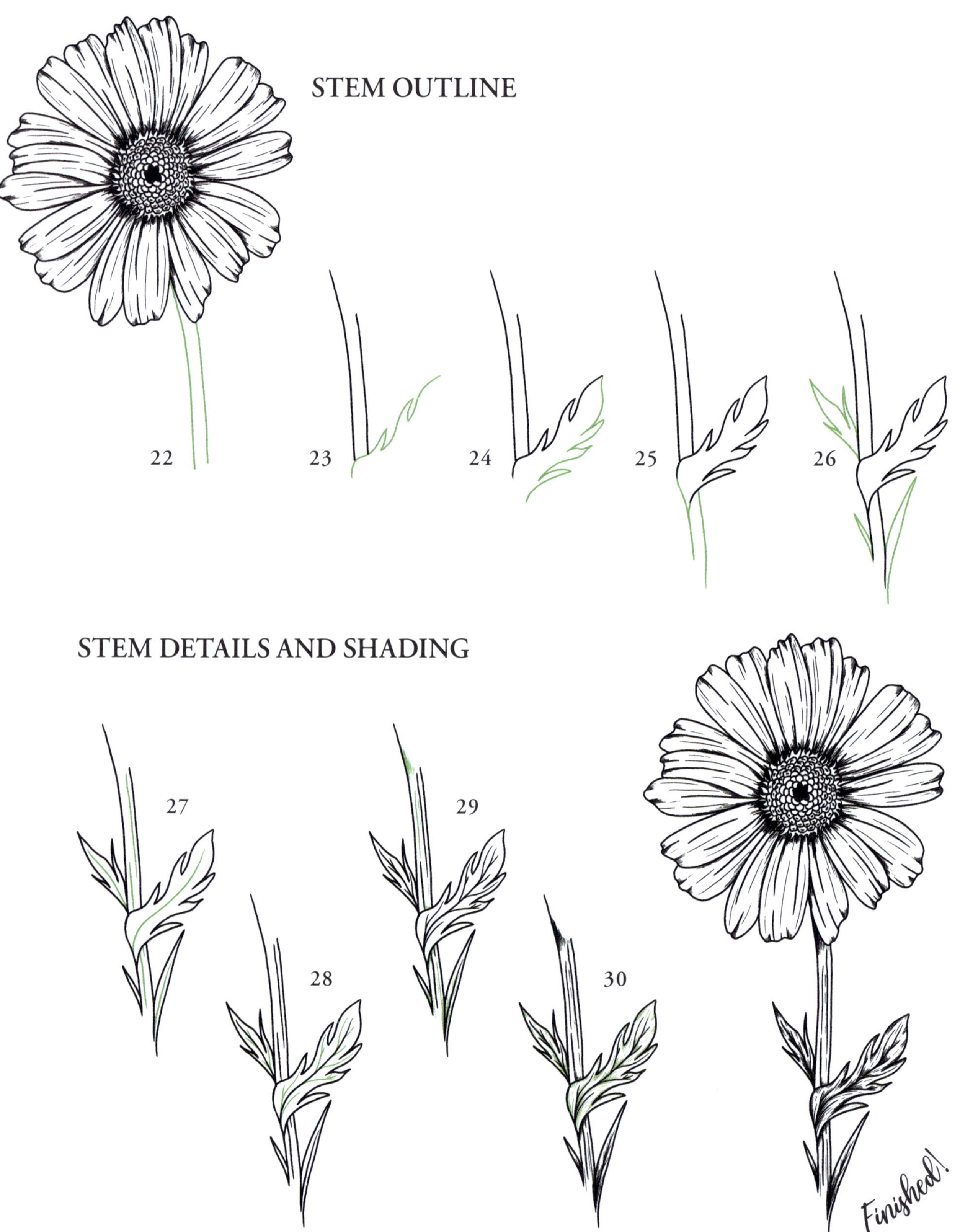

STEM DETAILS AND SHADING

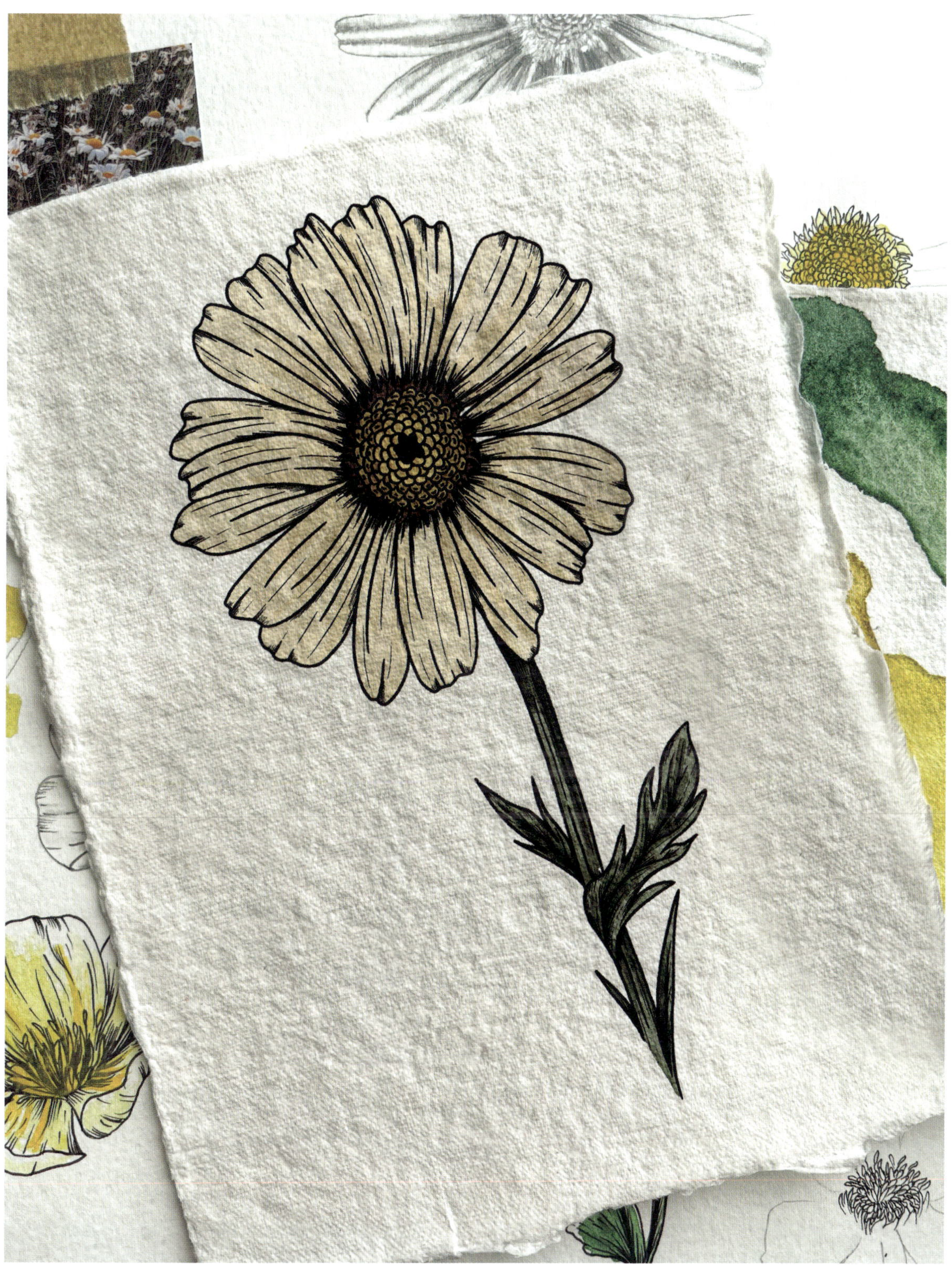

Geranium

The geranium is the first flower where I'll show you how to create two different outcomes from the same outlines, just by changing some decorative details.

Again, because this one is a head-on view, we will start from the centre of the flower and work outwards.

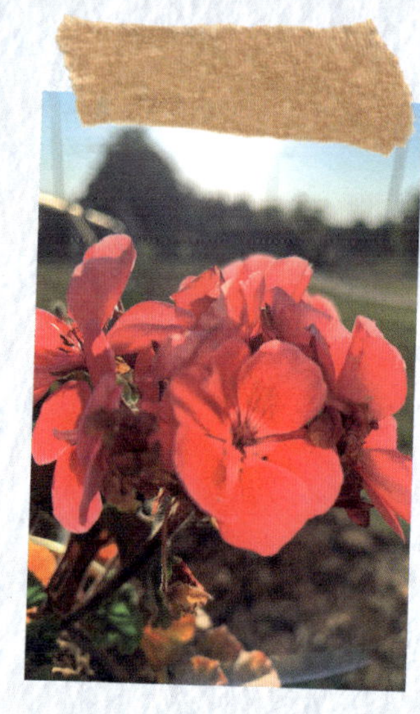

Colour petals in white, red, pink, purple, mauve or orange.

VARIATION 1
Simpler details, suitable for a more solid colour.

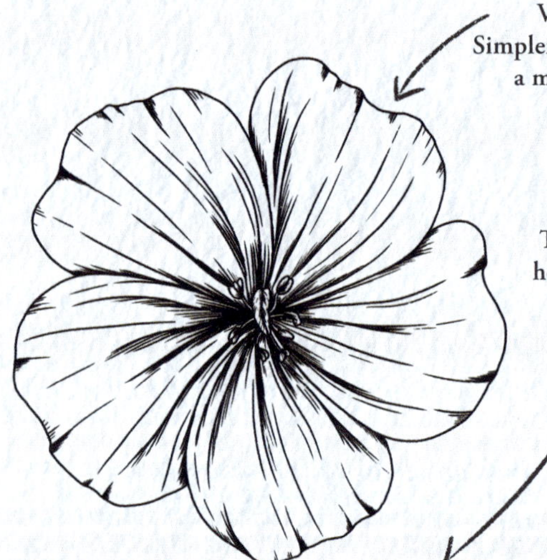

Try drawing a few flower heads together in a cluster in your experiments.

VARIATION 2
Extra details that make for a great base to use an ombré effect when colouring.

Leave enough white space in the centre so the detail stands out.

Try adding colour

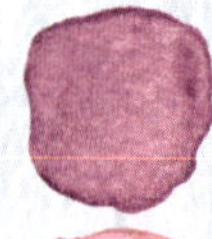

Mauve

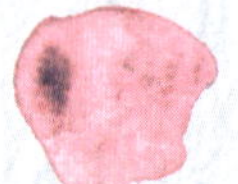

Purple lake + Chinese white

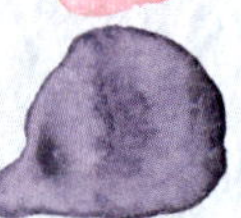

Dioxazine violet + Chinese white

FLOWER HEAD OUTLINE

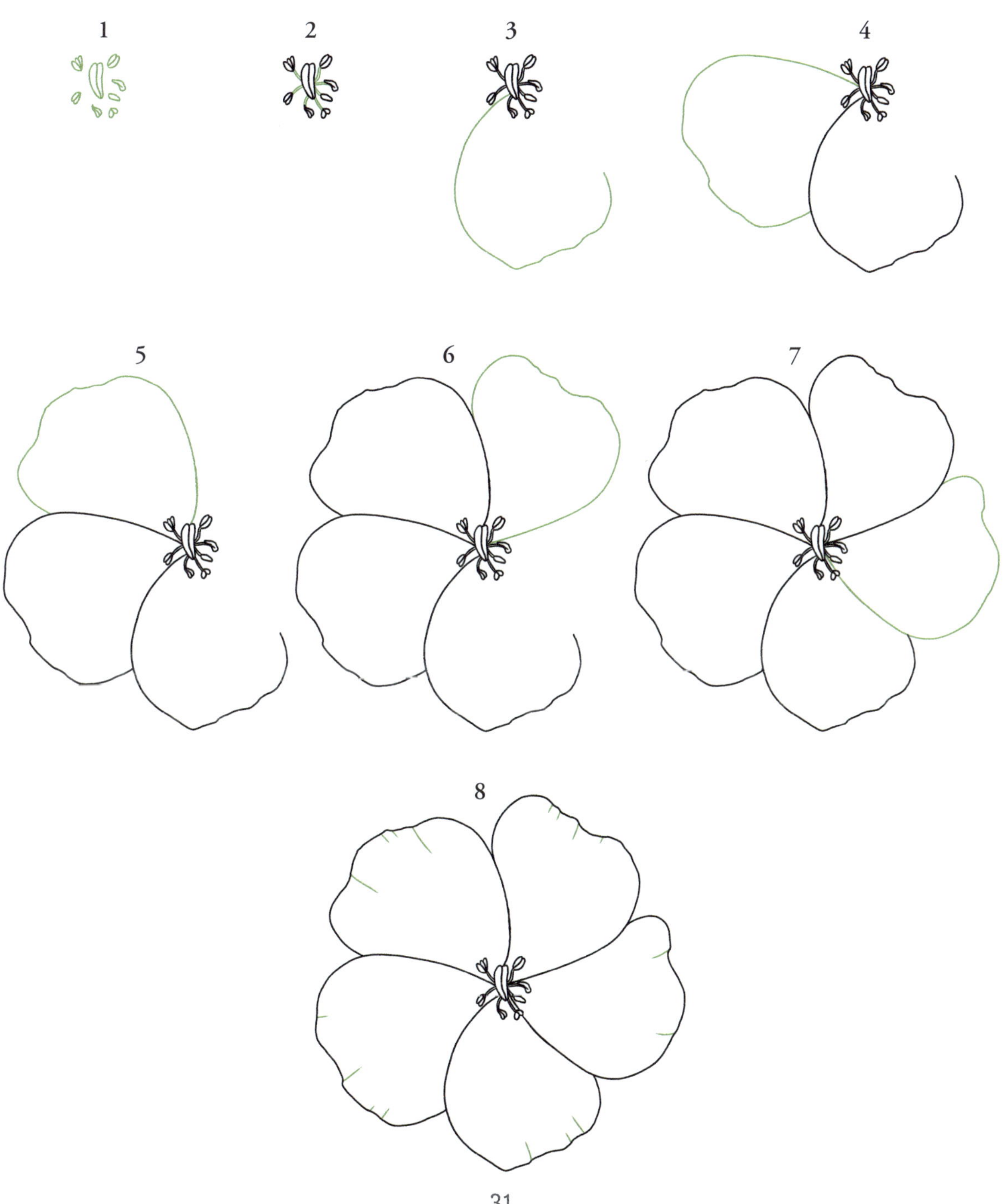

SHADING

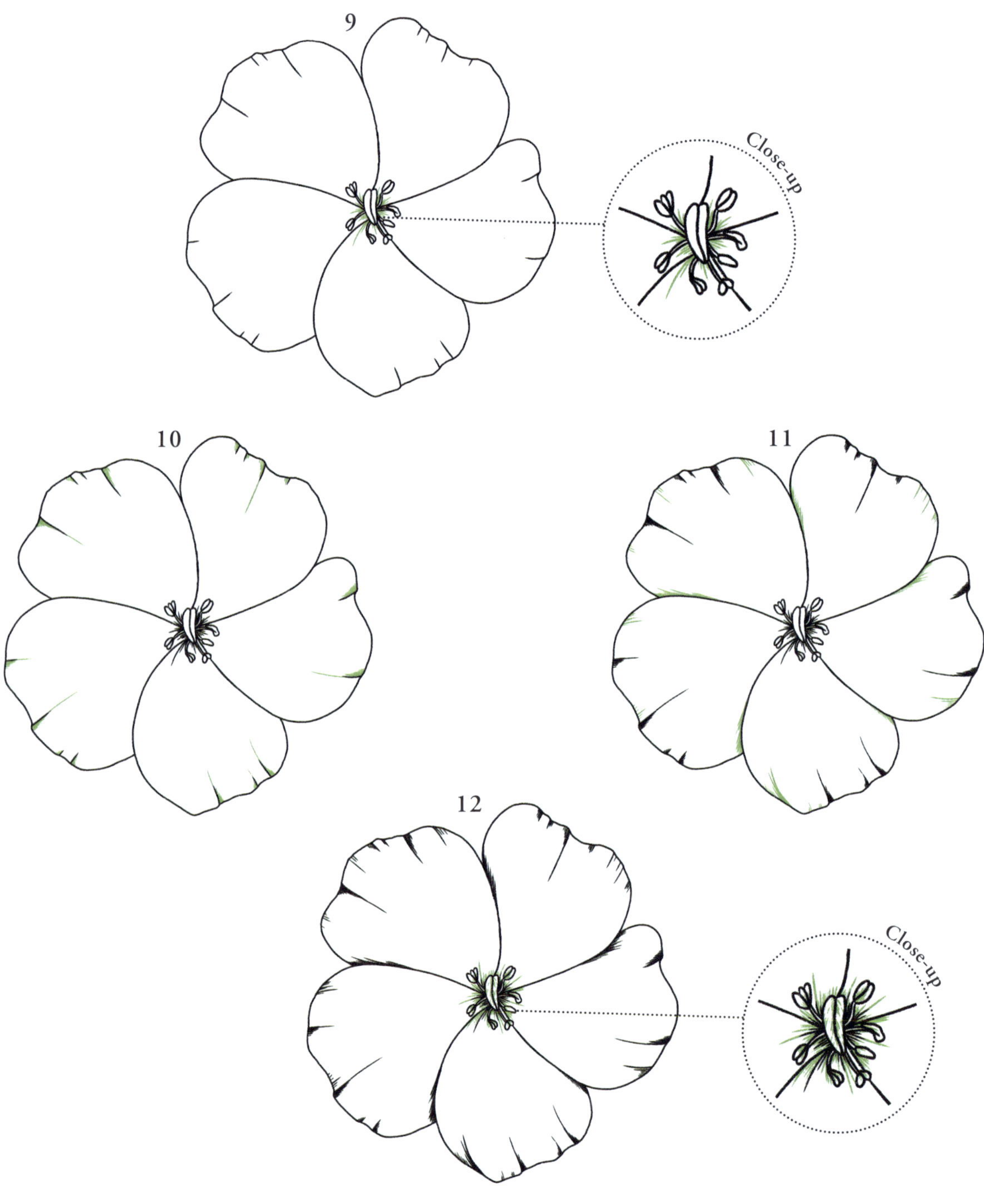

VARIATIONS

Idea 1

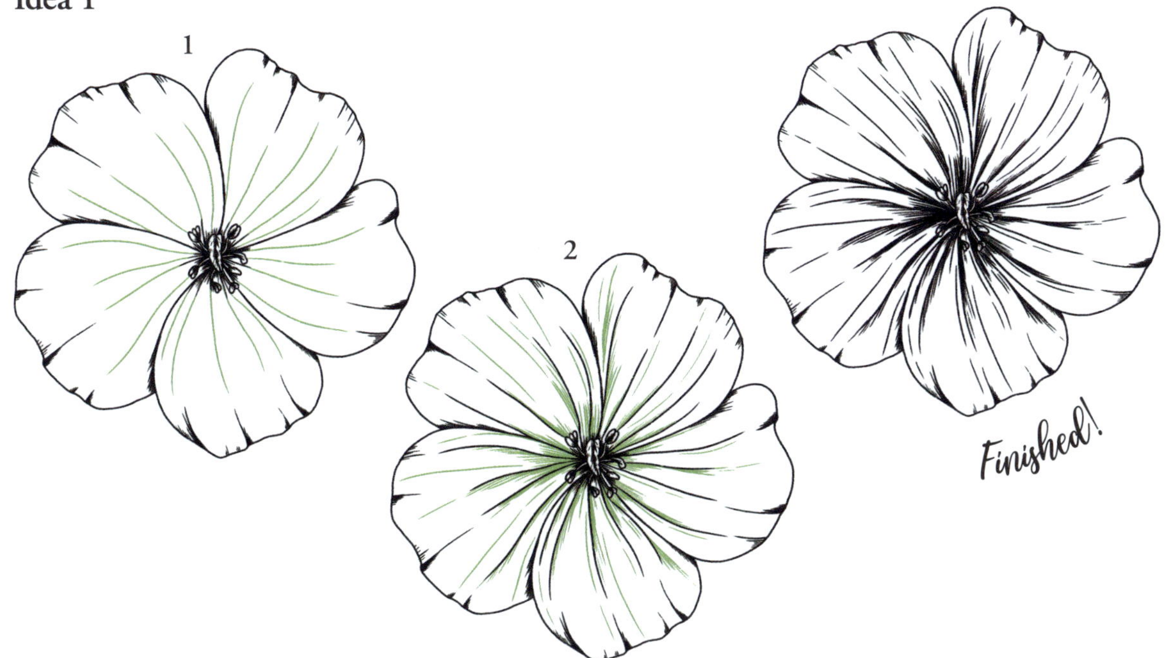

Idea 2

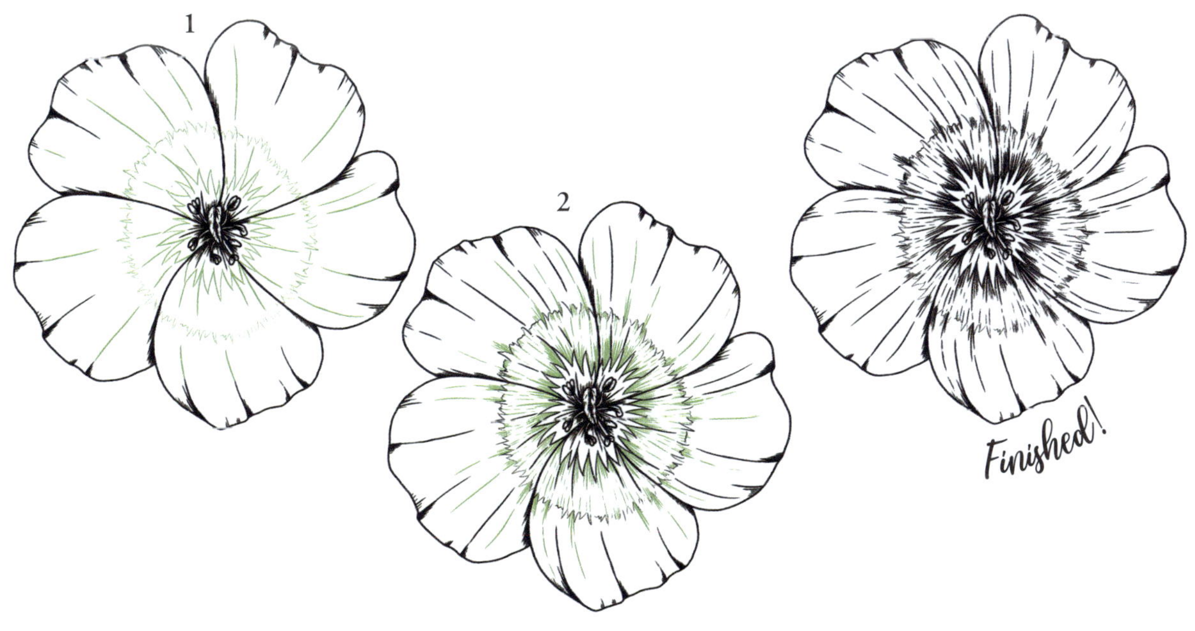

Camellia

Now we've practised a few flower heads, let's try a camellia.
This flower has a few more intricate details in the centre, which will
help to develop what we've covered so far.

You'll have the option to draw just the flower head for this one, or
you can add some spiky leaves at the end to create a bit more detail.

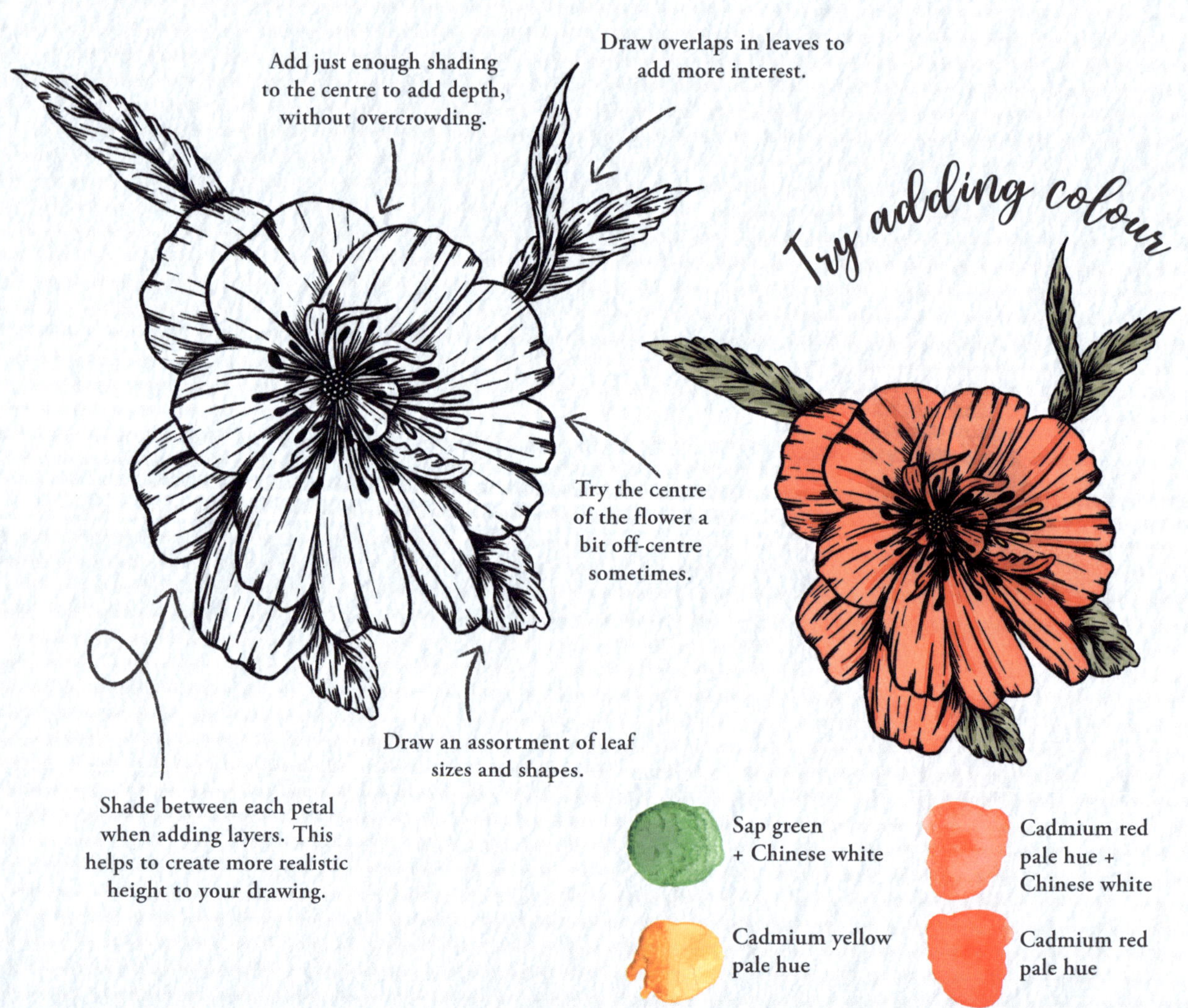

FLOWER HEAD OUTLINE

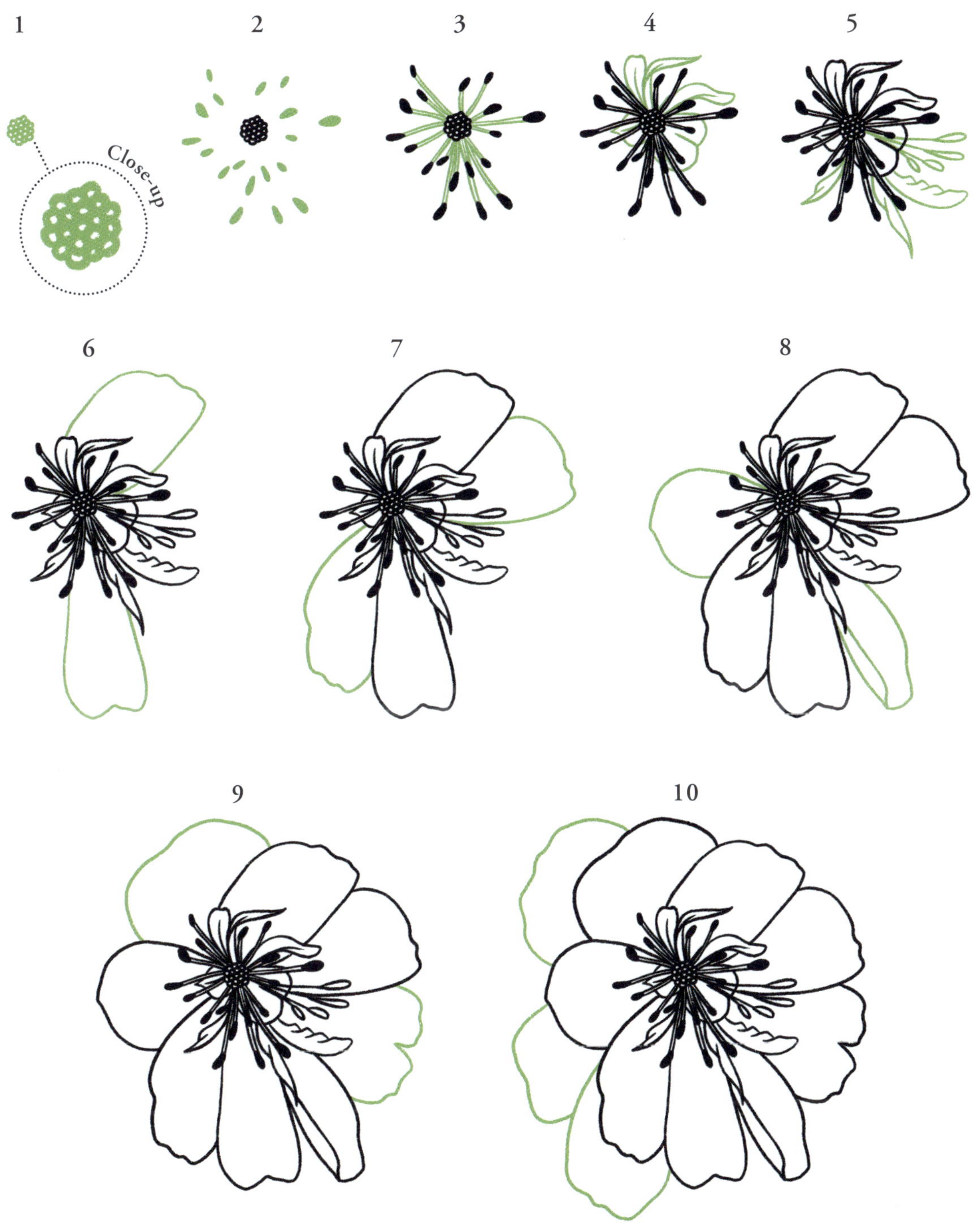

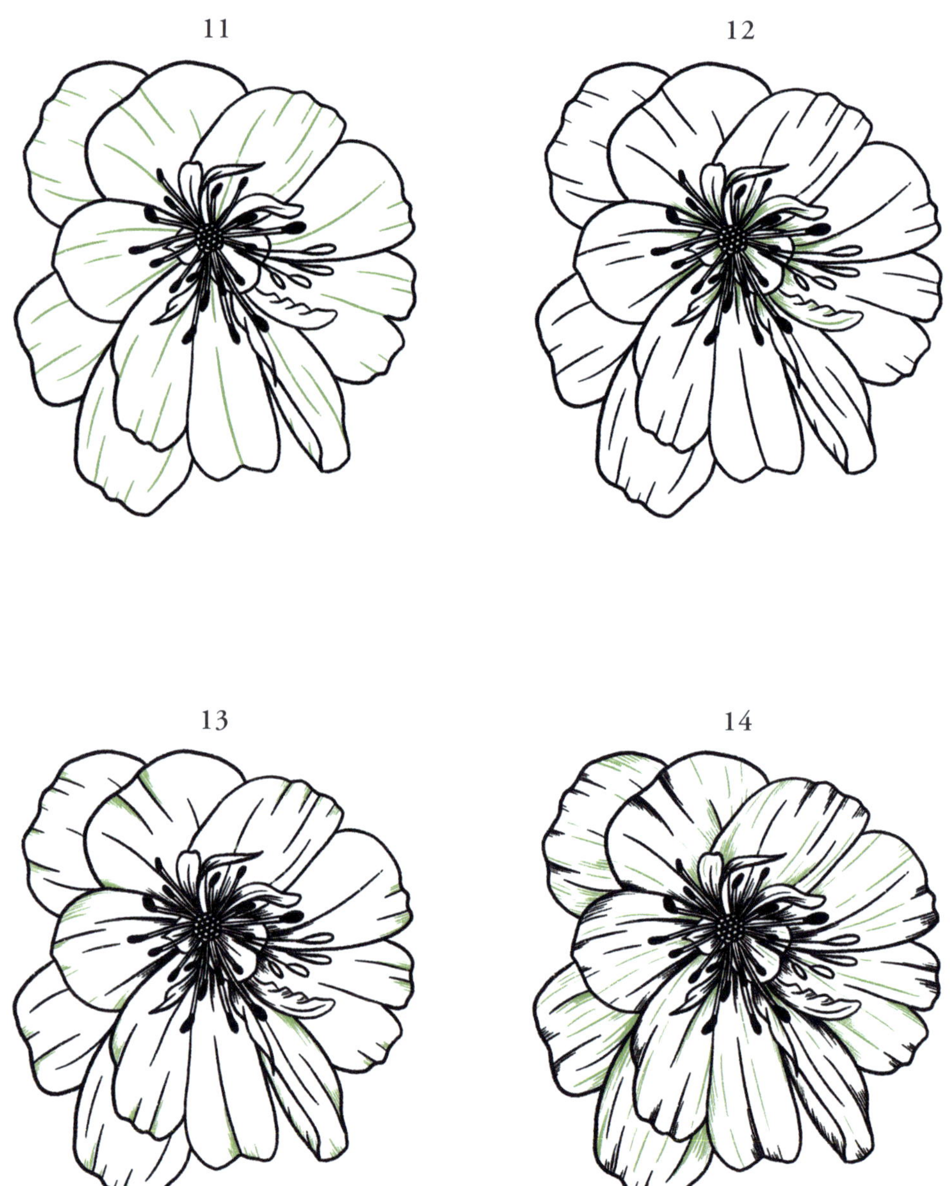

11
12
13
14

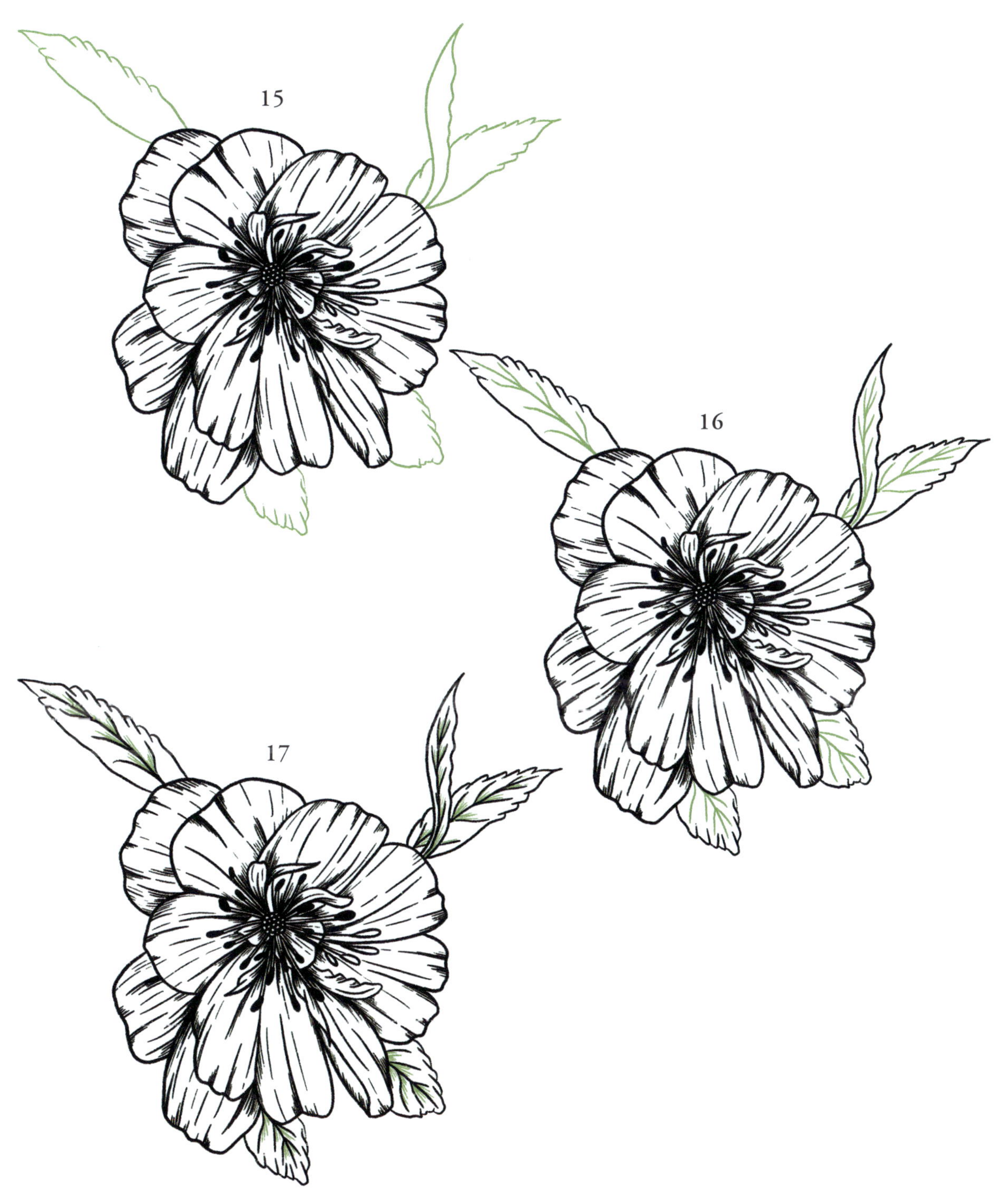
15
16
17

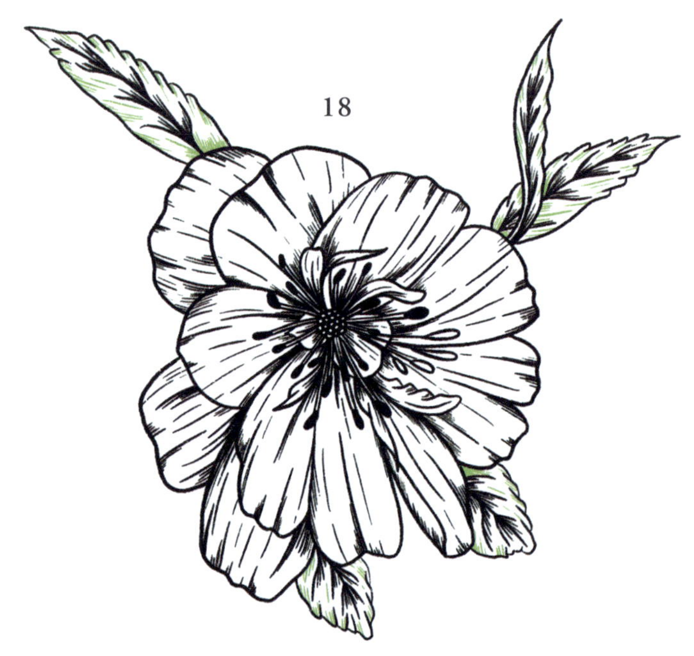

18

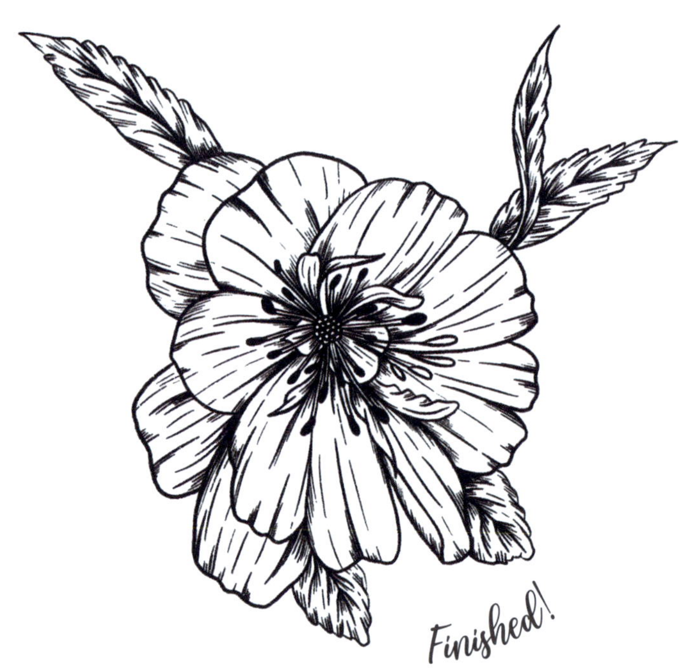

Finished!

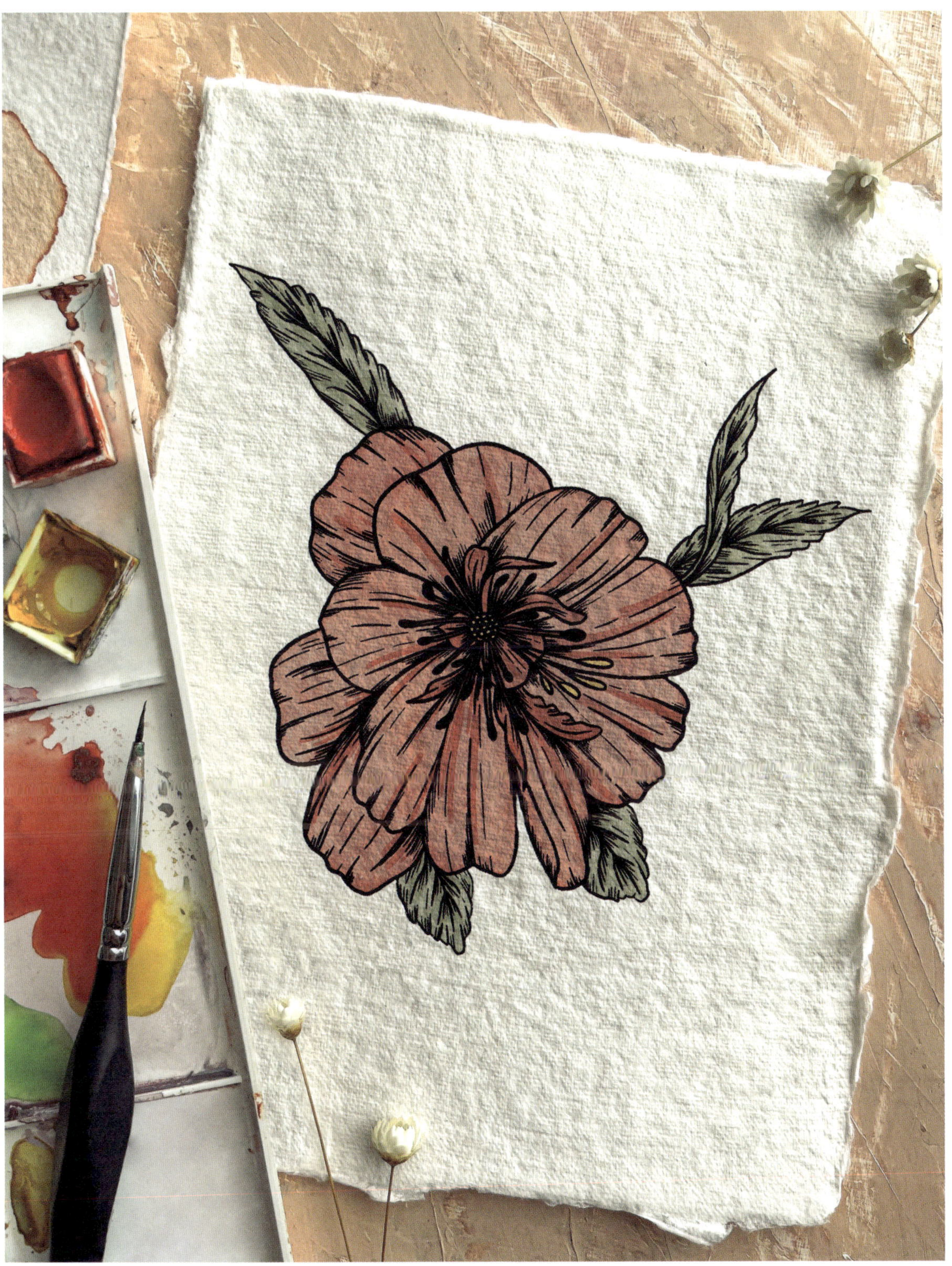

Lavender

Stems of lavender are always handy to pop among any floral compositions you may draw, so I'll show you how to draw this bunch, stem by stem. Starting with a single stem, you can add on as many as you like until you have a bunch of four, like below.

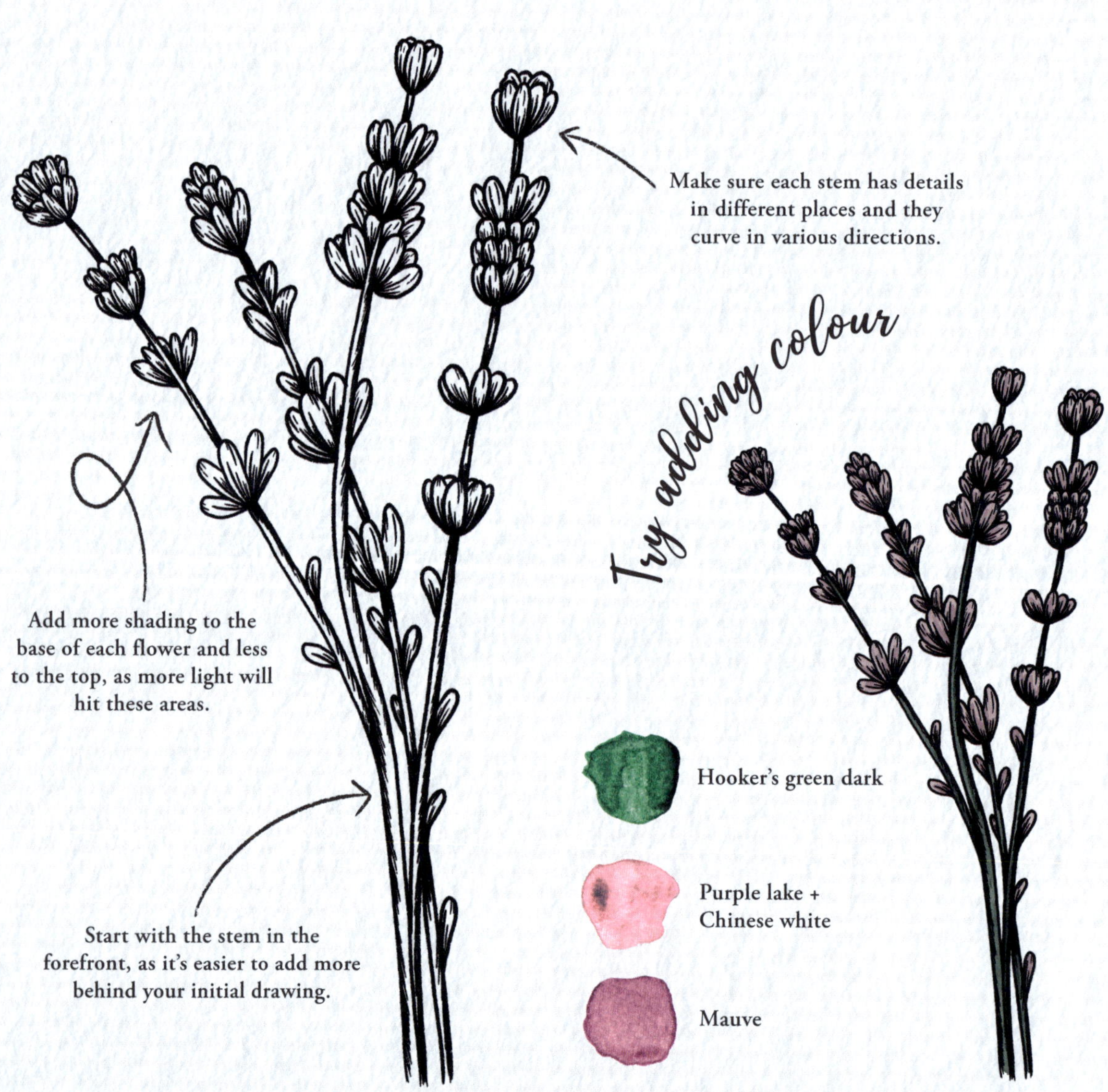

FIRST STEM

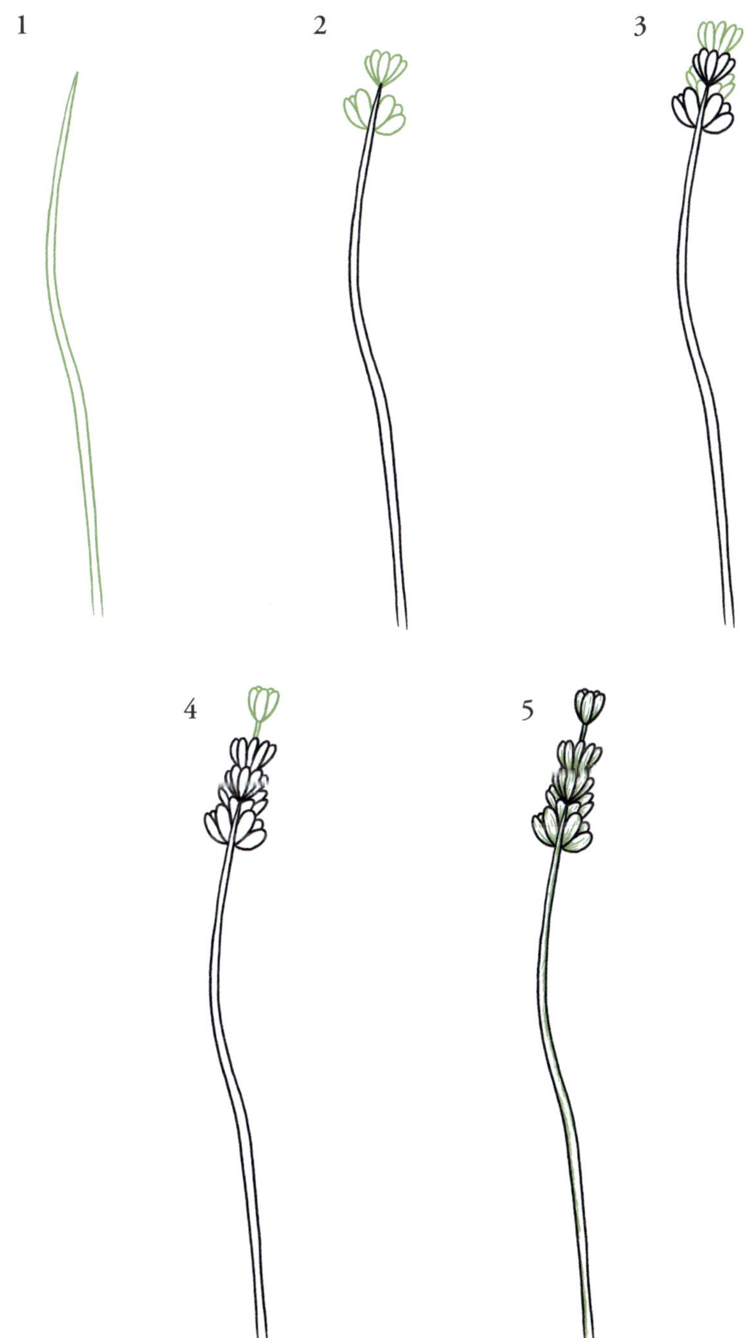

SECOND STEM

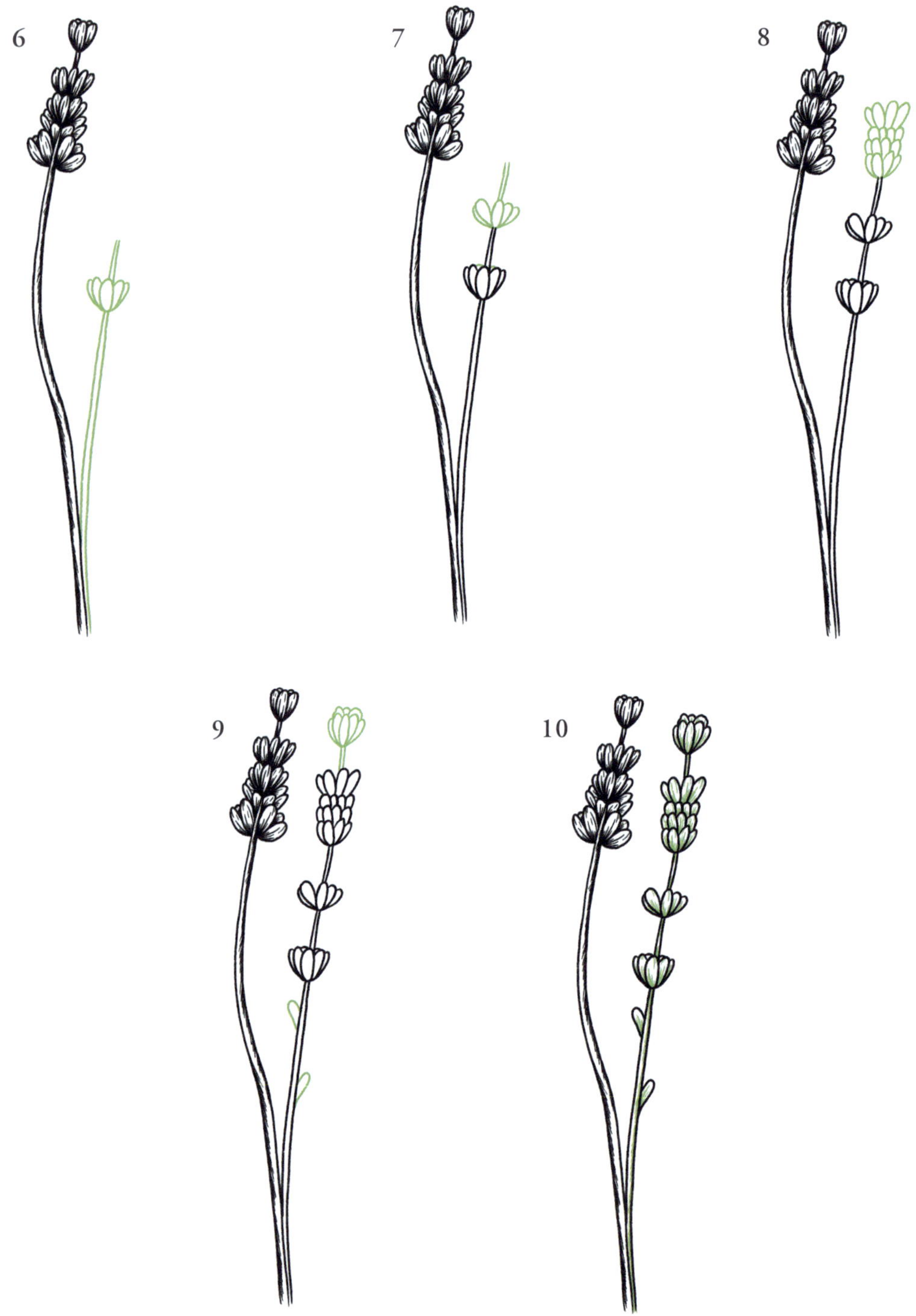

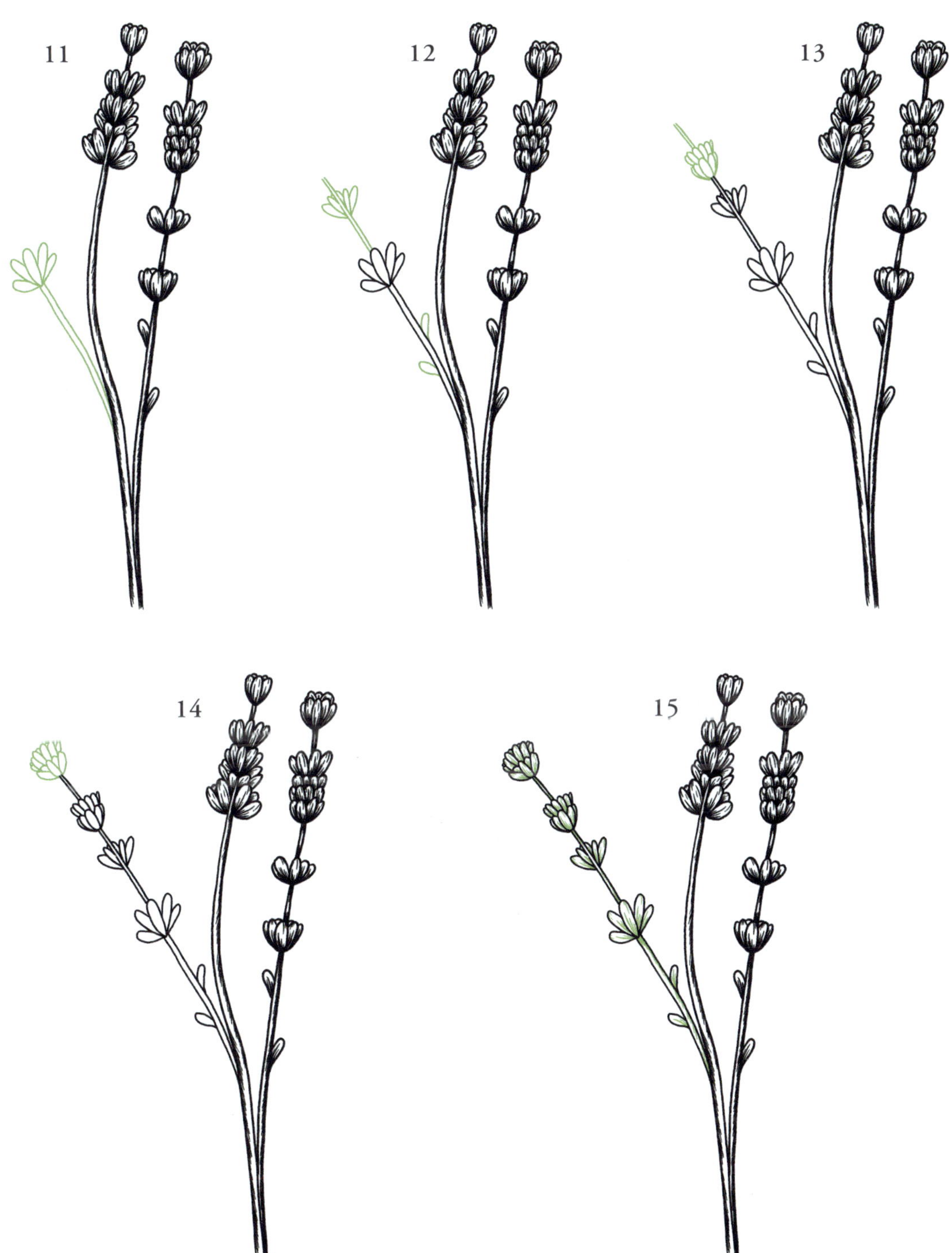

FOURTH STEM

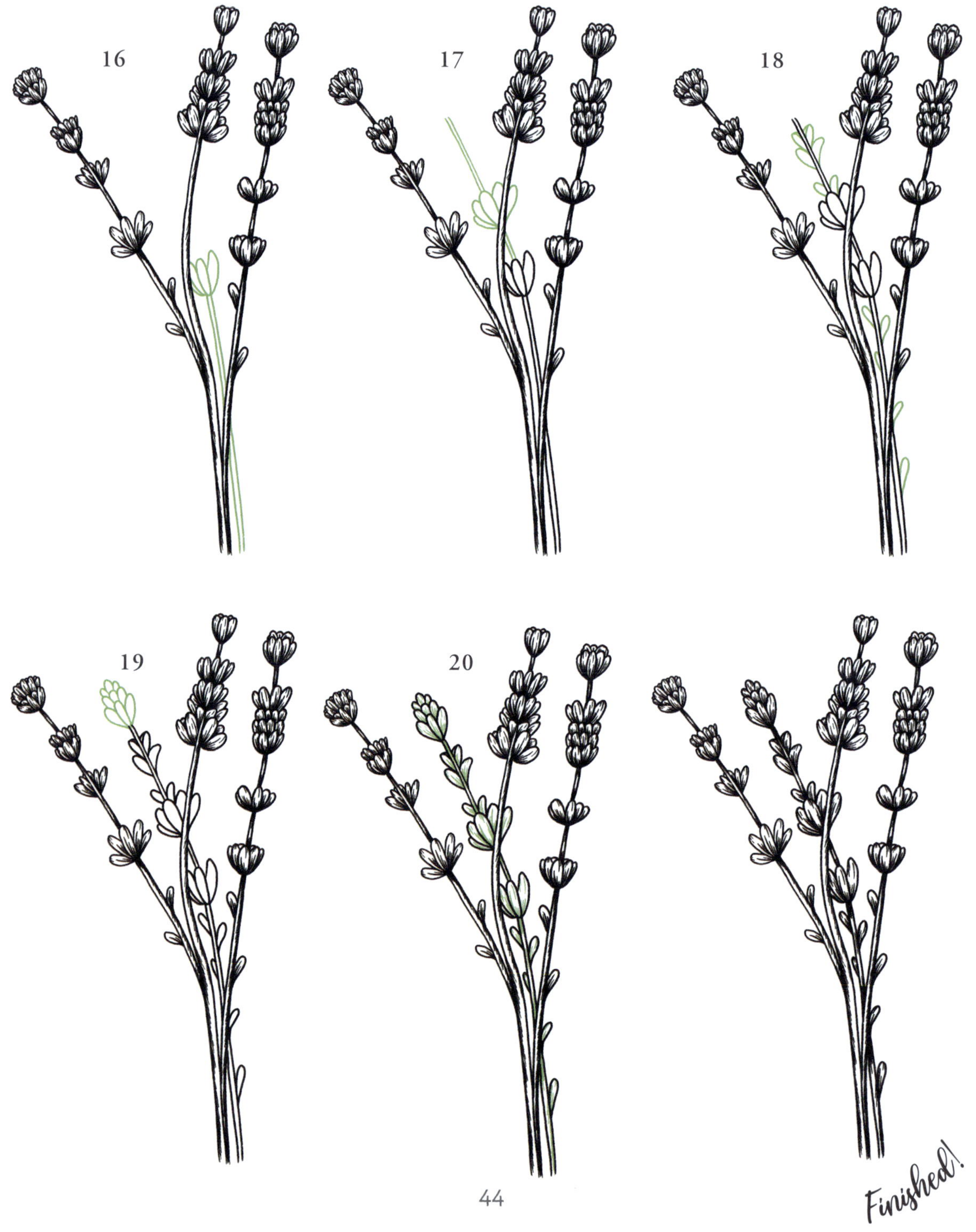

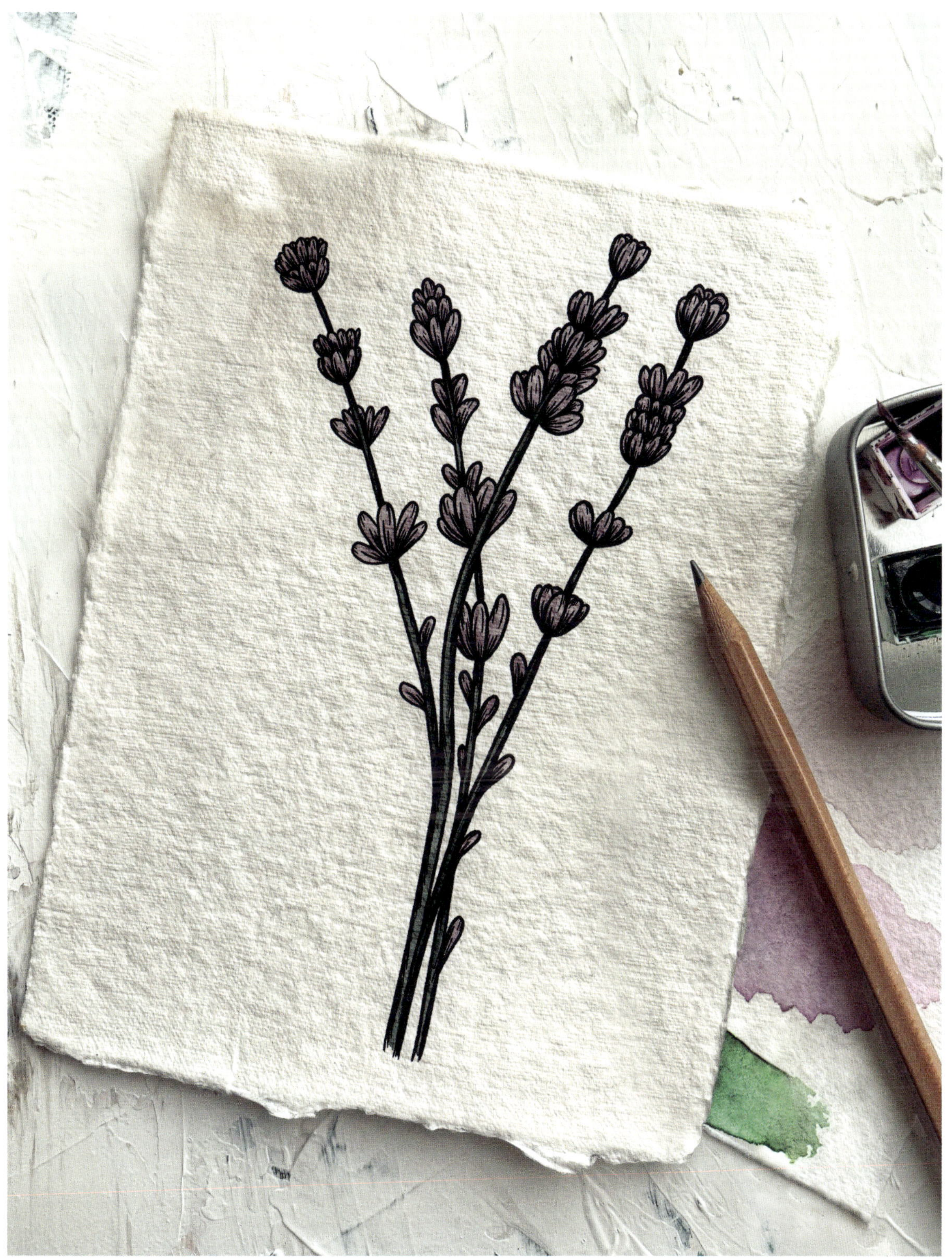

Lily

This is a more complex flower head, with two variations from the same outlines. Variation 1 is a perfect joy lily (shown in the picture to the right) with more subtle details in the form of shading to emphasize the white centre. Variation 2 is a stargazer lily with its signature spots.

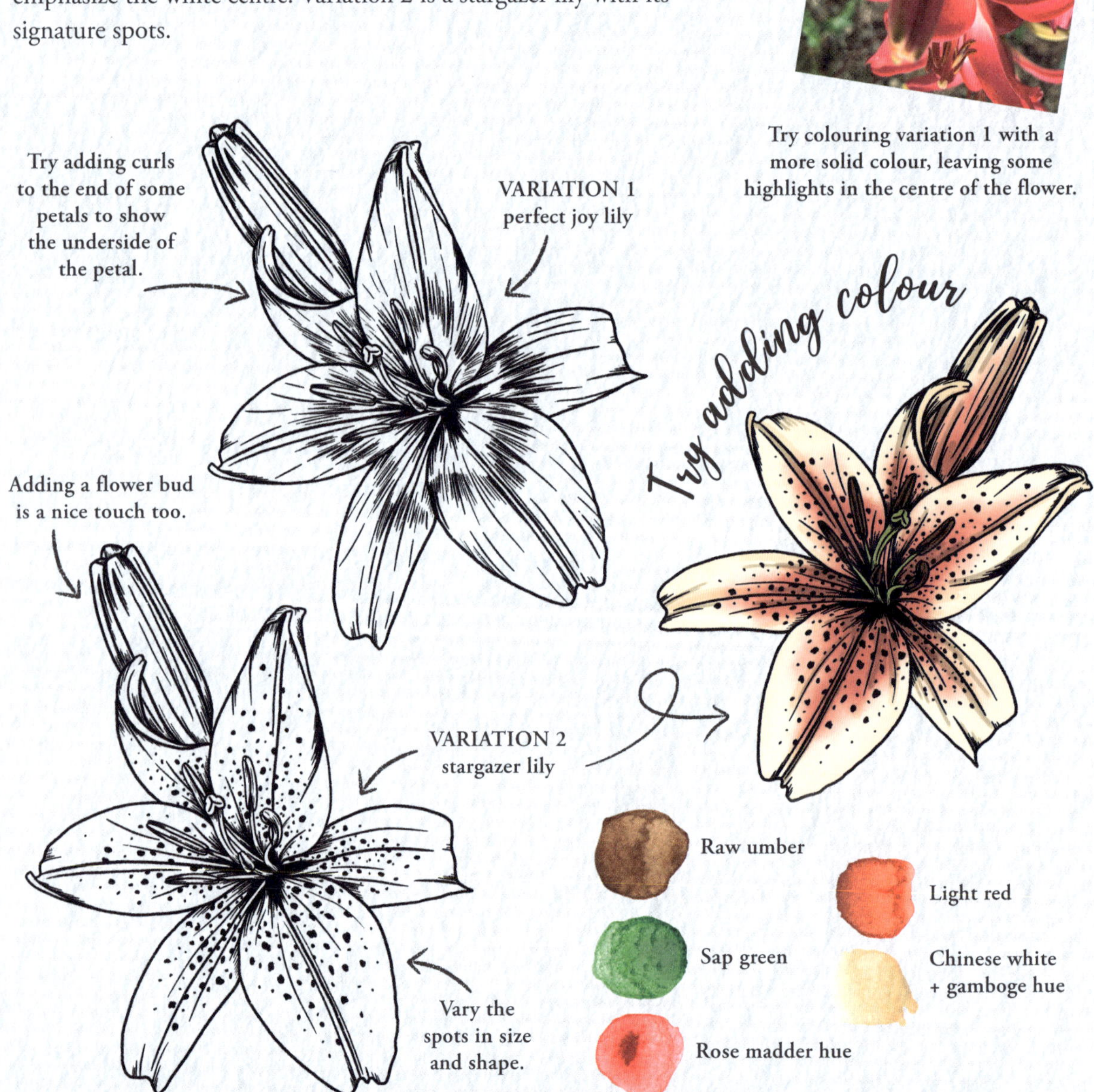

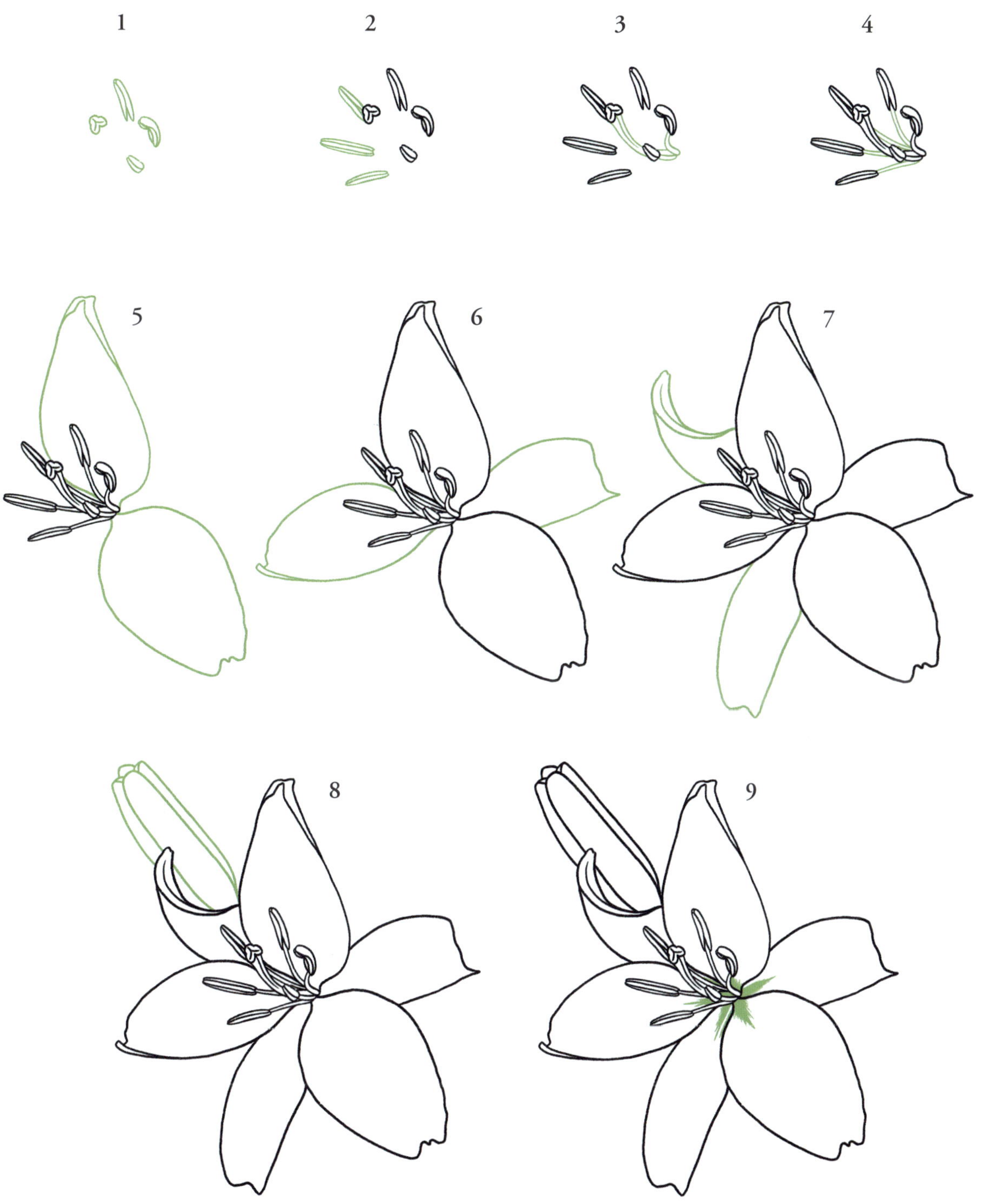

FLOWER HEAD DETAIL

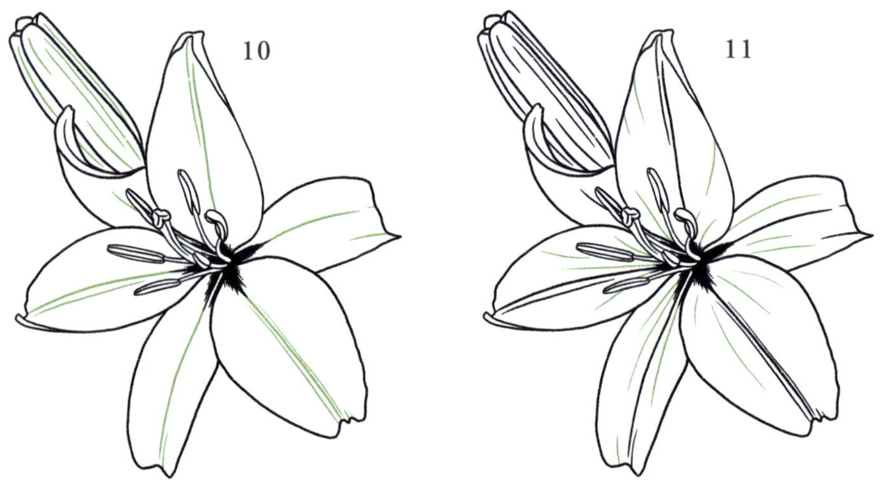

FLOWER HEAD SHADING

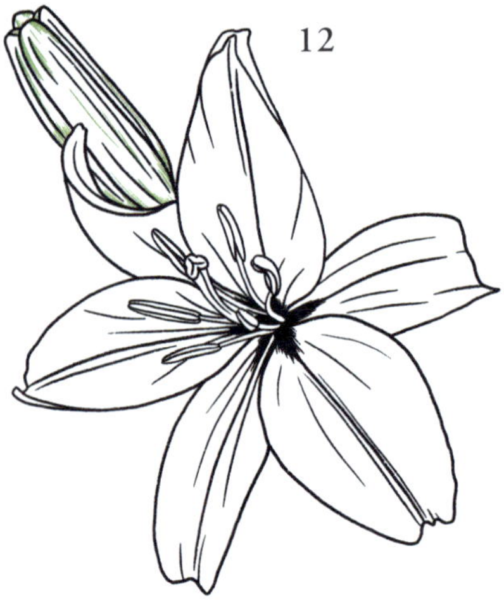

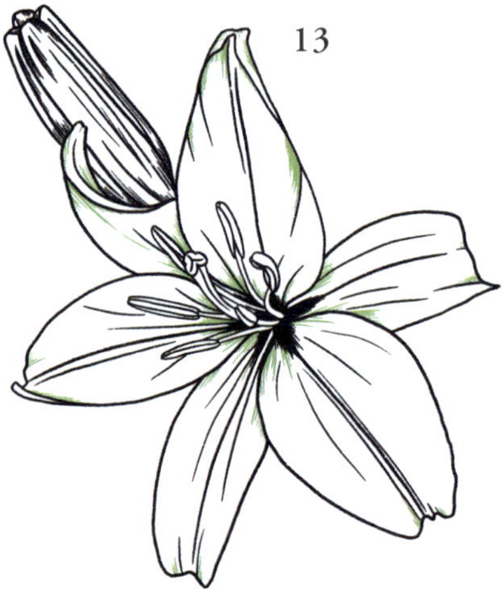

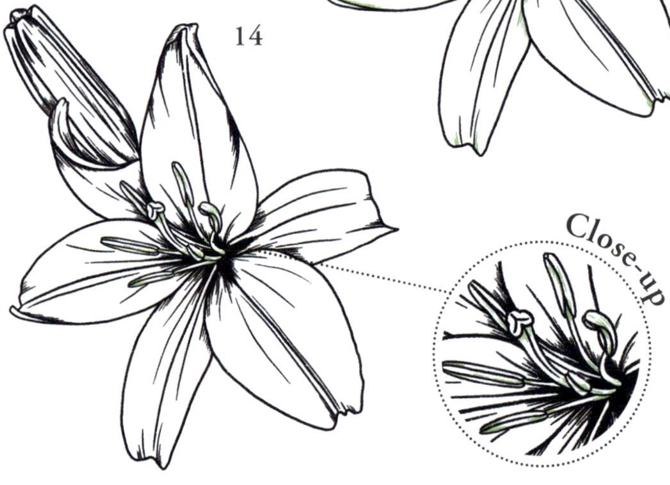

VARIATIONS

Idea 1

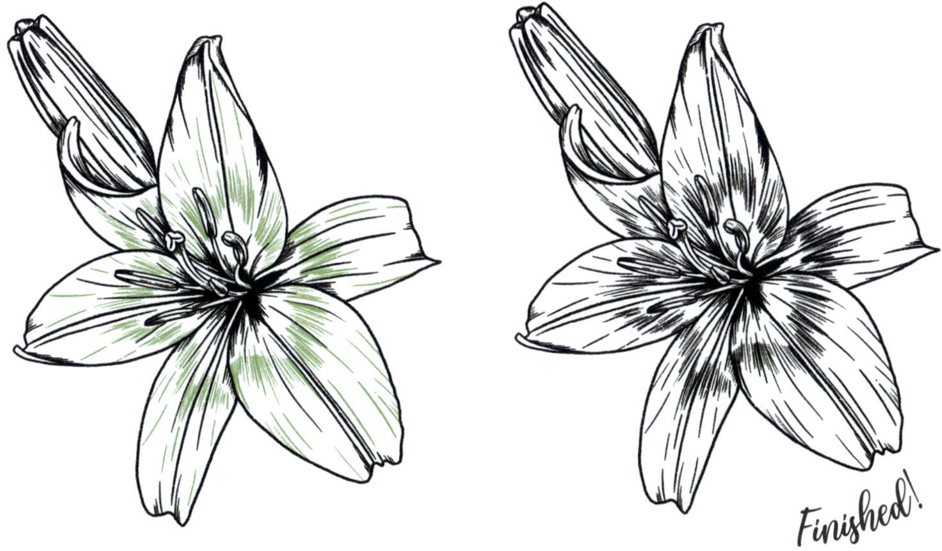

Idea 2

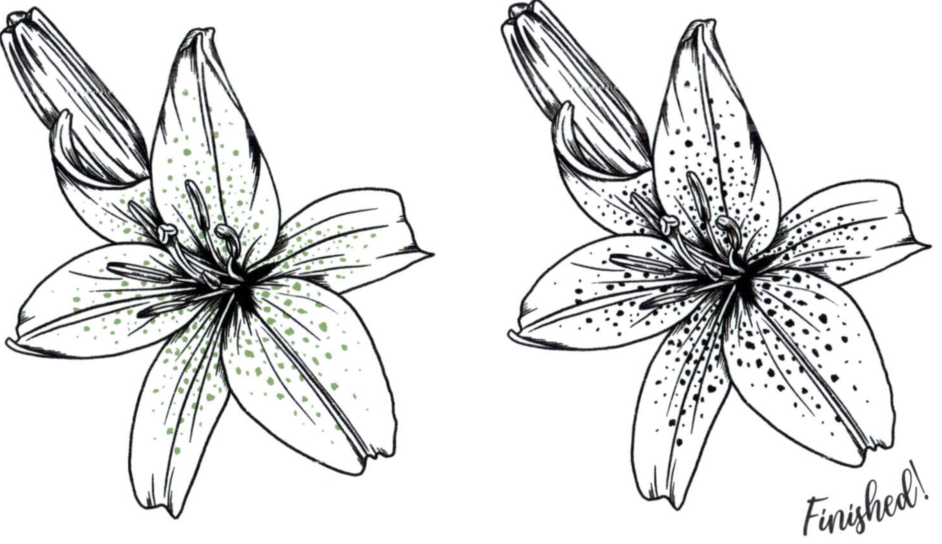

Peony

Peonies are one of my favourite flowers, partly because of how much I enjoy painting and drawing them. What I love most is how flowy and organic each petal is.

Again, I'll show you how to draw just the flower head, followed by the addition of the leafy stem and lastly the flower bud.

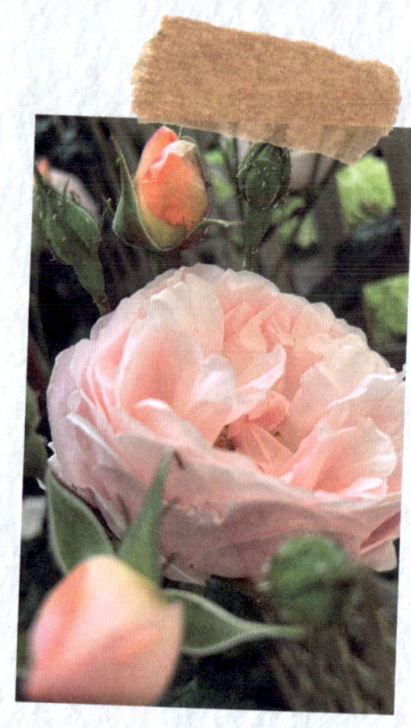

The most common peony colours are white, blush, pink and red.

Make sure to always connect any extra stems back to the main stem.

Create a better balance by adding larger details like bigger leaves and flower buds to the opposite side your flower head leans to.

Try adding colour

Hooker's green light

Sap green

Alizarin crimson hue + Chinese white

Cadmium orange hue + Chinese white

FLOWER HEAD OUTLINE

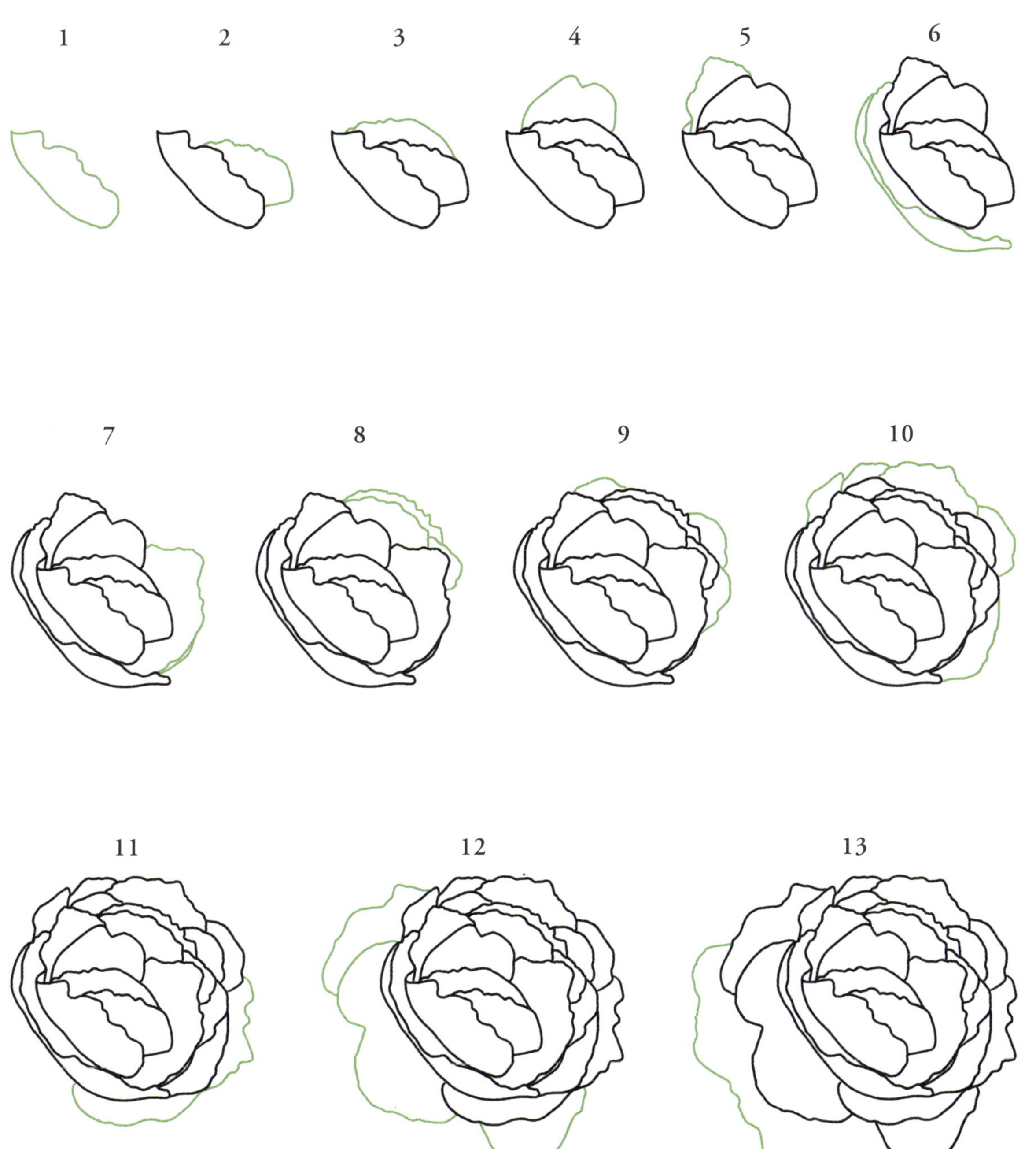

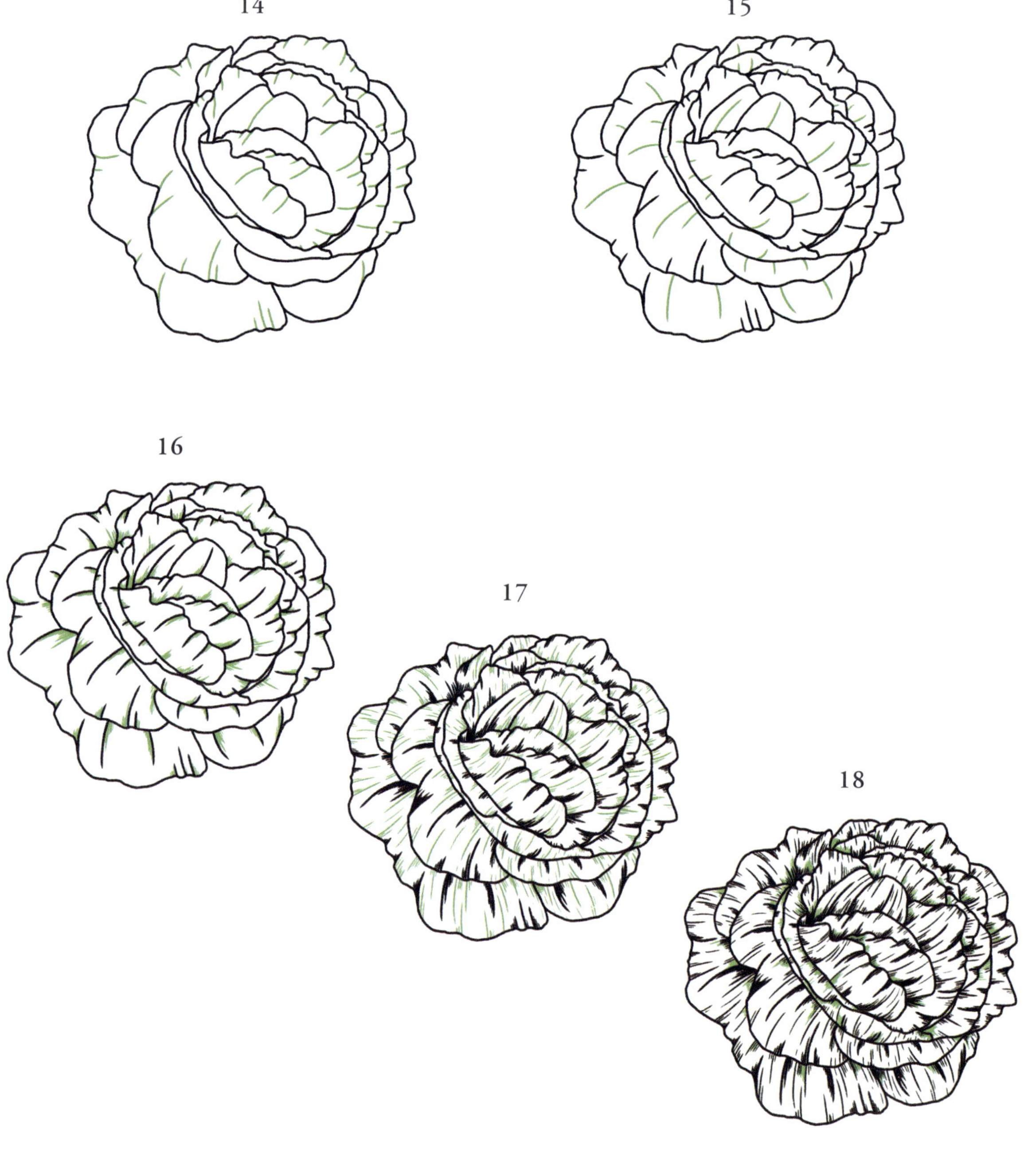

19　　　　　　　　　20

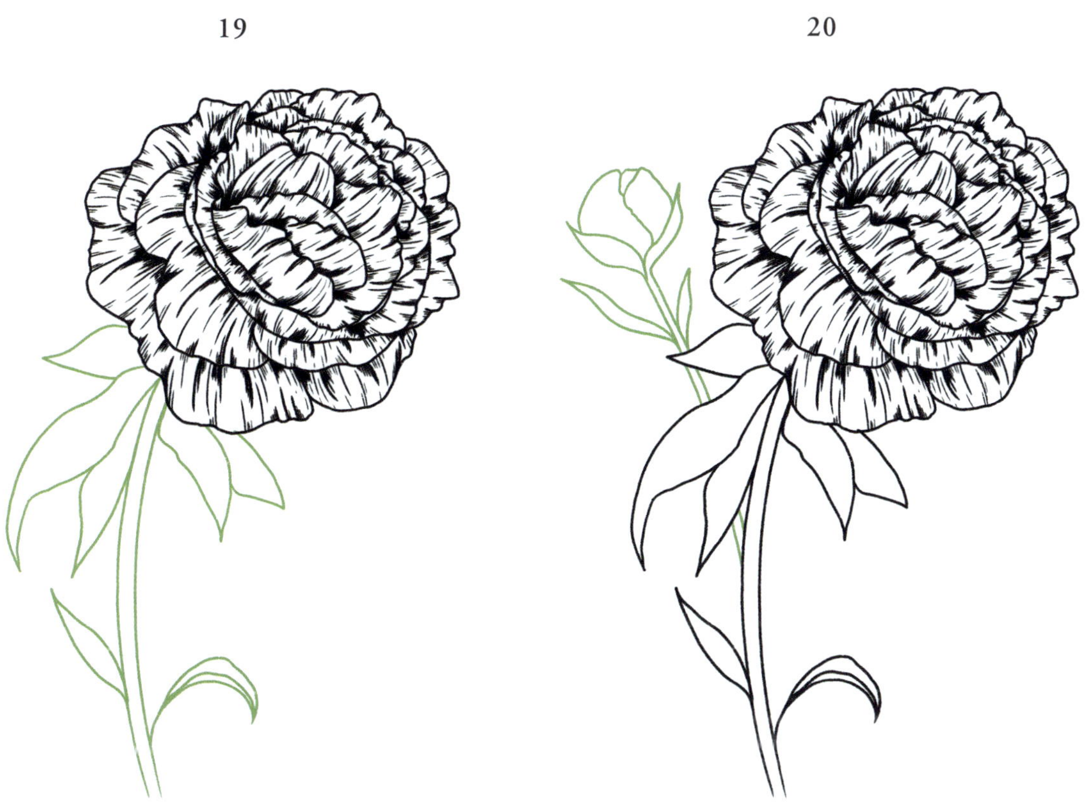

21
22

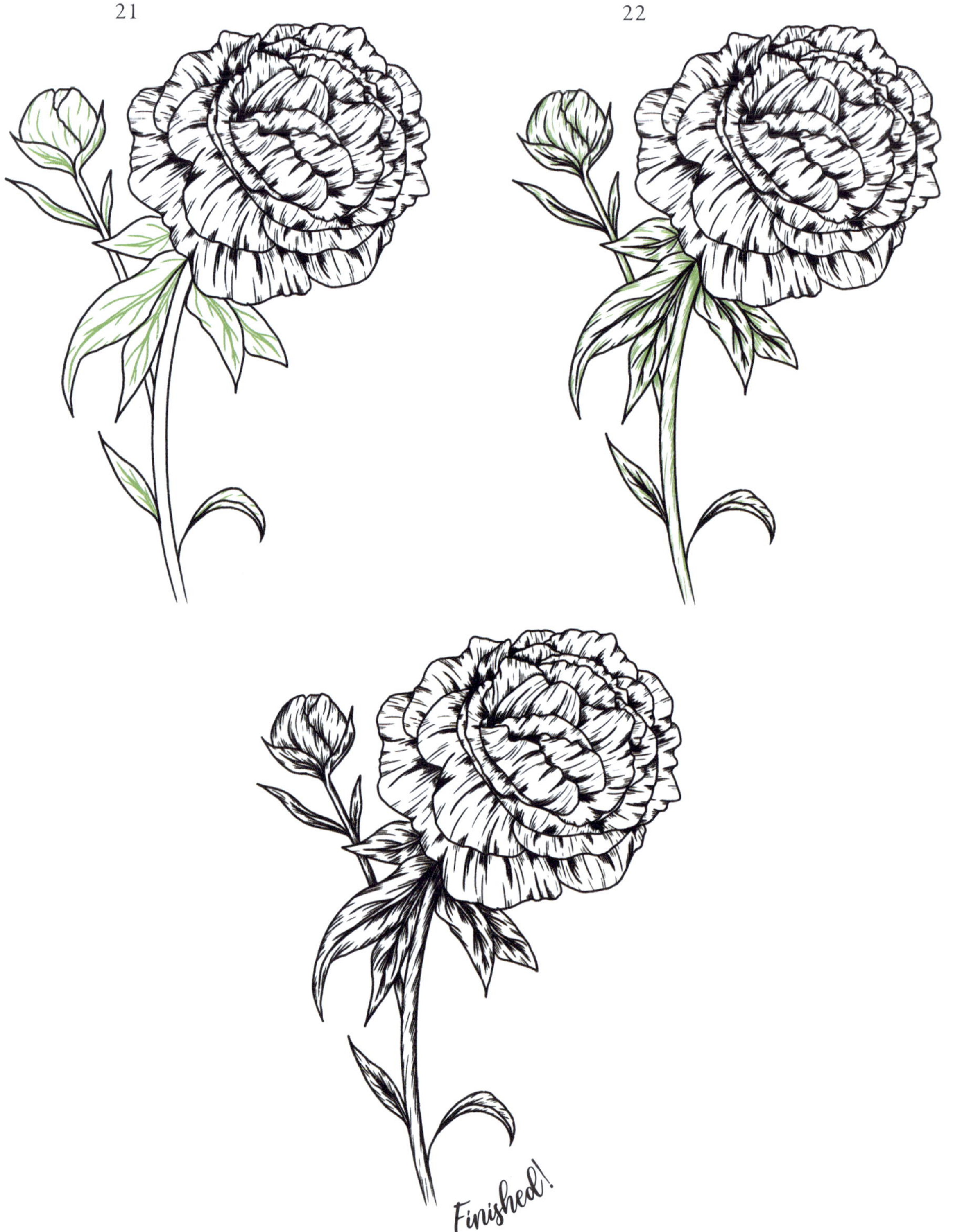

Finished!

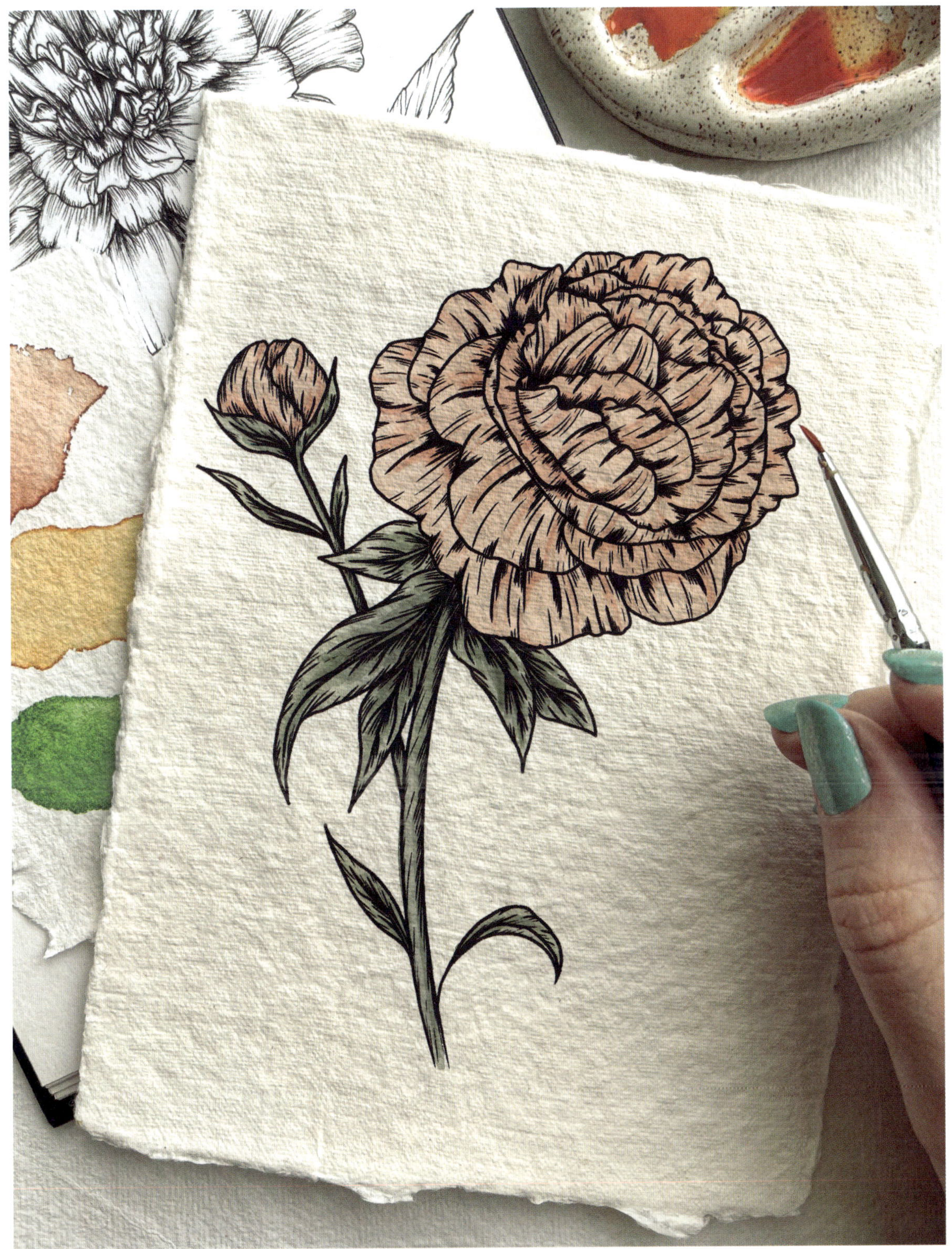

Cherry blossom

I always love the spring, when blossom season comes around and the trees start to come back to life!

Broken up into four stages, learn how to draw a cluster of cherry blossom flower heads, before optionally adding the leaves and then the branches with small flower buds.

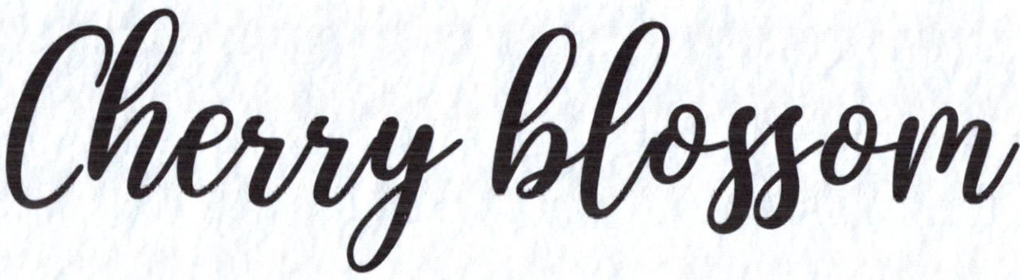

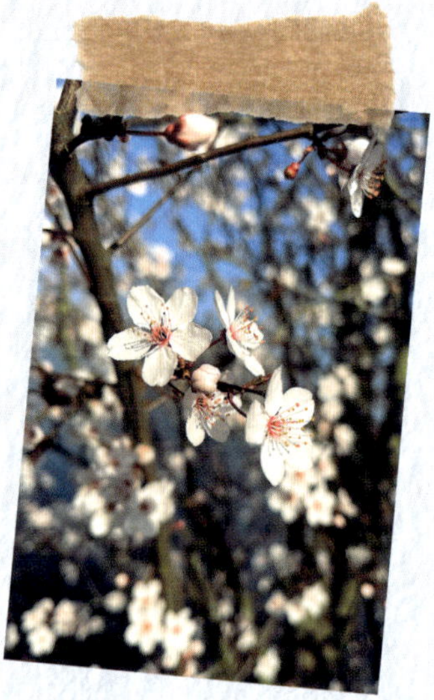

Spread out additional elements like branches, leaves and flowering buds randomly between your flower heads. Try to avoid any kind of symmetry.

Make sure to add just enough shading where petals overlap.

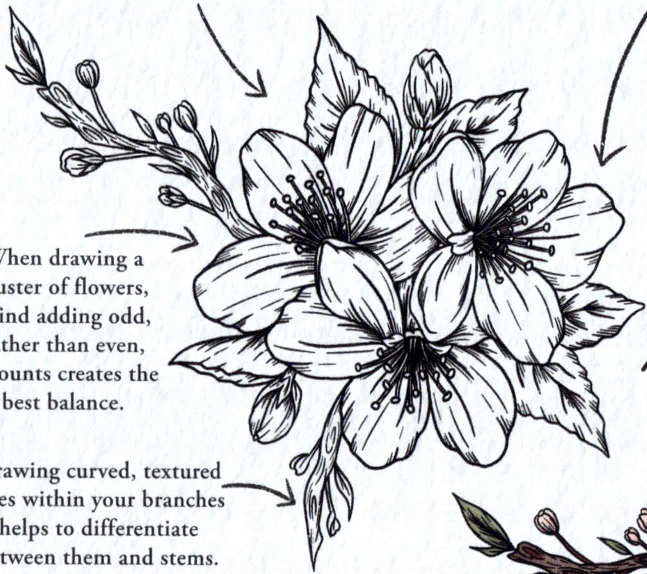

Colour flower heads in pink or white.

When drawing a cluster of flowers, I find adding odd, rather than even, amounts creates the best balance.

Drawing curved, textured lines within your branches helps to differentiate between them and stems.

Try adding colour

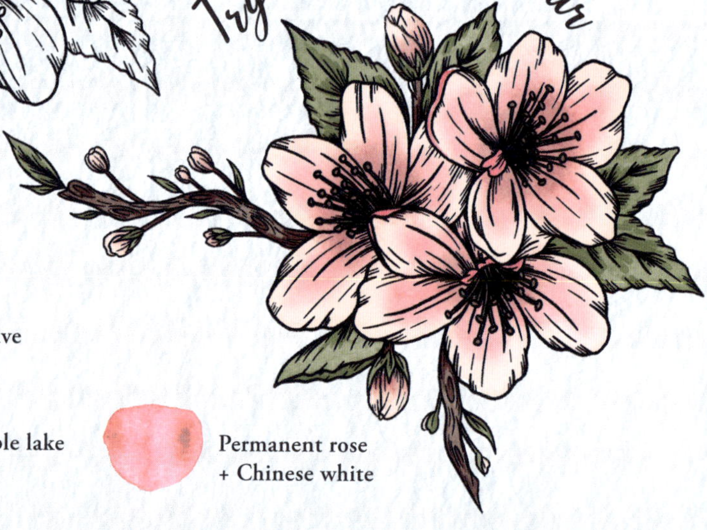

Sepia		Mauve
Sap green		Purple lake
		Permanent rose + Chinese white

FLOWER HEAD OUTLINE

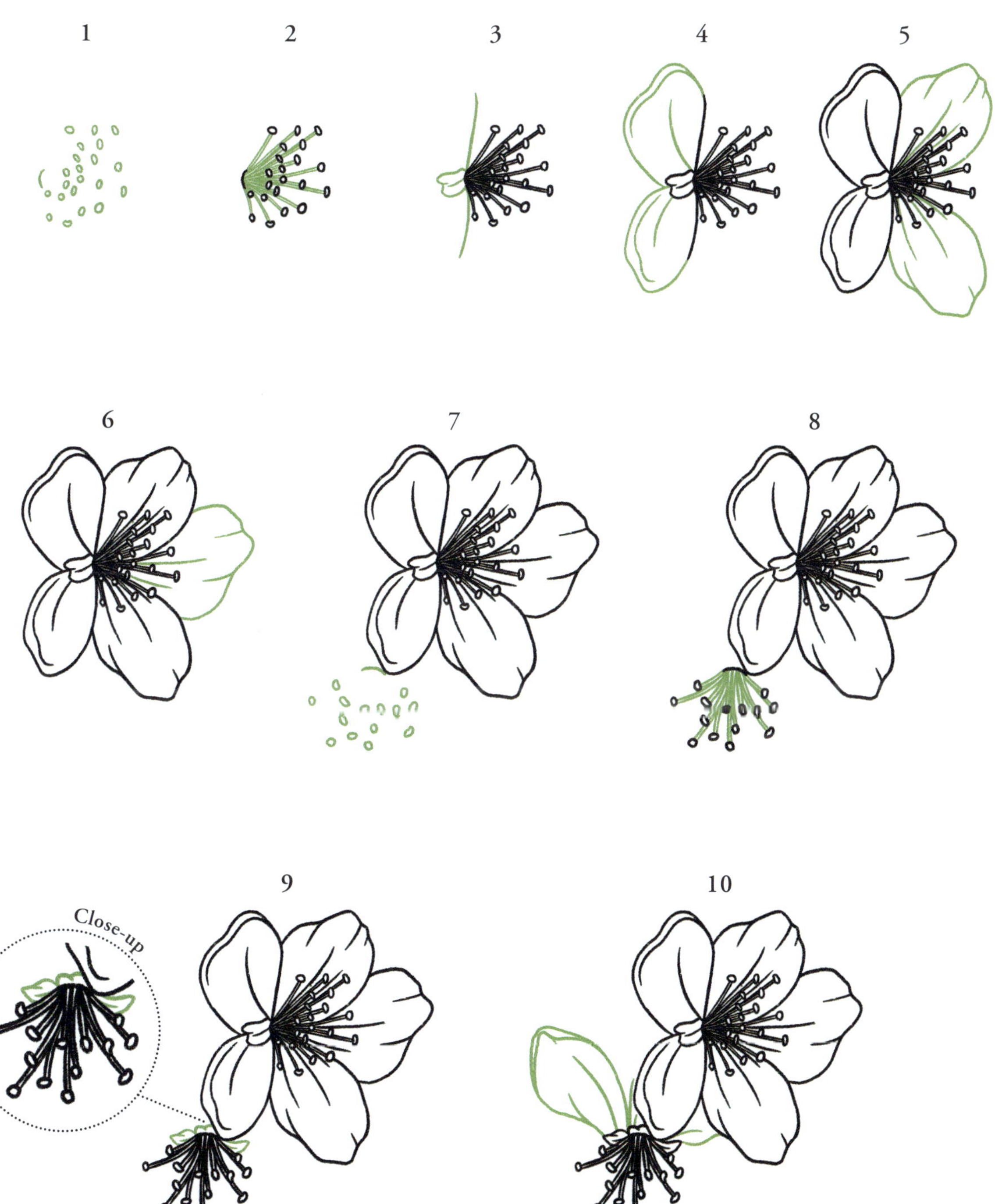

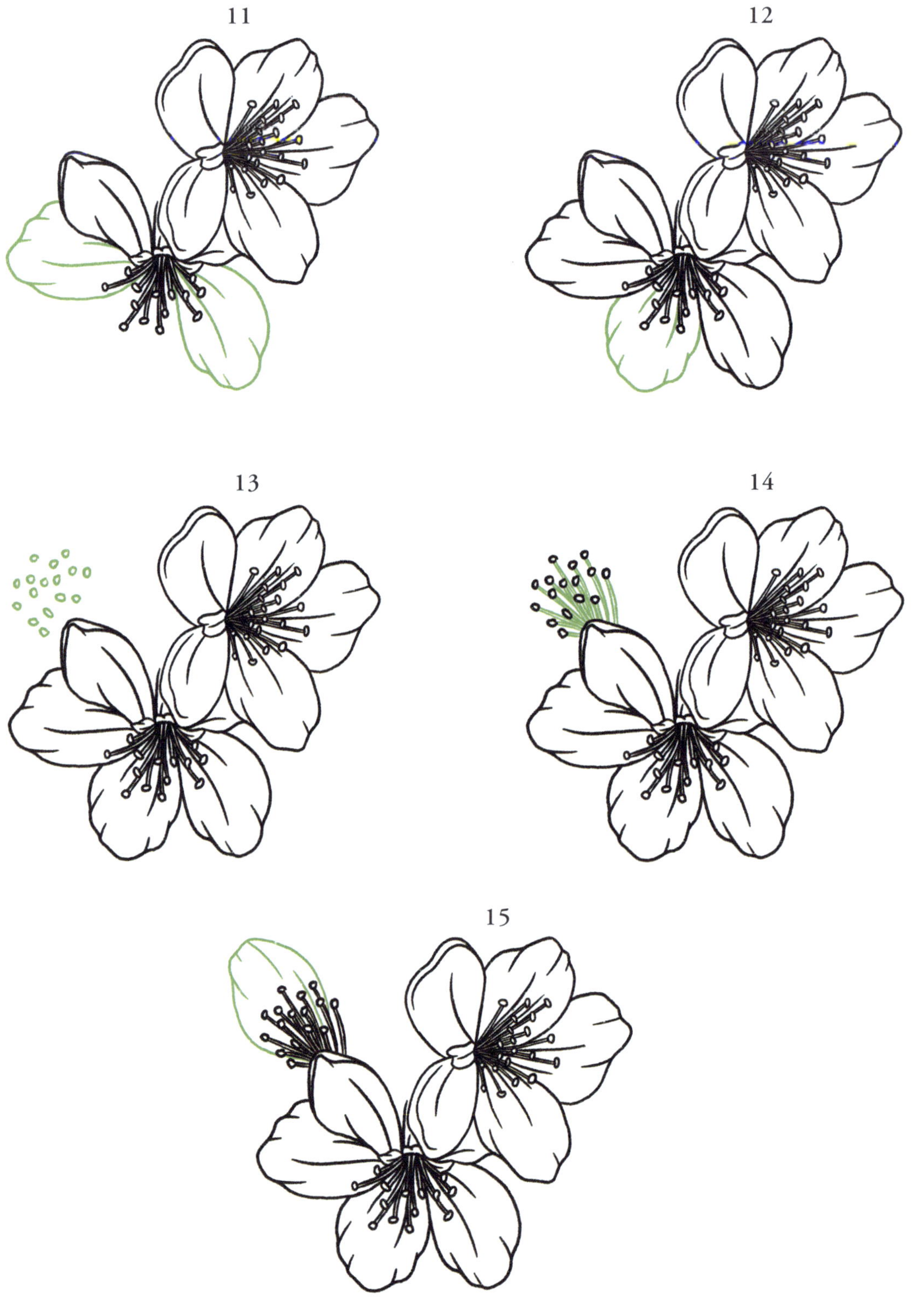

11
12
13
14
15

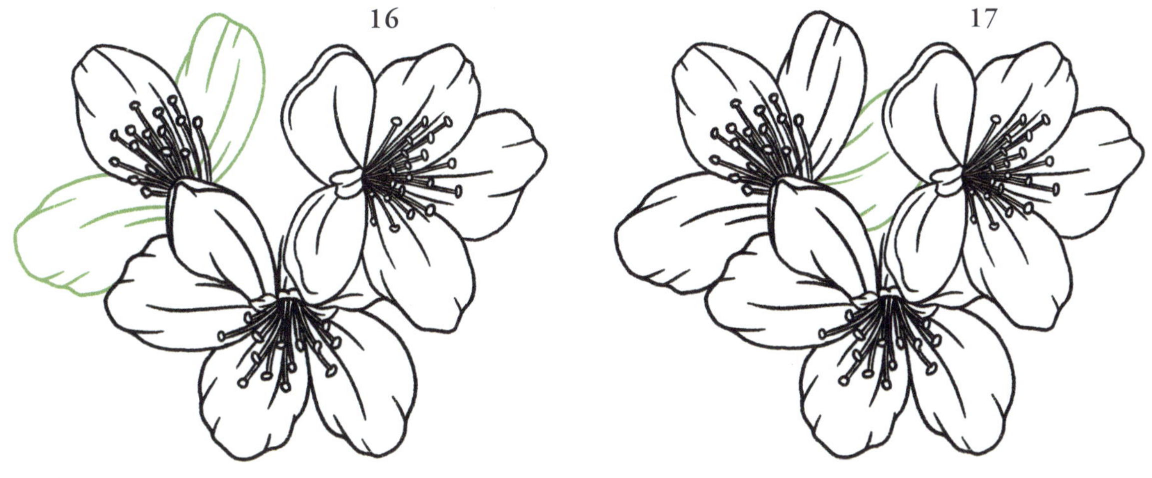

SHADING

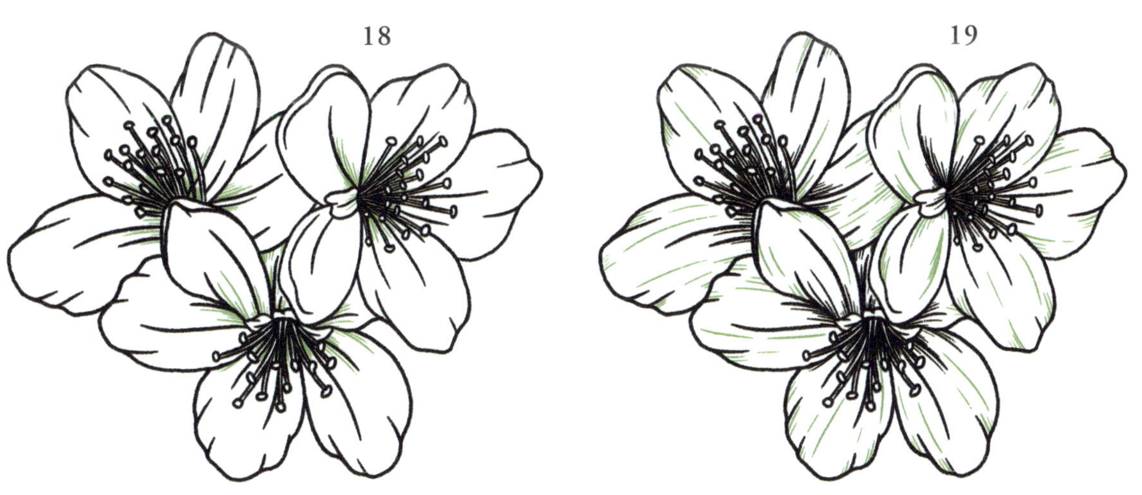

LEAVES

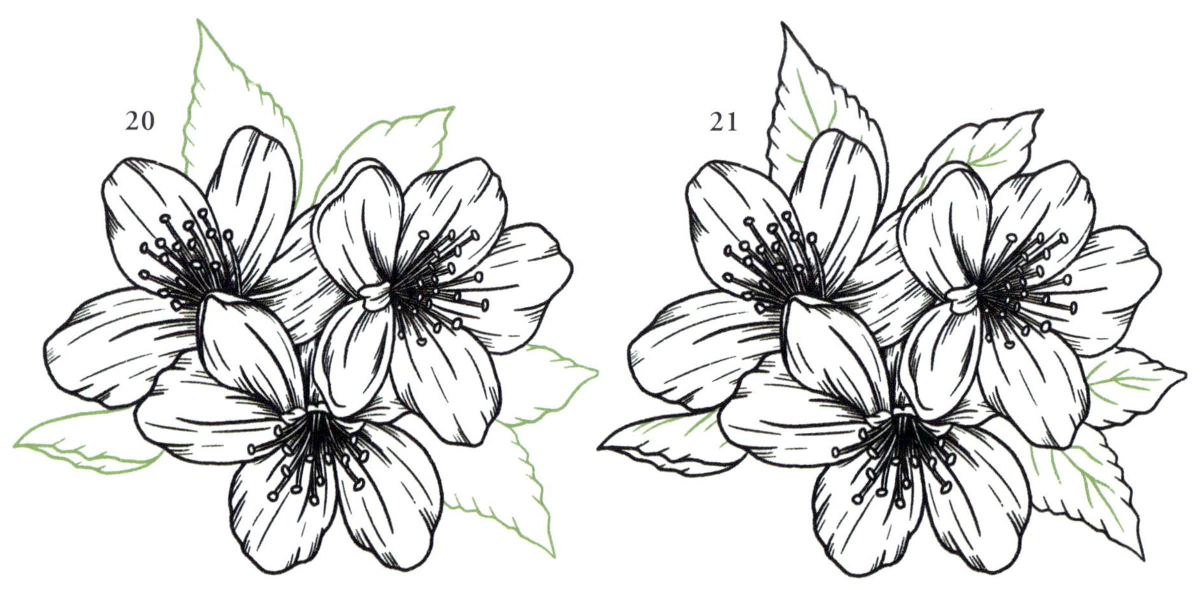

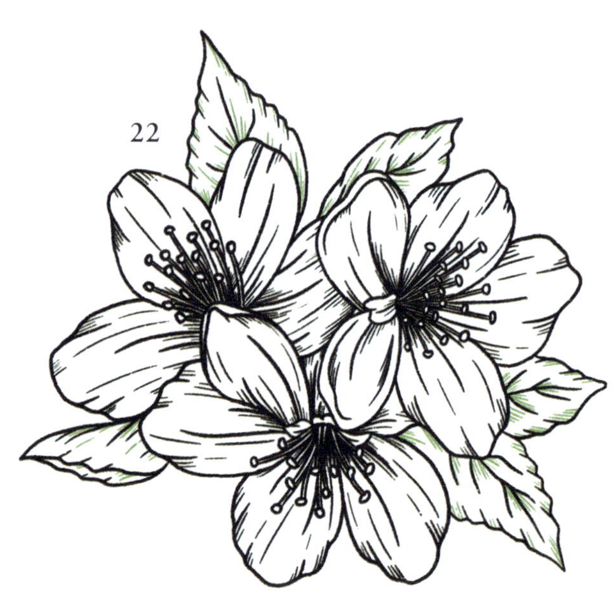

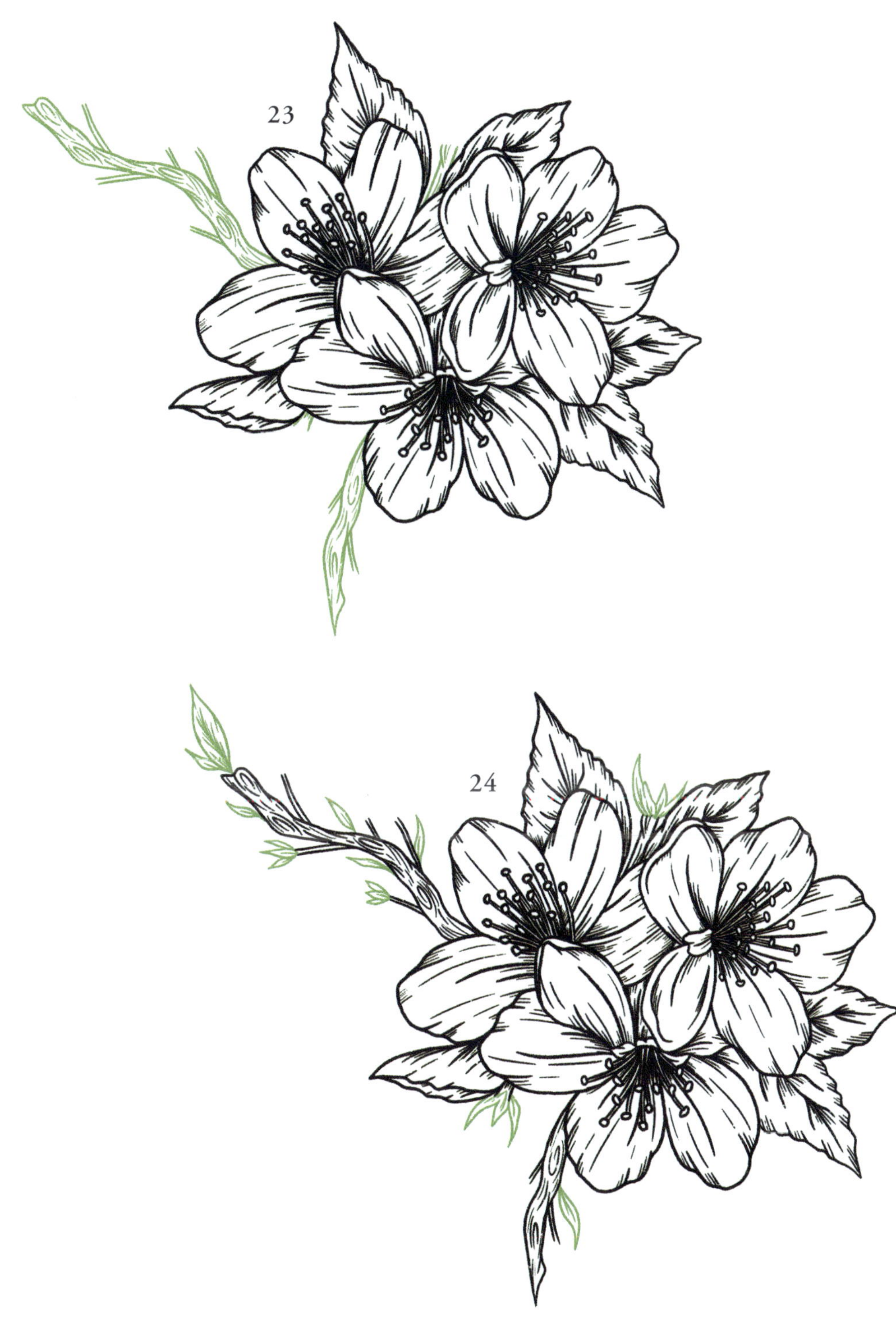

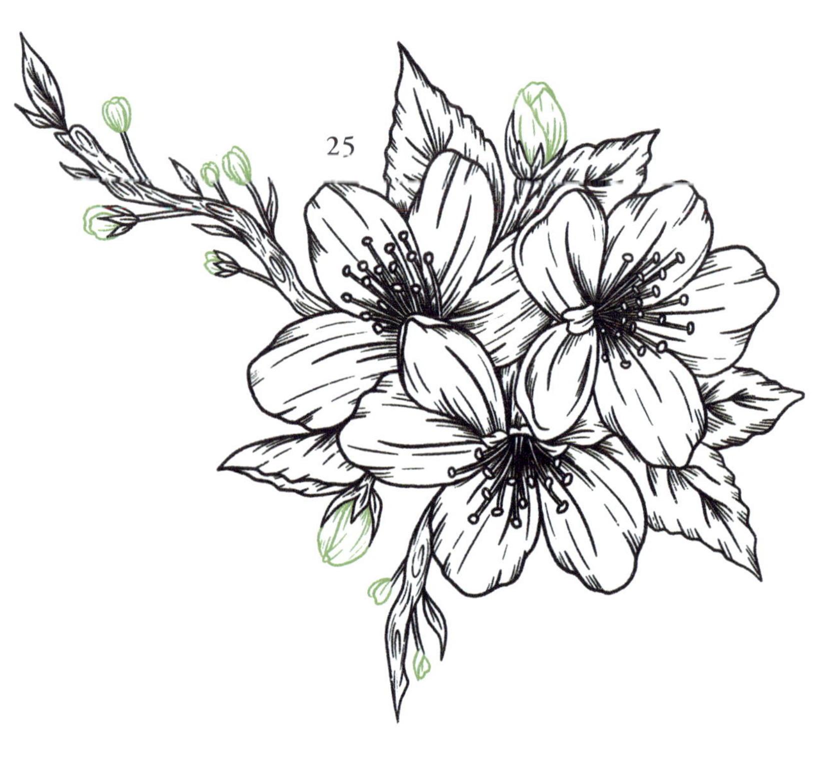

25

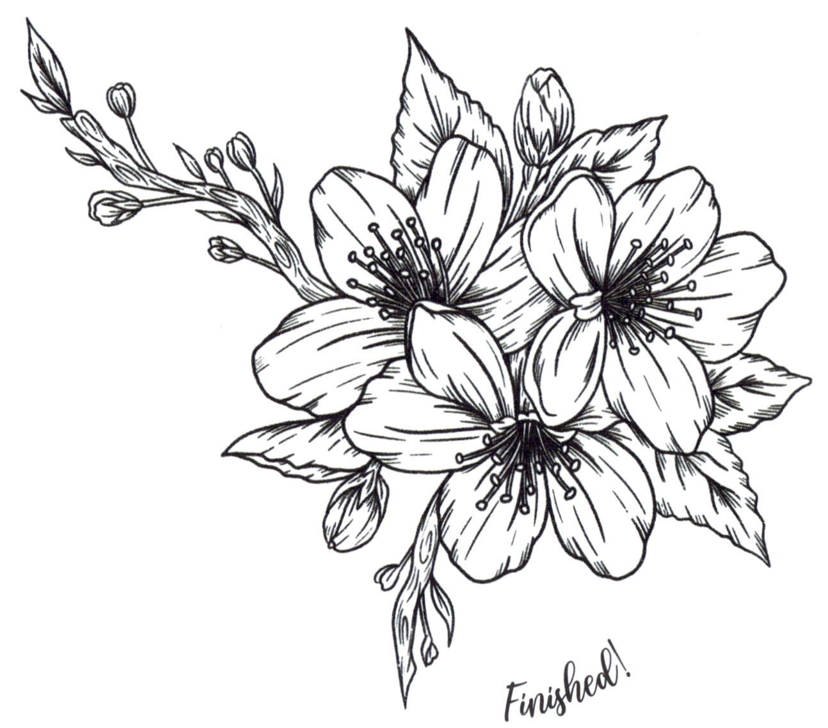

Finished!

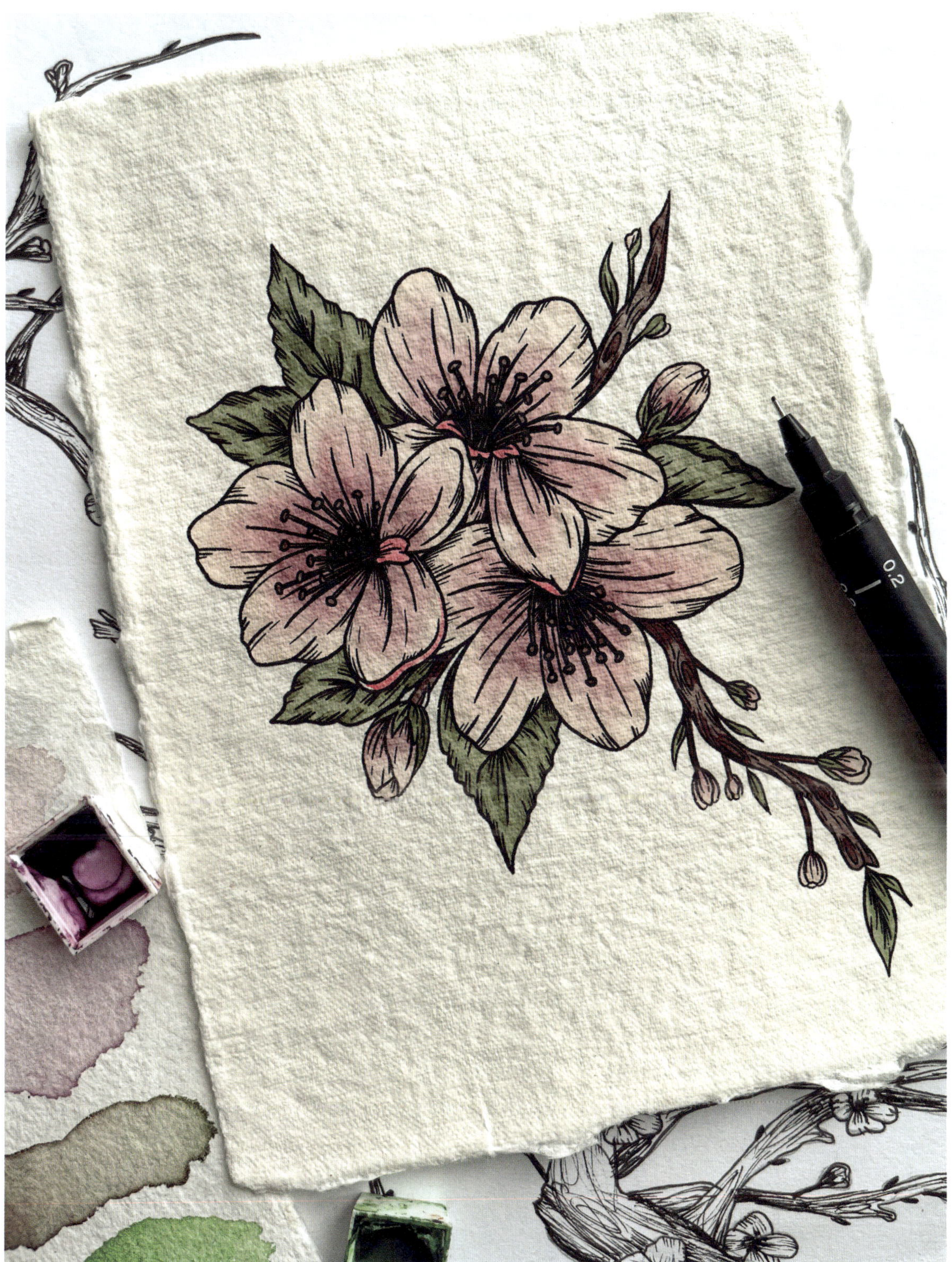

Dahlia

I thought a dahlia would be a good place to end the flower section, with its densely packed flower head that looks almost mandala-like. It's a little more time-consuming to draw, due to the amount of petals.

Once you get into the flow of adding the smaller petals around the centre point, it's actually quite a relaxing flower to draw.

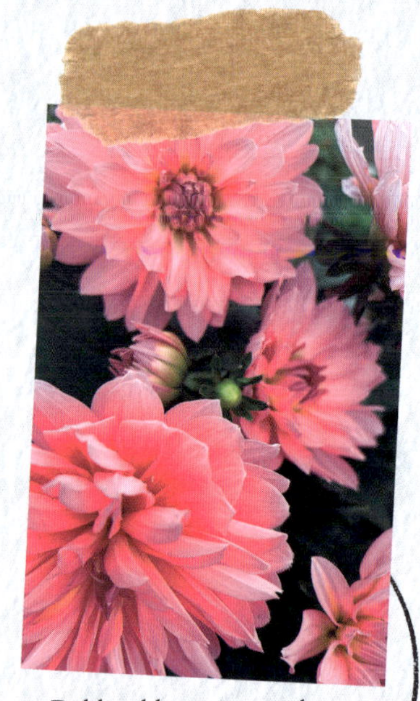

Dahlias bloom in a wide range of hues, so experiment with colour!

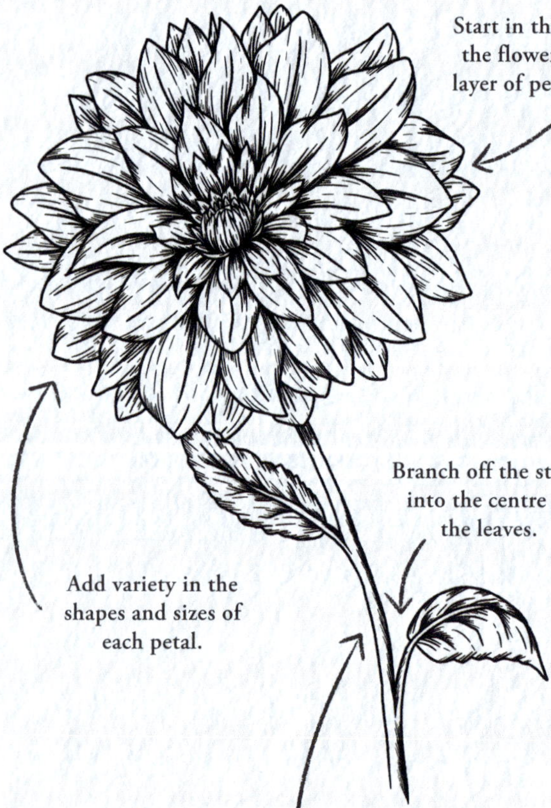

Start in the very centre of the flower and add each layer of petals from there.

Add variety in the shapes and sizes of each petal.

Branch off the stem, into the centre of the leaves.

Draw a slight curve in the stem, to emphasize the weight of the flower head.

Try adding colour

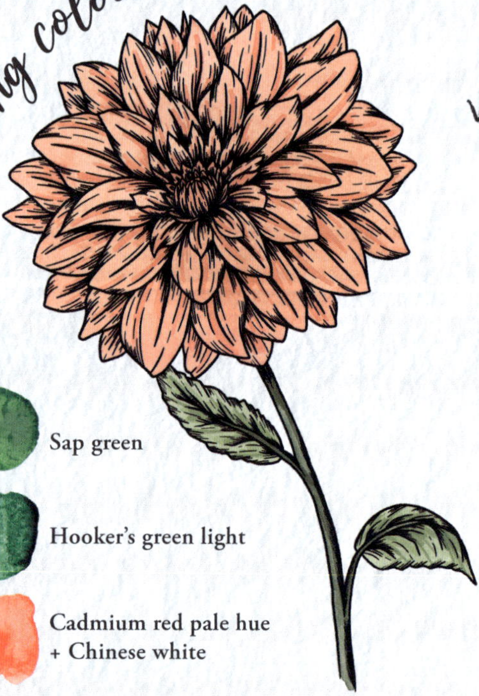

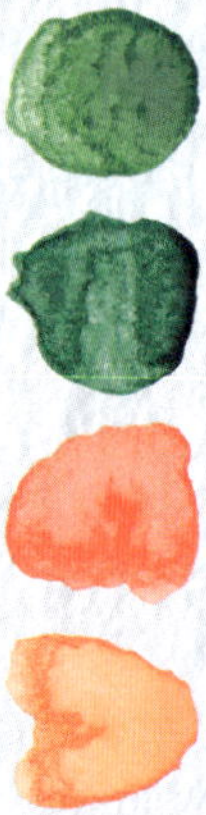

Sap green

Hooker's green light

Cadmium red pale hue + Chinese white

Cadmium orange hue + Chinese white

FLOWER HEAD OUTLINES

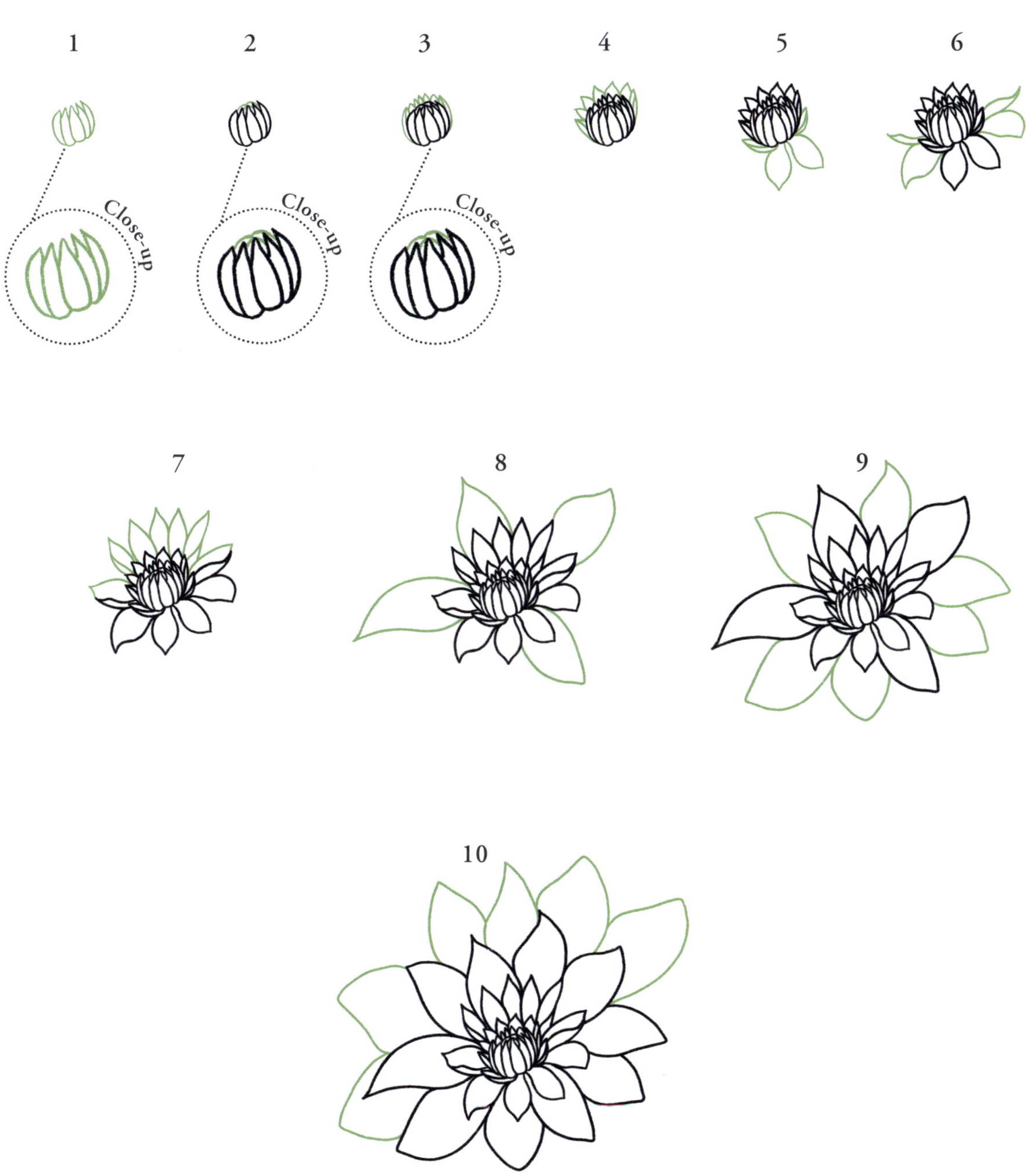

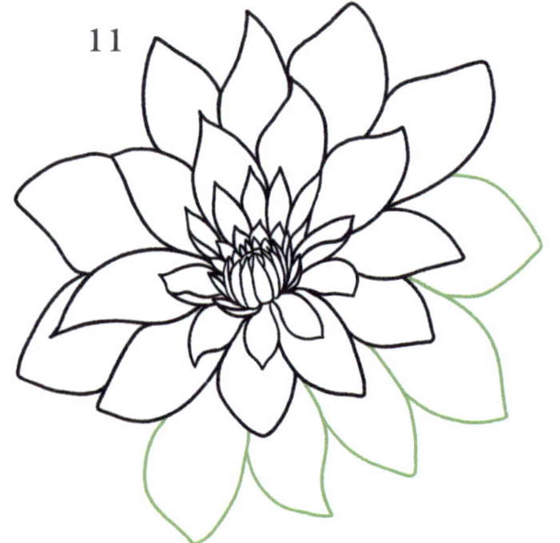

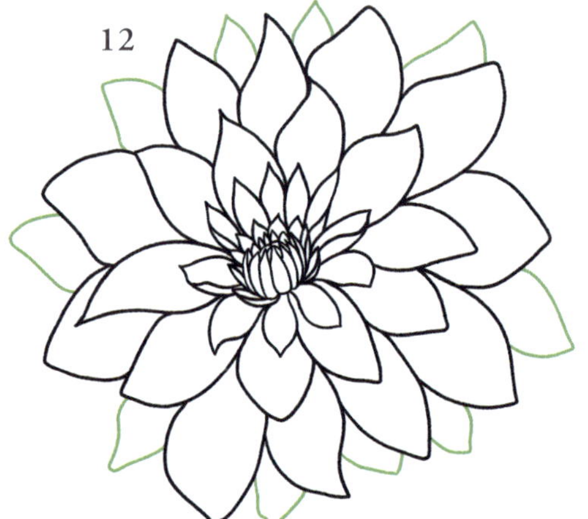

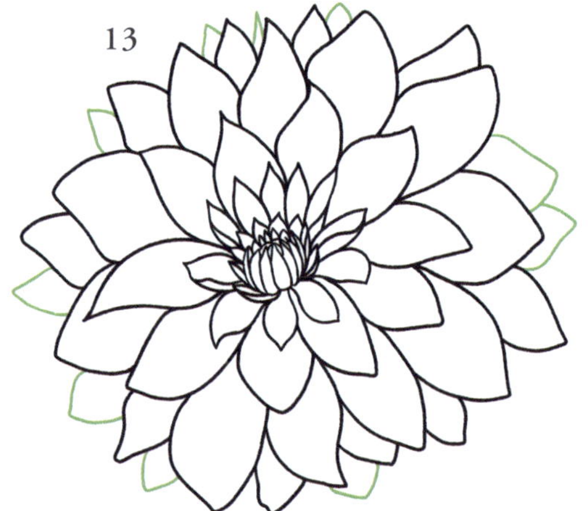

FLOWER HEAD DETAIL

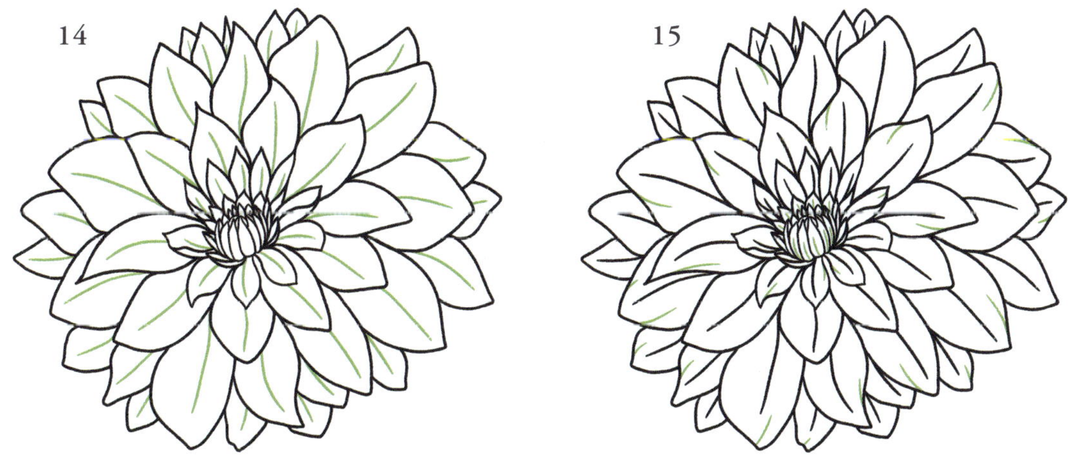

FLOWER HEAD SHADING

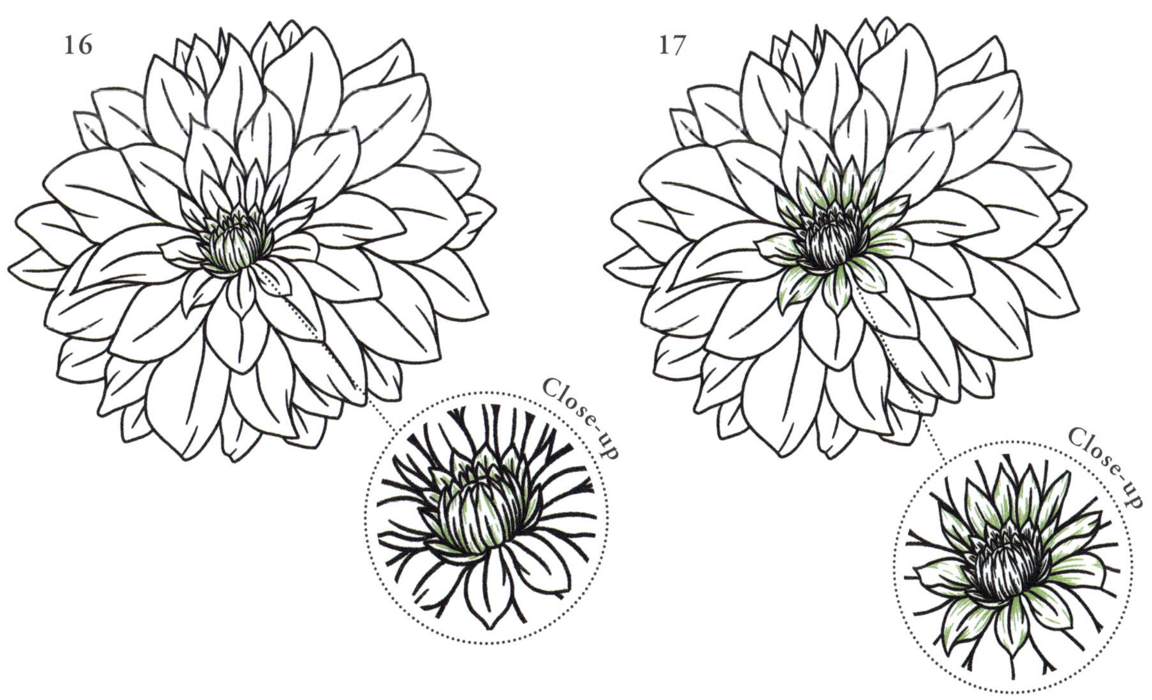

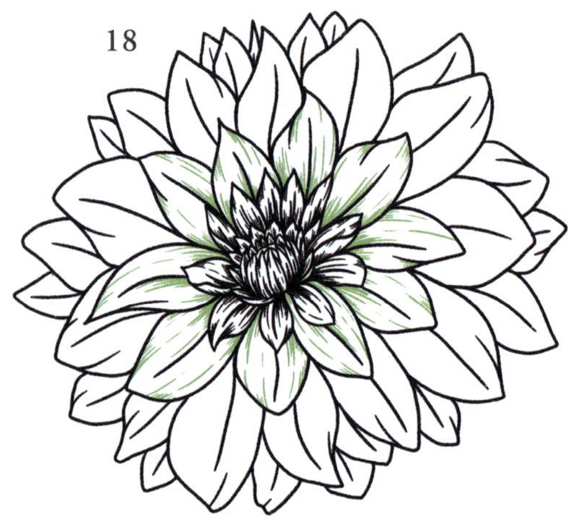

18

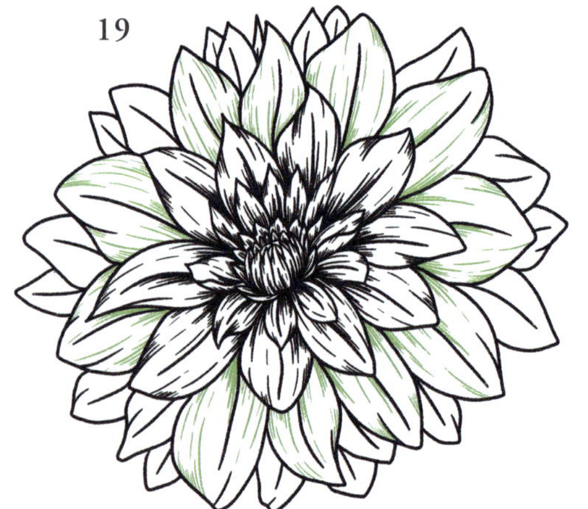

19

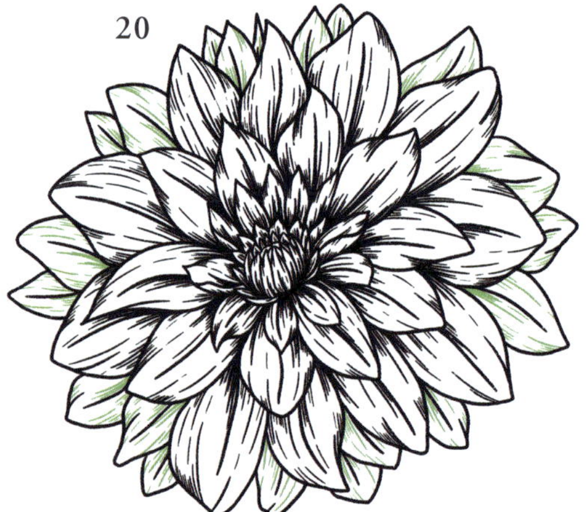

20

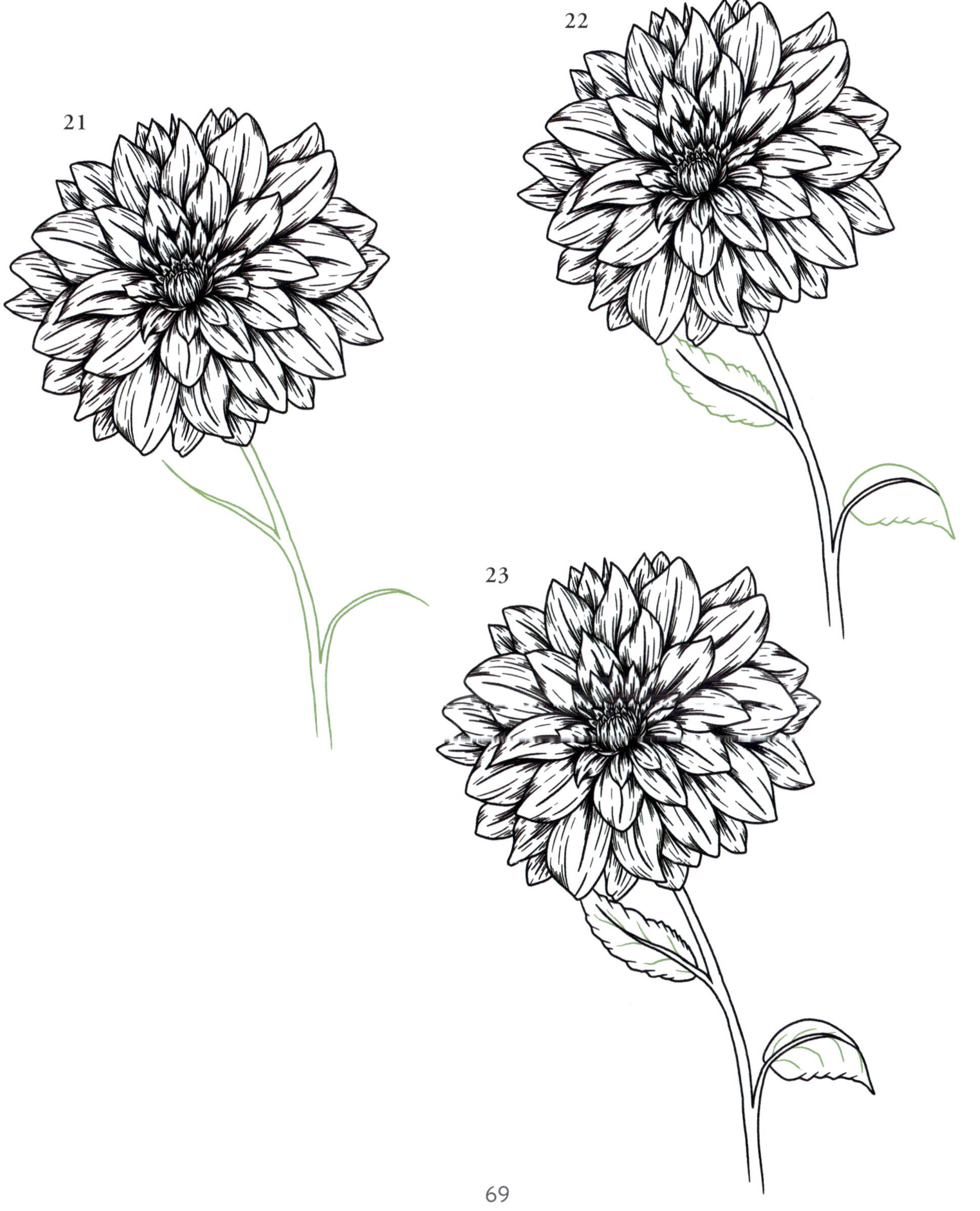

21
22
23

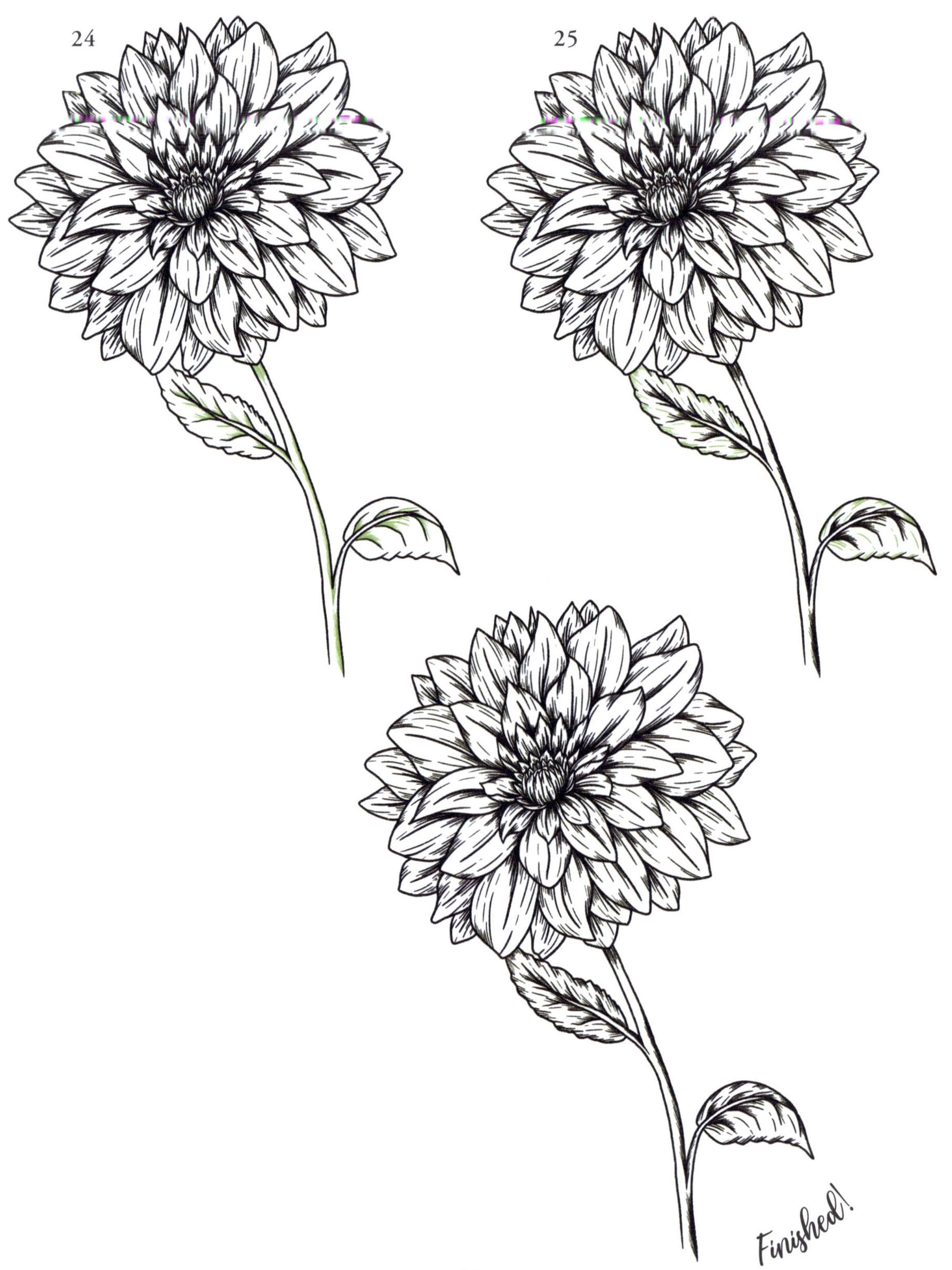
24
25
Finished!

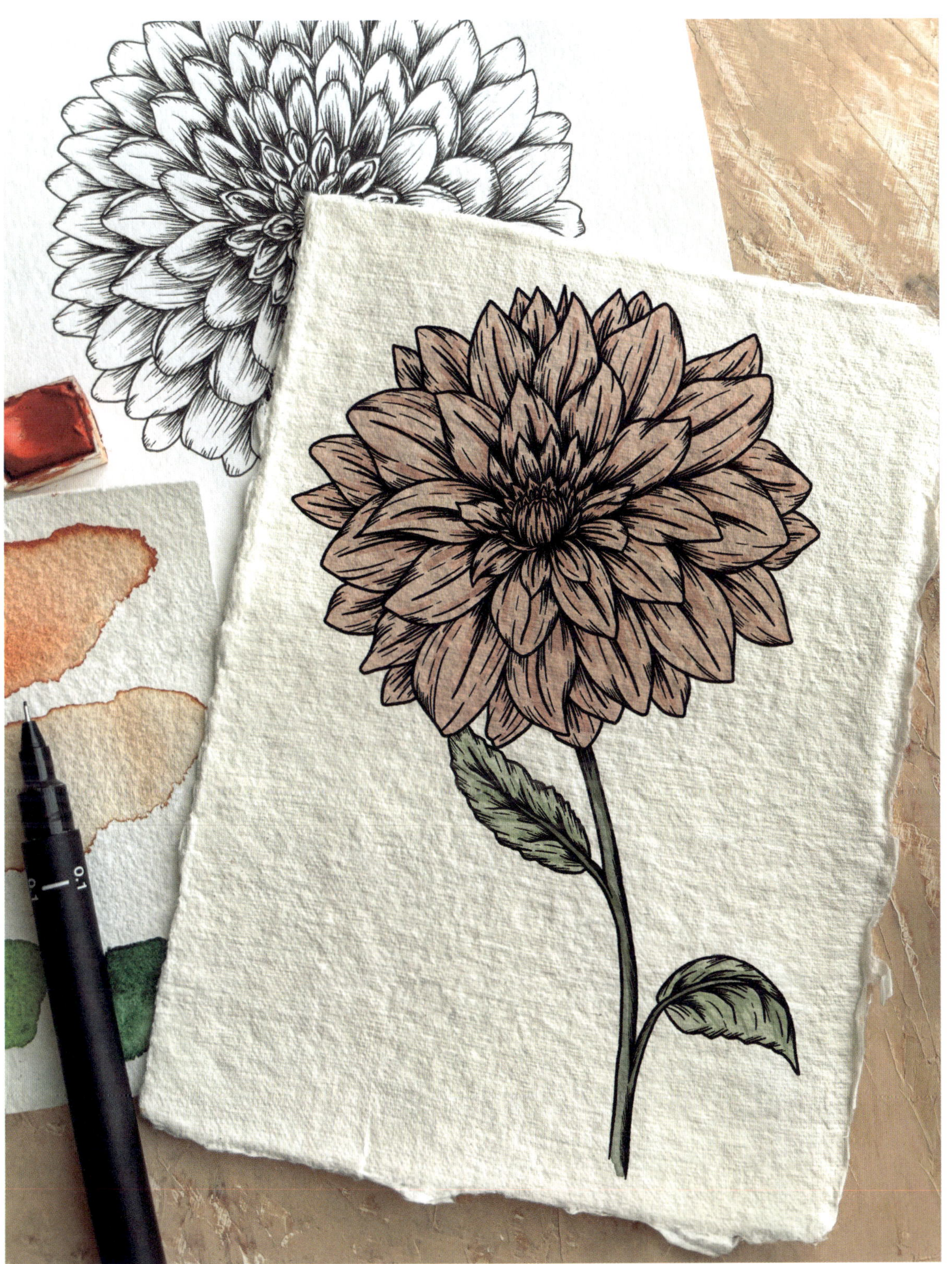

Insects

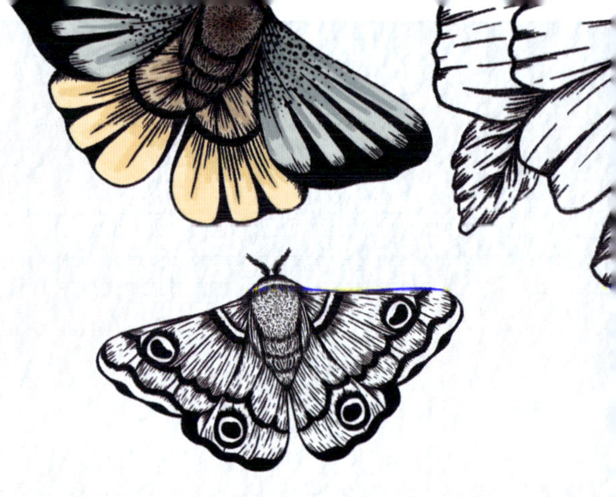

Insects are a great way to bridge the gap between drawing flowers and starting to develop towards birds and animals. They're also a great way to start learning limbs, smaller details and textures.

Within this section you'll start to learn techniques to draw textured details and wings, ahead of progressing onto drawing birds, which are a little more complex.

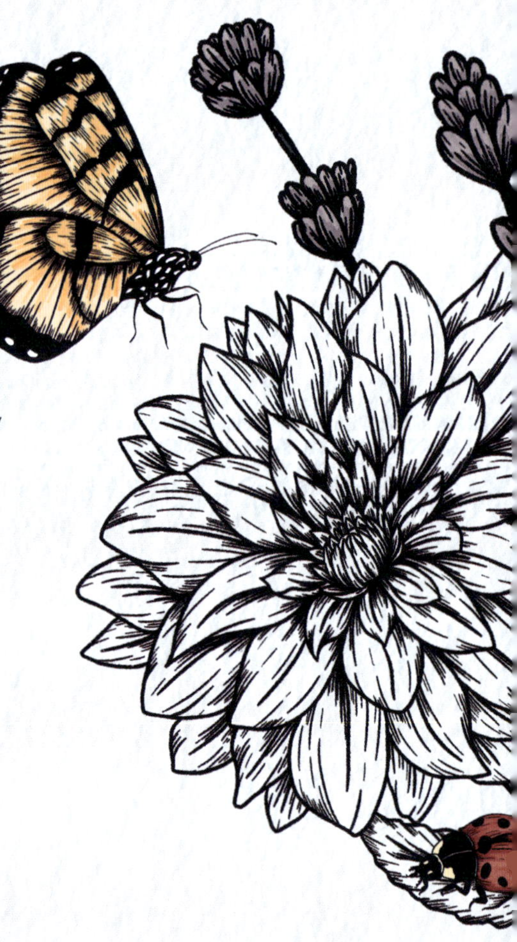

Top tips for drawing insects

- ◆ Once you're ready to get a bit more creative with your style of drawing, you can end up with so many different outcomes – just by changing some details after drawing your outline.

- ◆ Try drawing just the outline and playing around with the details on the body and especially the wings. Draw anything in these spaces that you can dream up to enjoy a unique outcome each time.

- ◆ If you're drawing digitally, making use of symmetrical drawing functions can be a fun way to draw insects from a top-down perspective, making them same on both sides, such as the beetle and moth.

Insect drawing techniques

Practise your shading pen strokes

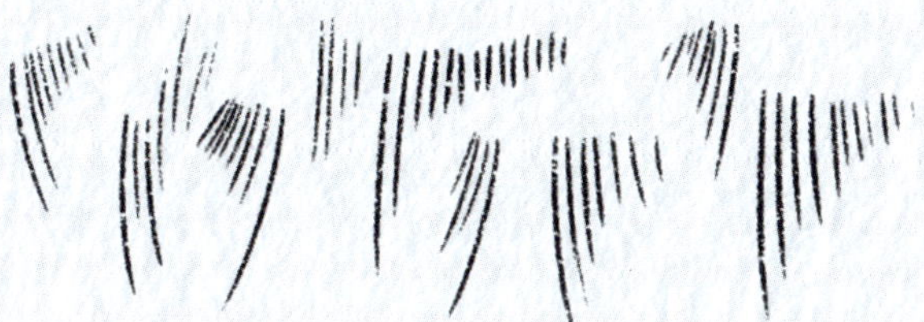

Using the tapered pen strokes learnt when drawing flowers (see page 10), loosen your hand and practise drawing these even quicker. Try a range of angled directions, curving from the left and the right, as well as straight lines.

Think about where shading would be most natural

As a general rule, envisage where the least amount of light would hit the insect. This would usually be closest to any joints in the limbs or overlaps in sections of the body. These areas would naturally be darkest and are a good place to add your shading pen strokes.

Be sure to follow the curvature of the area when adding pen strokes, to make the shading blend in and look as natural as possible. The green lines shown on the beetle opposite, illustrate the general areas to focus your darkest shaded points.

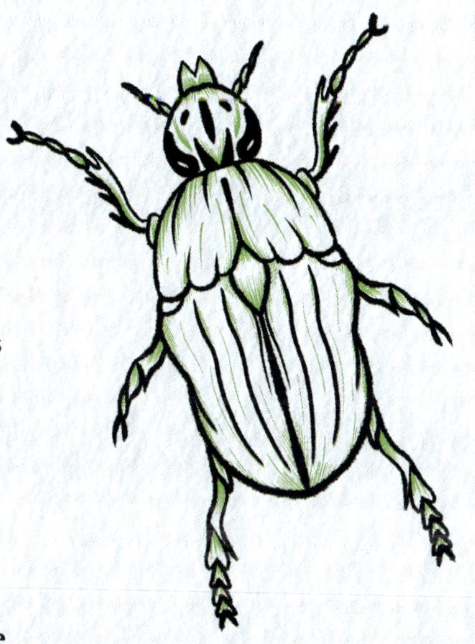

Add new textures and details with a stippling technique

Stippling is an easy way to add more natural shading, while also adding variations in texture and detail. For a fairly simple technique, the results can look a lot more complex.

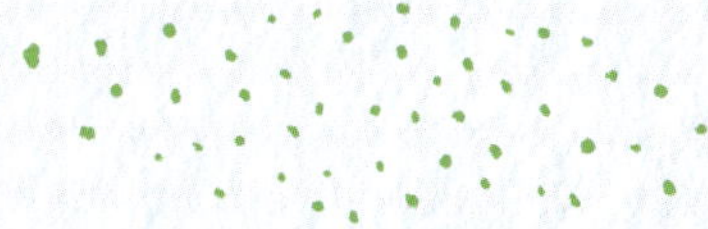

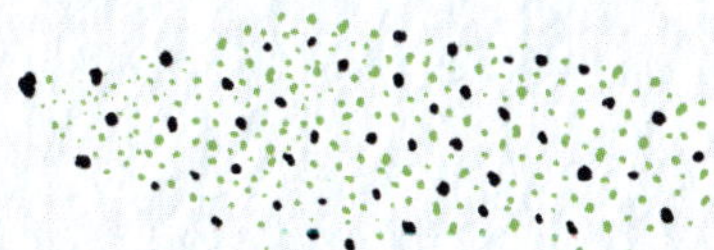

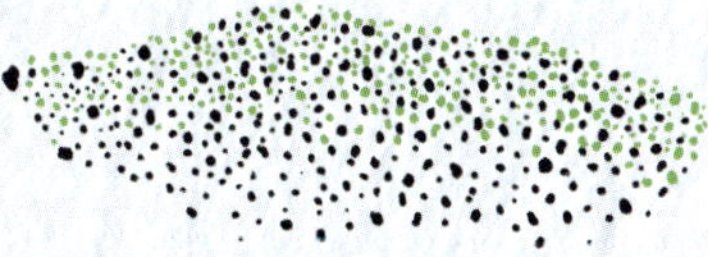

1. Start with a few dots that vary in size, across the whole surface area you wish to fill.

2. Add in more dots to fill the spaces in-between, making sure these are scattered randomly, not in a pattern.

3. Reduce the amount of dots towards the edges you'd like to be less solid to create a bit of a fade.

Ladybird

This ladybird project is a great place to start drawing insects and can be achieved in just 12 steps.

I like to add ladybirds to my floral compositions. A great place to add them is resting on the leaves of your flowers.

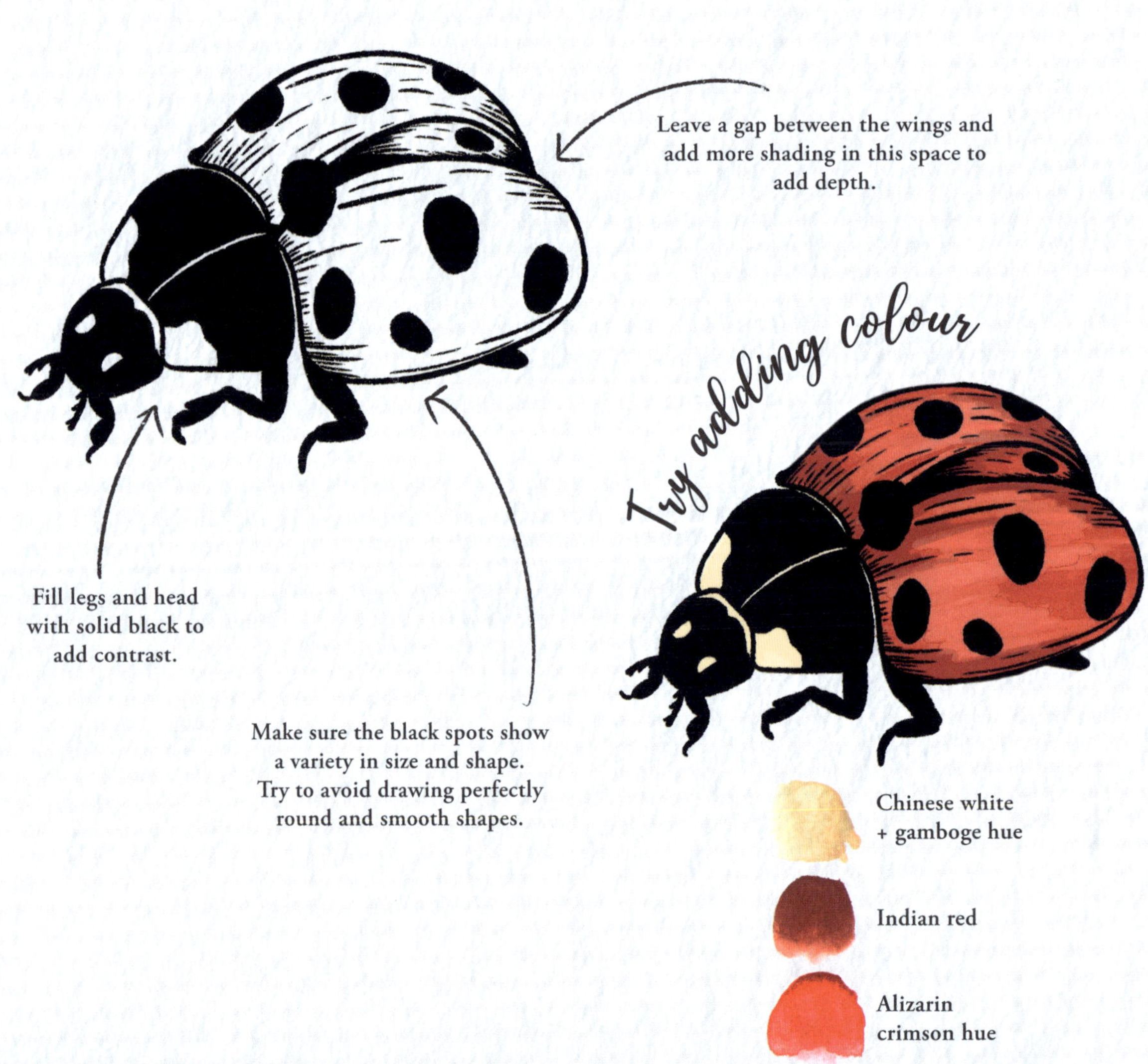

OUTLINE

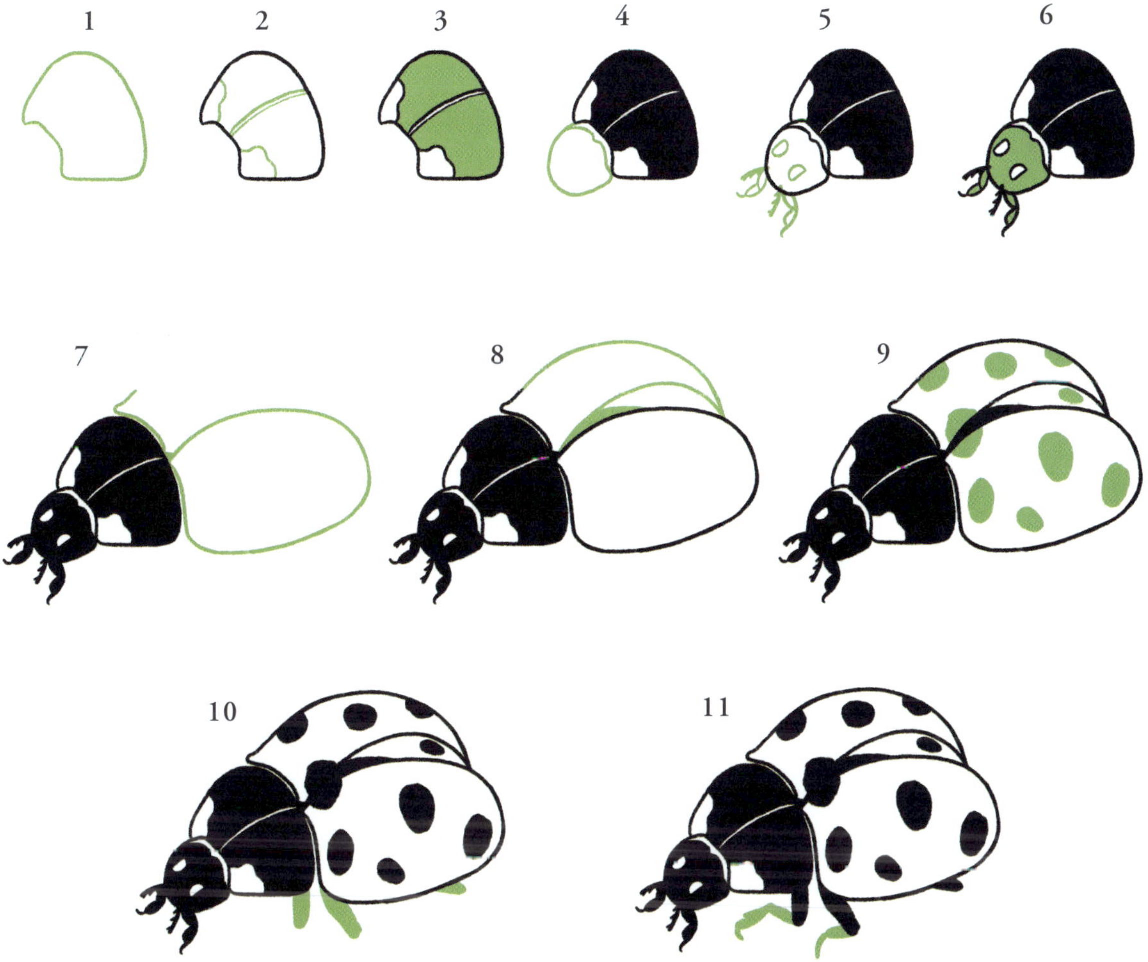

1 2 3 4 5 6

7 8 9

10 11

SHADING

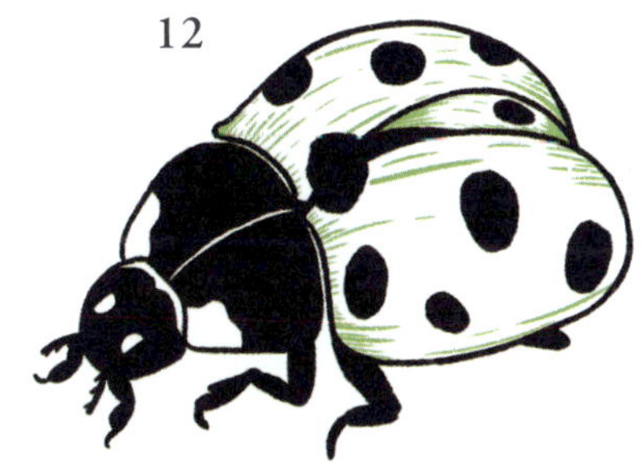

12

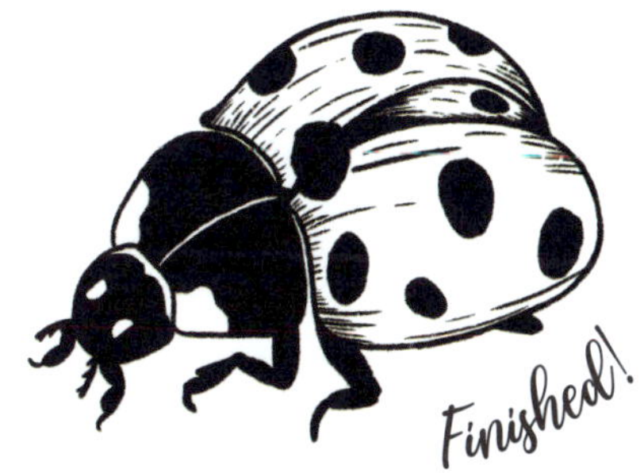

75

Beetle

Drawing a beetle from a top-down view is a fun angle to start to experiment with more illustrative, playful details. It does require you to keep a good balance with the symmetry though, which requires a bit of practice to mirror your lines.

I'll show you three variation ideas that you can try once you've drawn the outline. Feel free to experiment and fill the outline with your own details too.

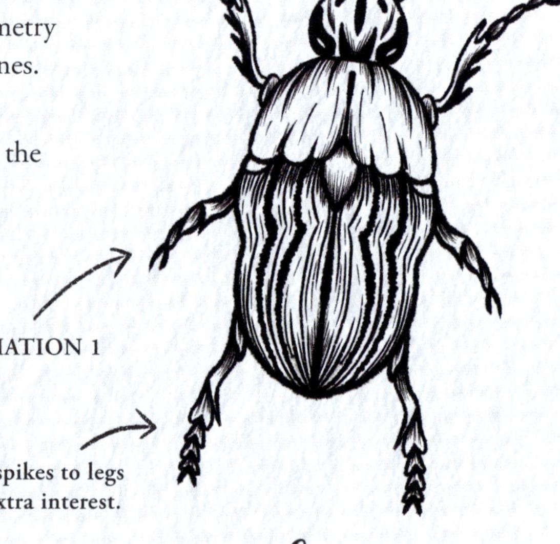

VARIATION 1

Add spikes to legs for extra interest.

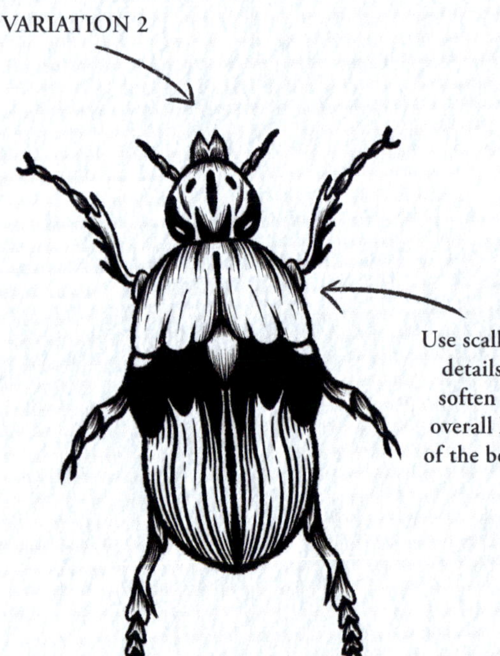

VARIATION 2

Use scalloped details to soften the overall look of the beetle.

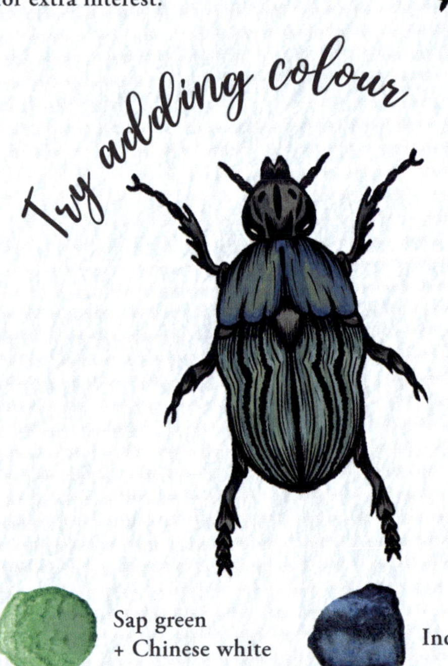

Sap green + Chinese white

Indigo

Prussian blue

Payne's gray

OUTLINE

1

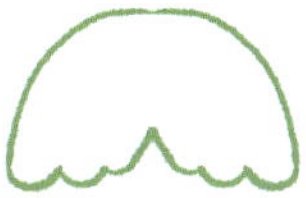

2

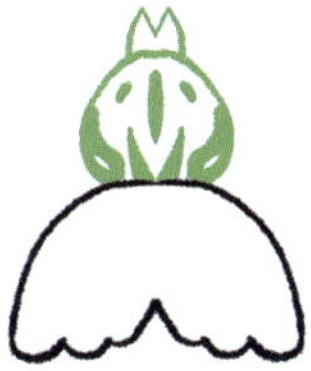

3

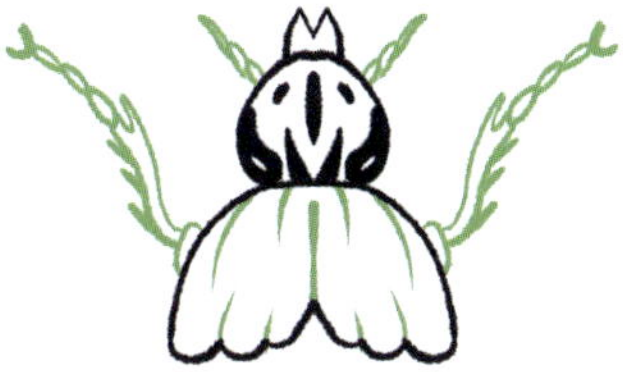

4

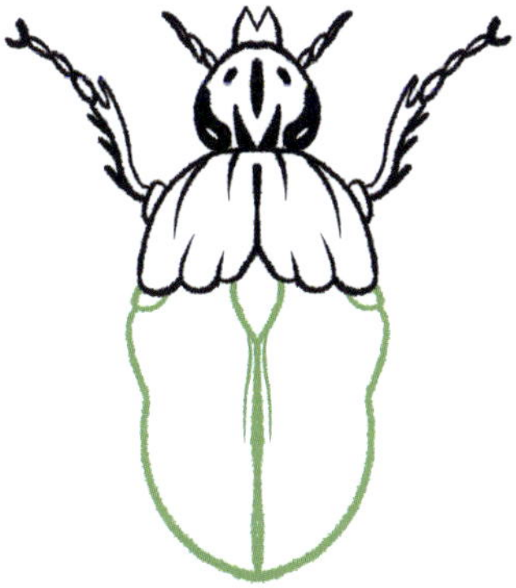

5

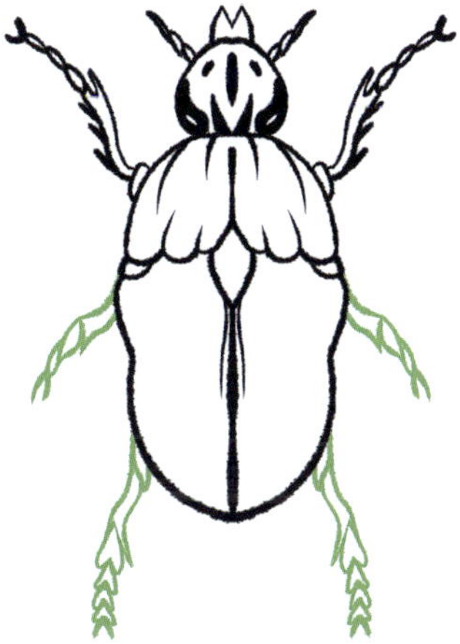

SHADING

6

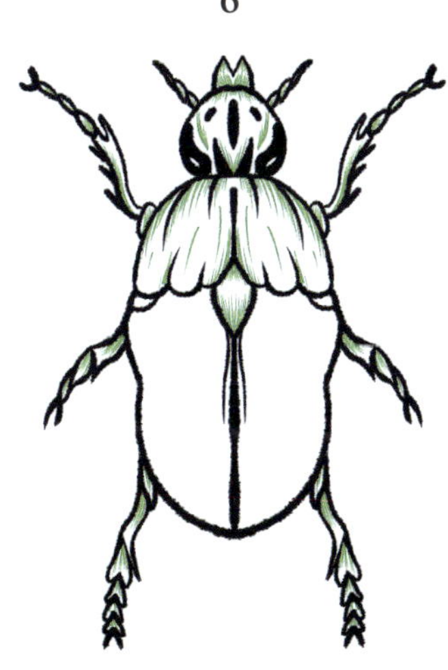

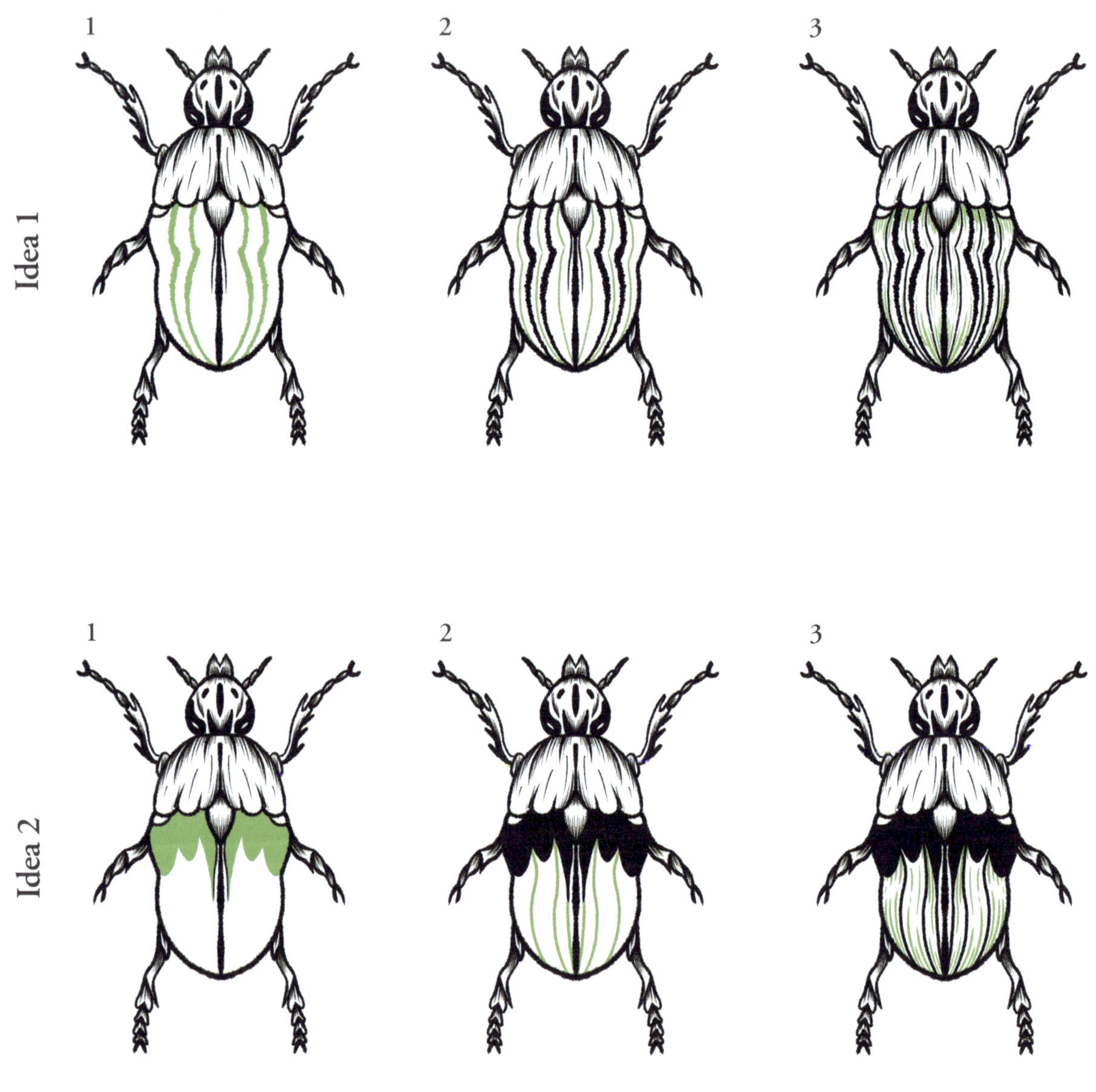

1
2
3
Idea 1
1
2
3
Idea 2

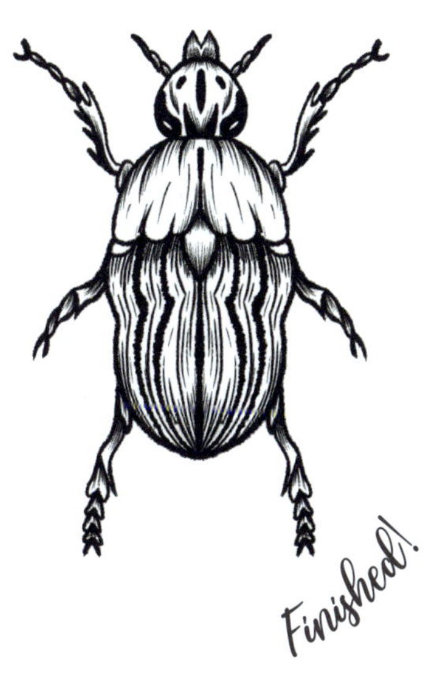

Finished!

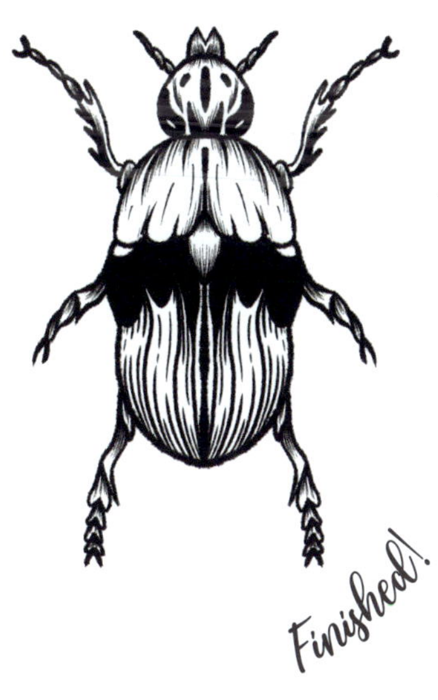

Finished!

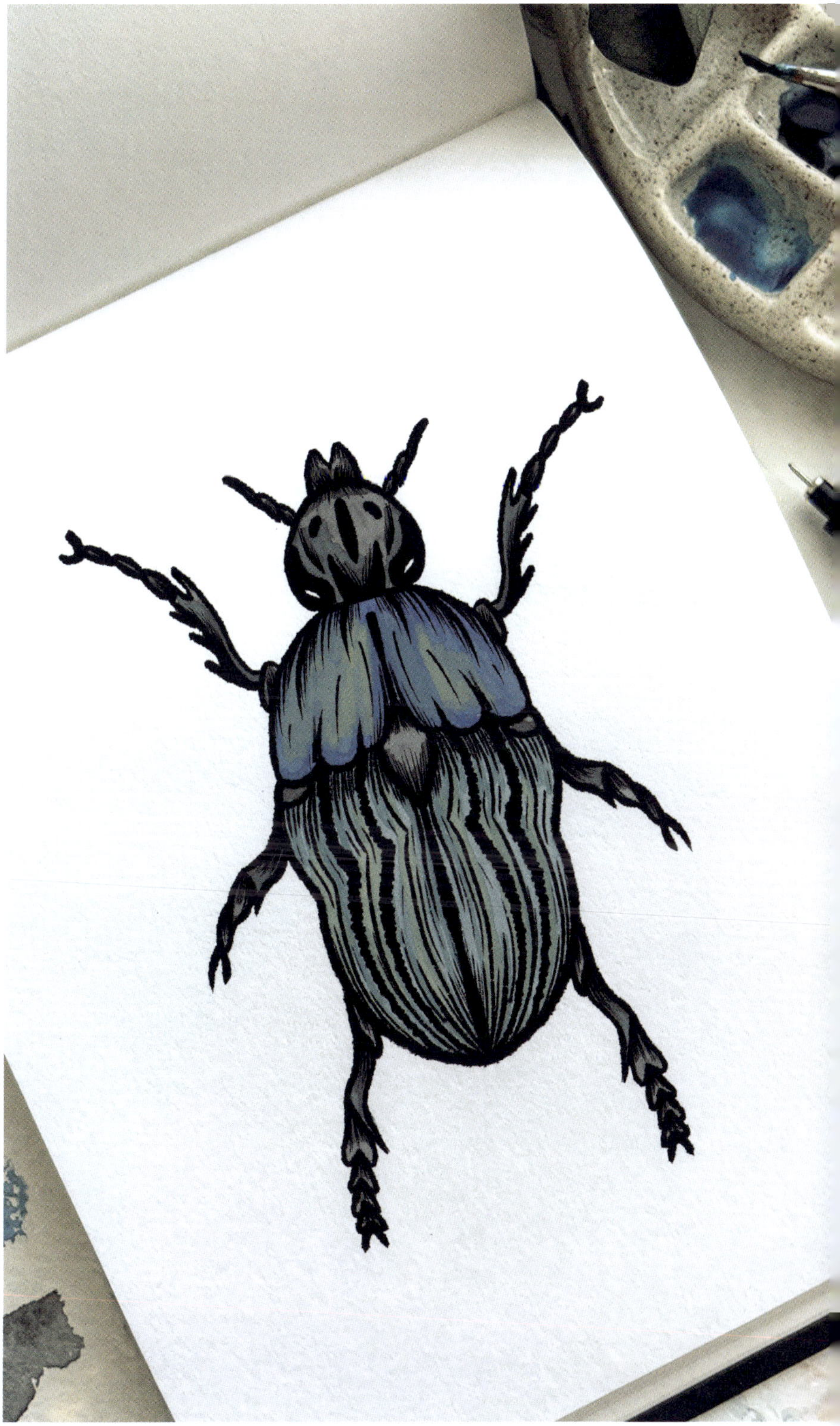

Butterfly

Now you've tried a couple of insect bodies, let's advance and try adding some wings to the features you've learnt so far.

Drawing a butterfly from a side profile first is a great way to learn its features, as the trickiest part of drawing a butterfly with both full wings visible is getting the symmetry accurate enough.

Feel free to experiment and add your own decorative elements inside the wings once the outline is drawn.

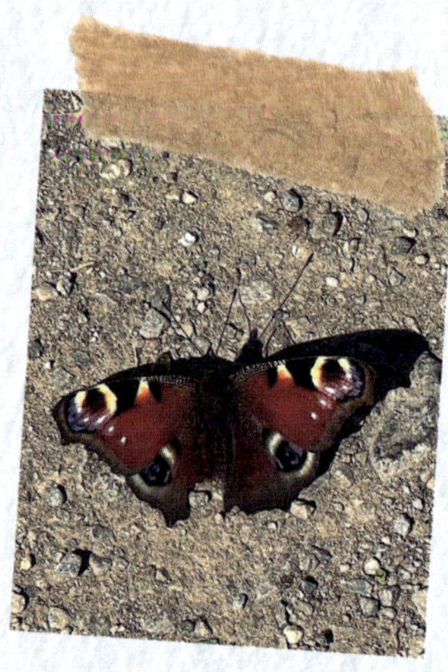

Experiment with different colours and shapes inside the wing outlines. I play with illustrative shapes and patterns when I want to draw something more dreamy.

Add shading within each of the panels.

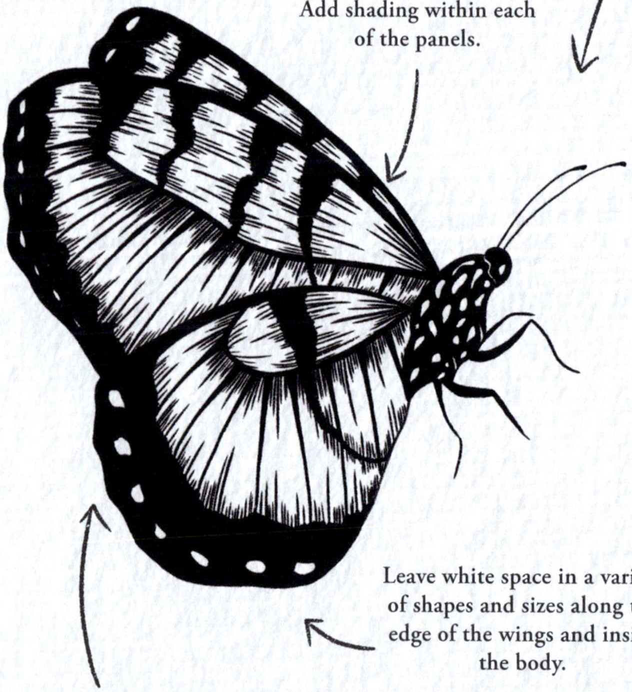

Try adding colour

Leave white space in a variety of shapes and sizes along the edge of the wings and inside the body.

Add scallops along the outside edges of the wings.

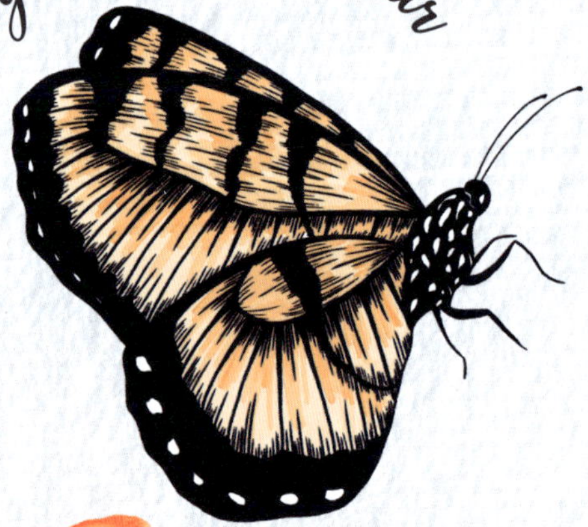

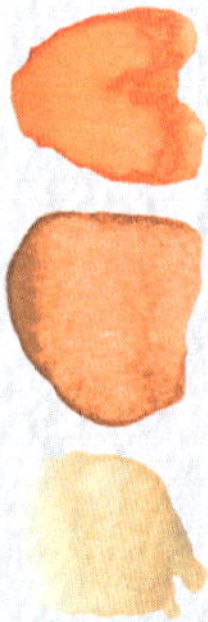

Cadmium orange hue

Burnt sienna

Chinese white + gamboge hue

OUTLINE

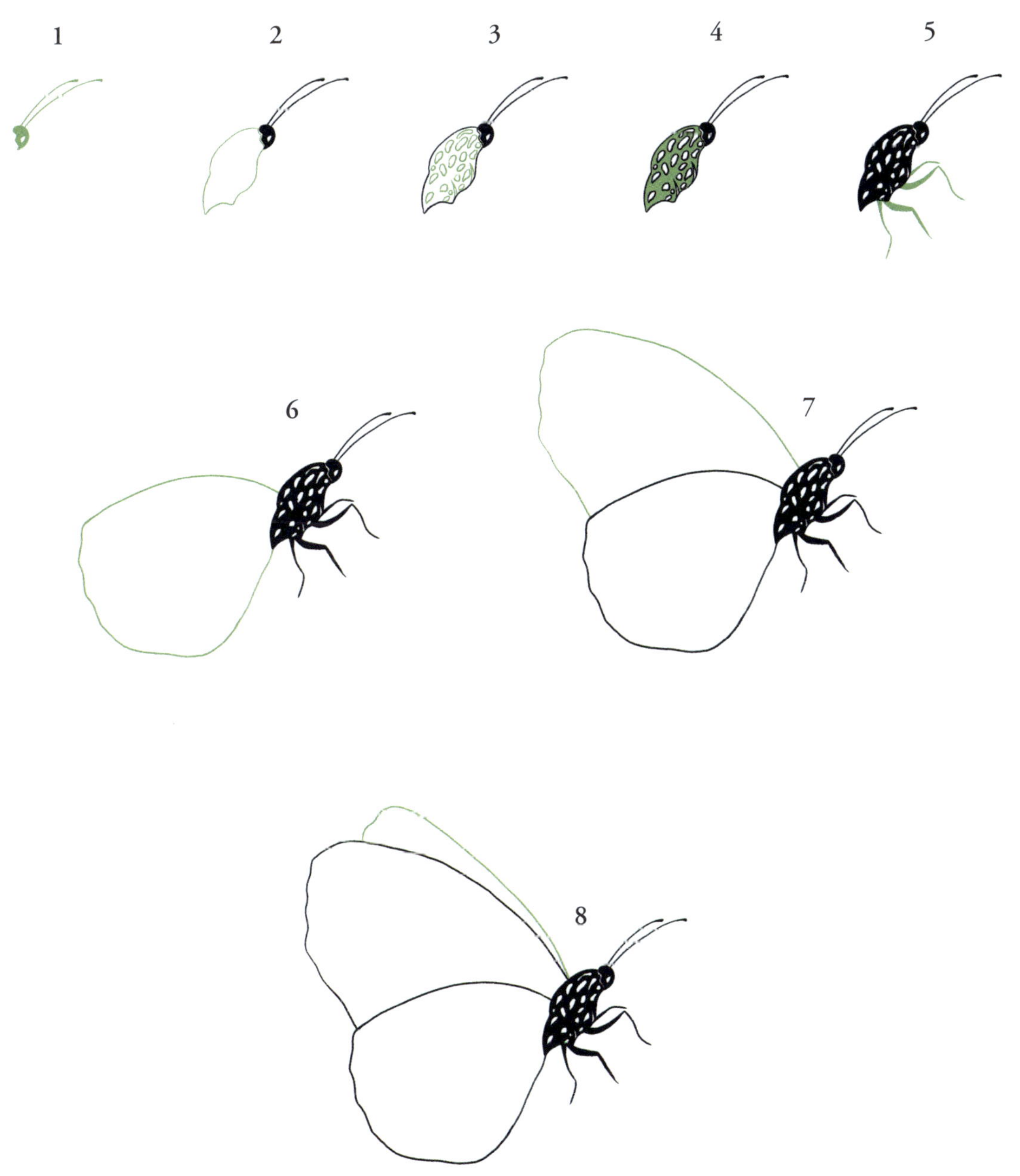

DETAILS

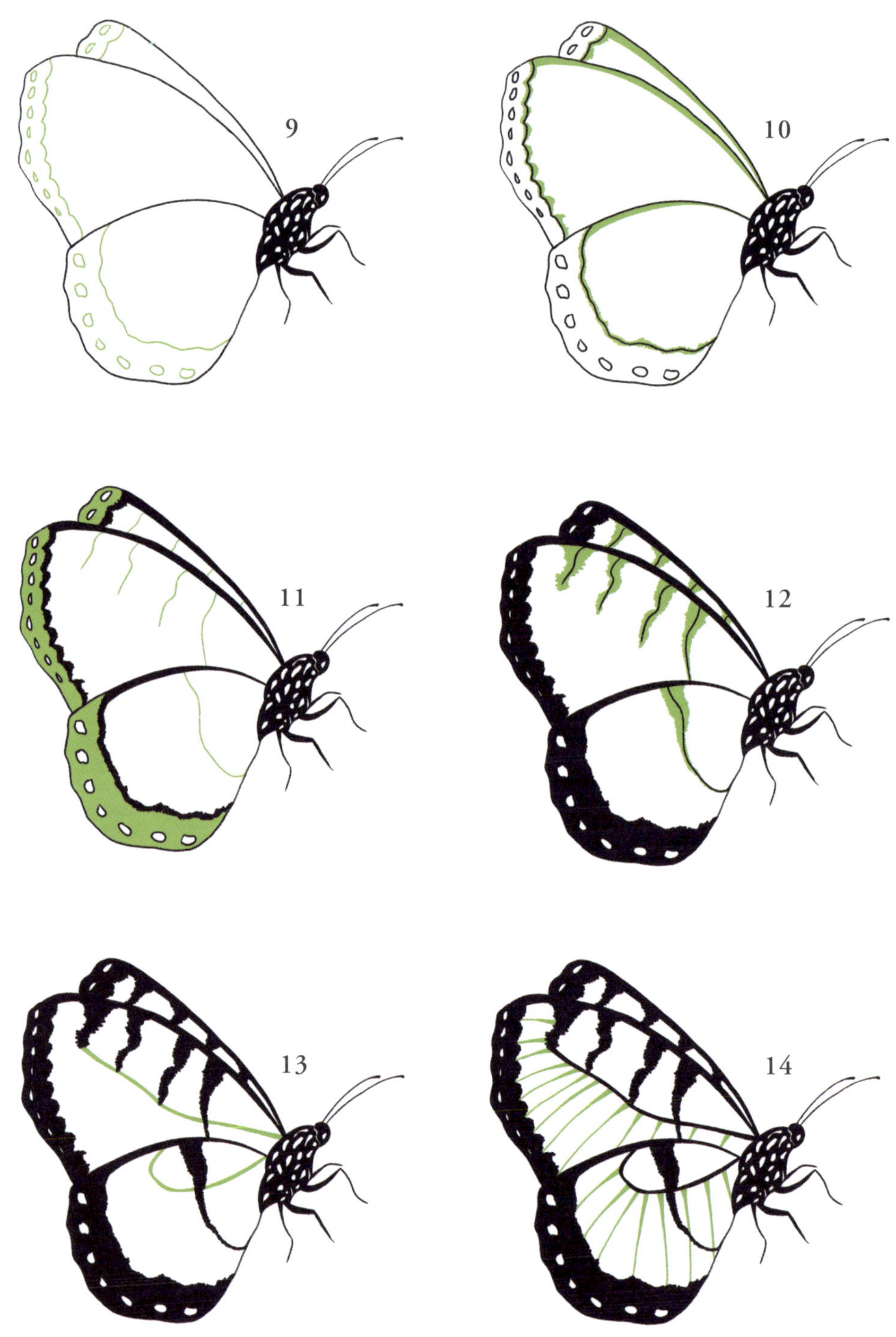

SHADING

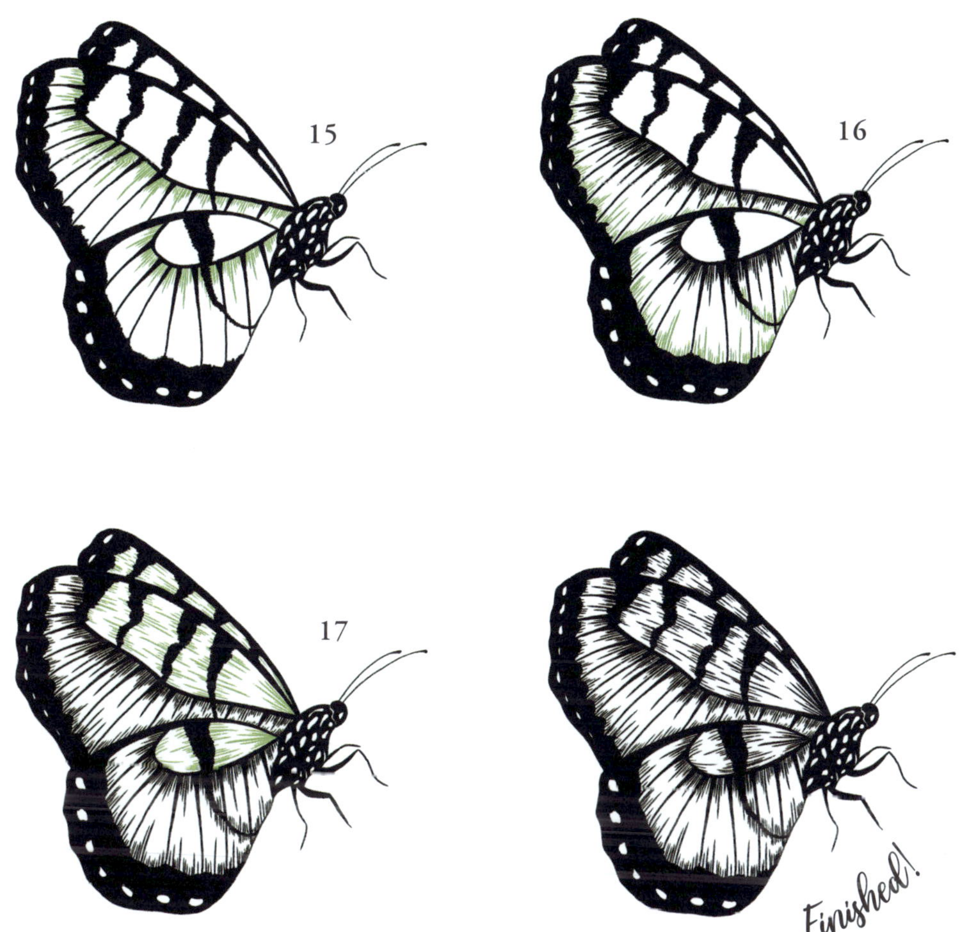

Moth

Now you've had a practice with the butterfly from a side angle, let's give a moth a try, with both wings fully visible.

I'll show you how you can experiment with the decorative elements inside the wing outlines, with two variations. We will also start to look at using pen strokes to add texture that looks furry.

If you draw digitally, try using a symmetry drawing tool to aid you while drawing insects like the moth. It's a lot of fun too!

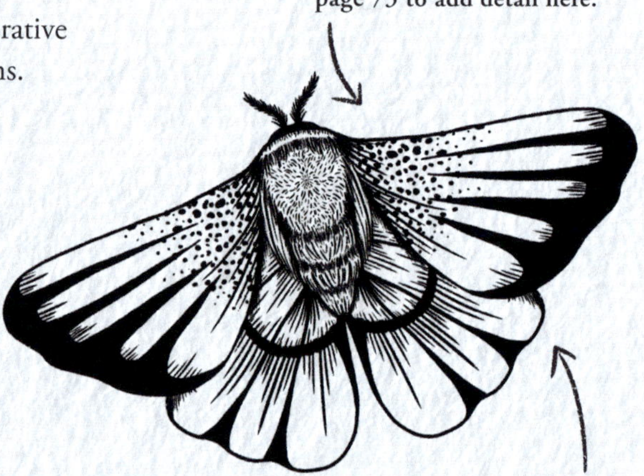

Use the stippling technique from page 73 to add detail here.

VARIATION 1

Use the short-length texture technique from page 93 for the body.

VARIATION 2

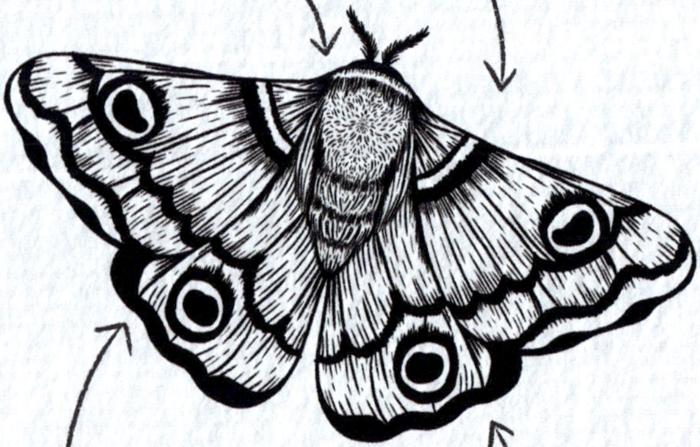

Try adding colour

Experiment with your own decorations inside the wing outlines.

Scallop the outside edges of each wing.

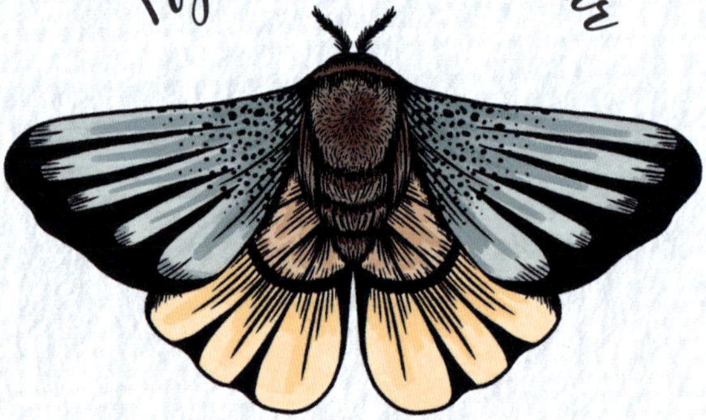

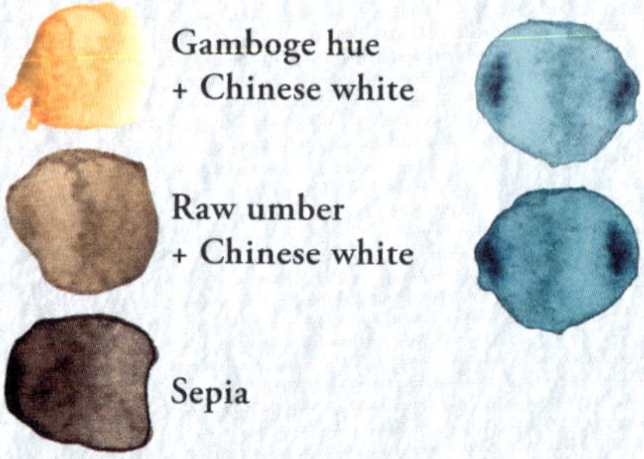

Gamboge hue + Chinese white

Raw umber + Chinese white

Sepia

Prussian blue + Chinese white

Prussian blue

BODY AND WING OUTLINES

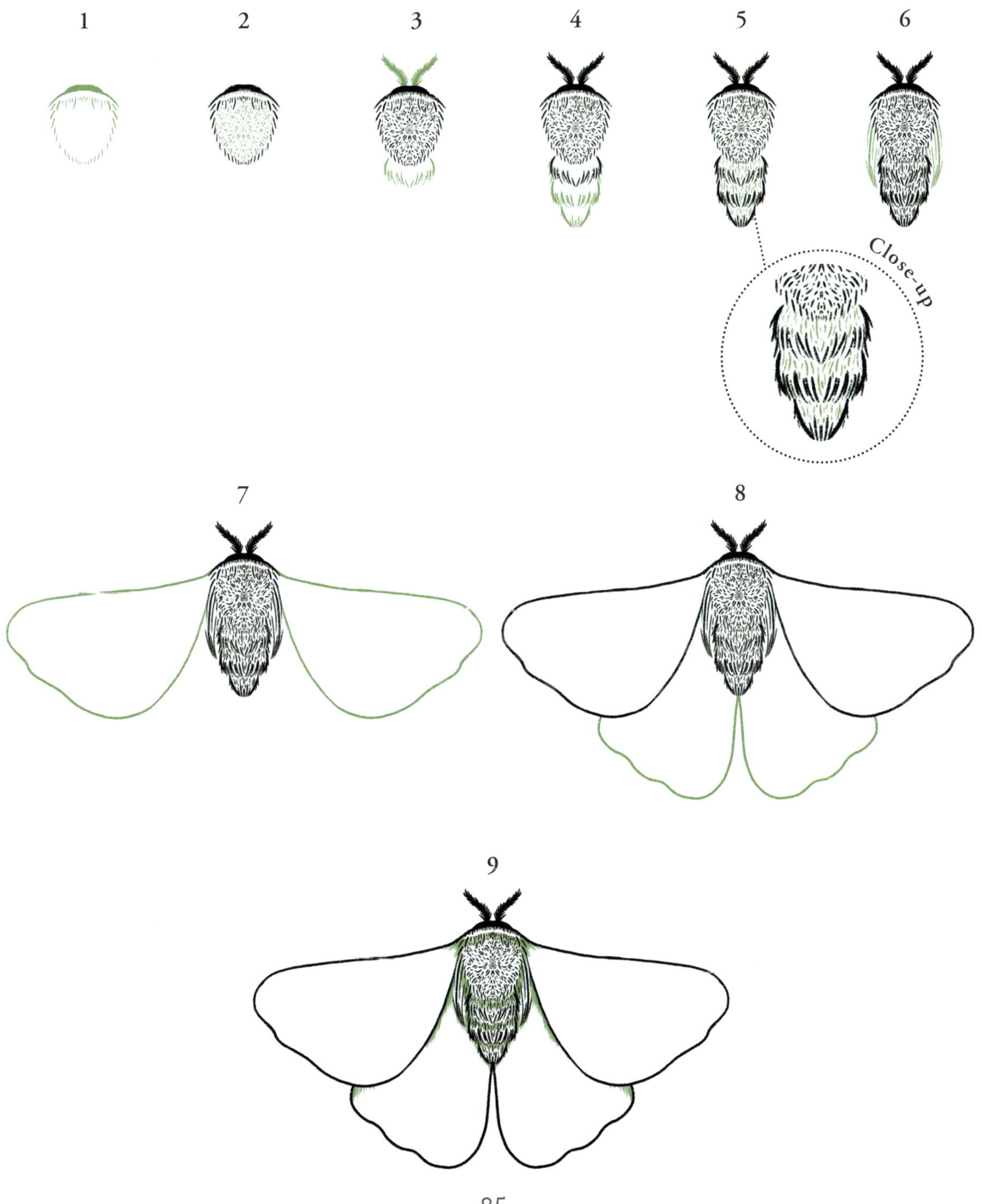

VARIATIONS

Idea 1

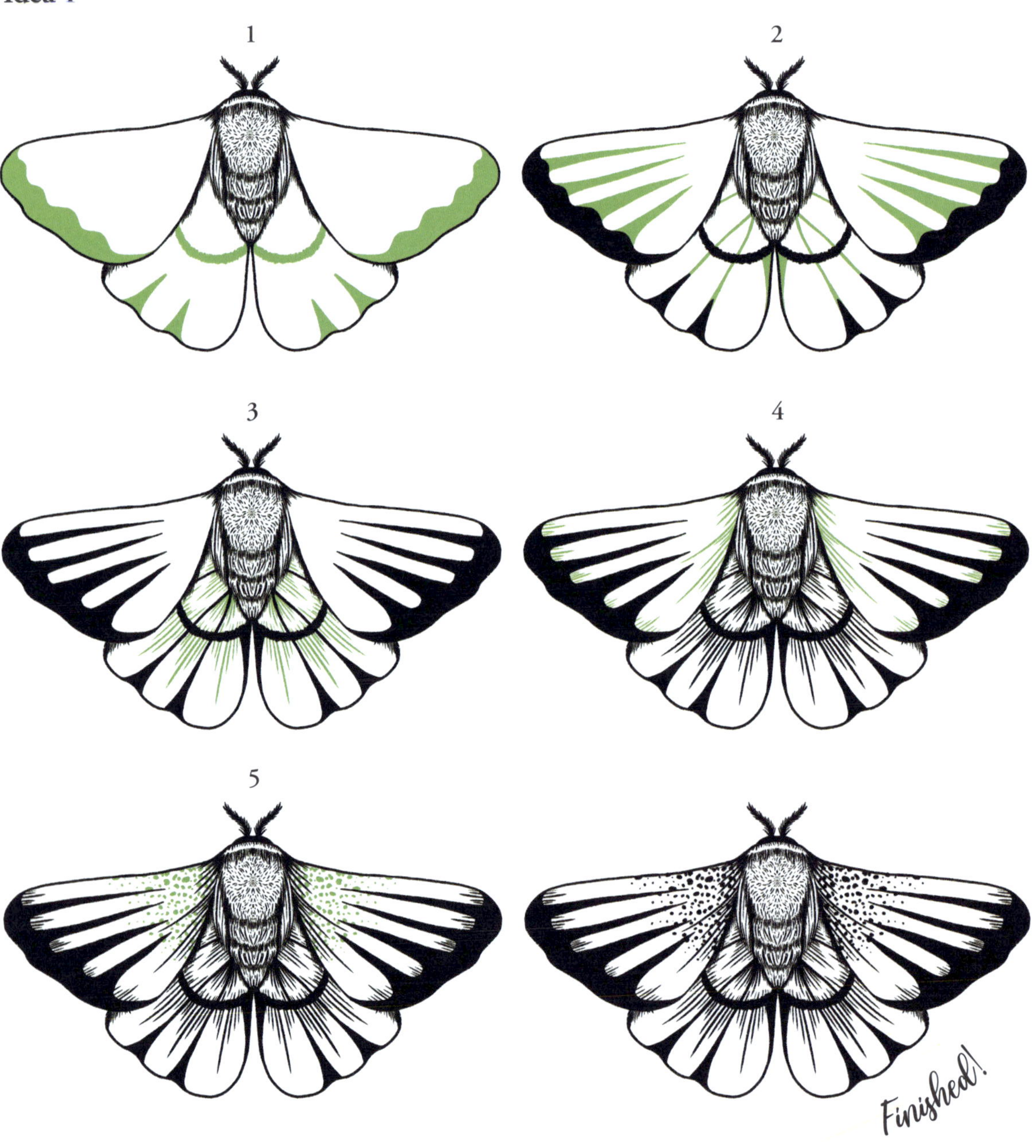

Idea 2

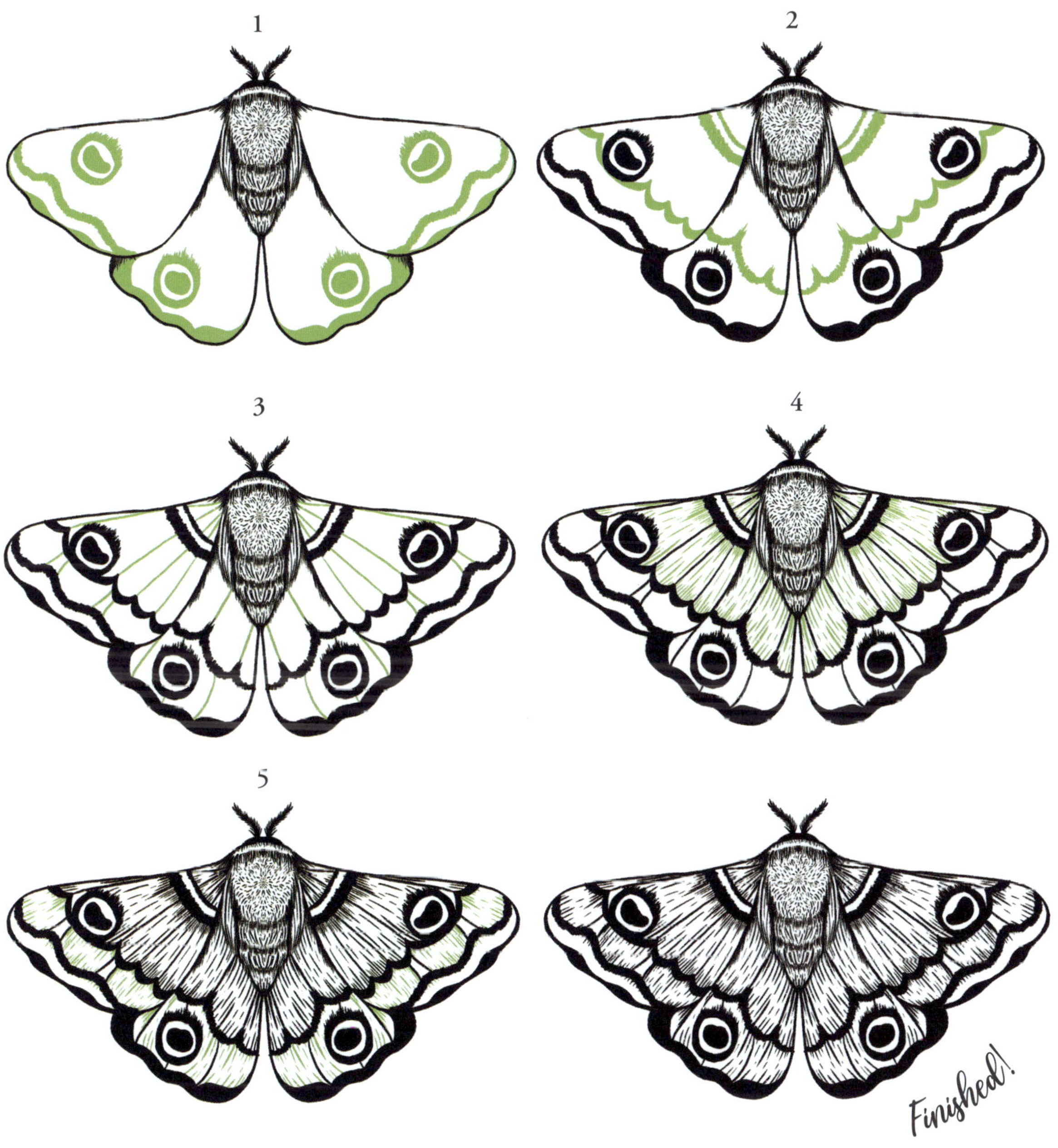

Bumblebee

The last insect we will try is a bumblebee, before advancing on to drawing birds. The small body means we need to try and pack a lot of fine details in to bring out its features.

We will start from the eye, to help shape the head, and draw the rest of the body from there. We will build on the texture pen stroke techniques introduced when drawing the moth, to create an even fluffier look, which we'll also use when drawing birds and animals.

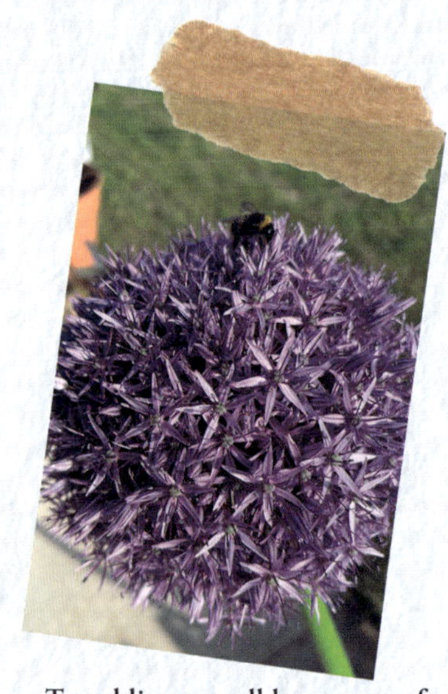

Use the long-length texture technique from page 107 for the top of the head.

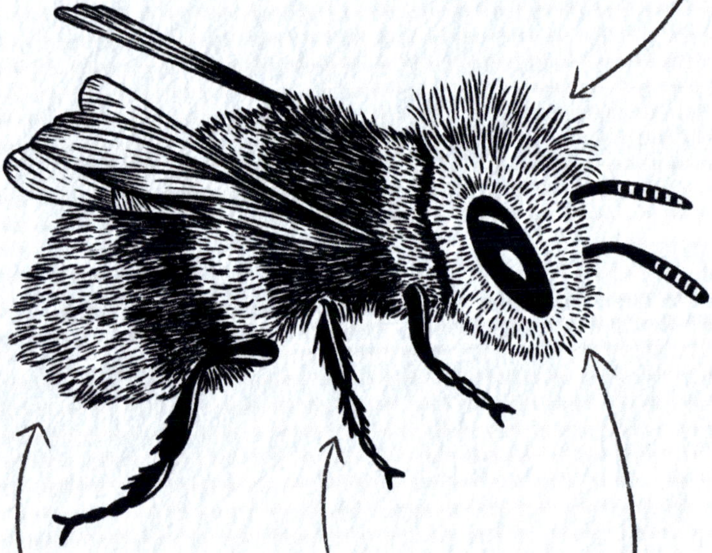

Try adding a small bee to one of your flower drawings. I love to add them flying away from or towards the flower.

Try adding colour

The legs have a similar structure to the beetle's (see page 76).

Use the rough textured technique from page 107 for the body.

Use the short-length texture technique from page 93 for the head.

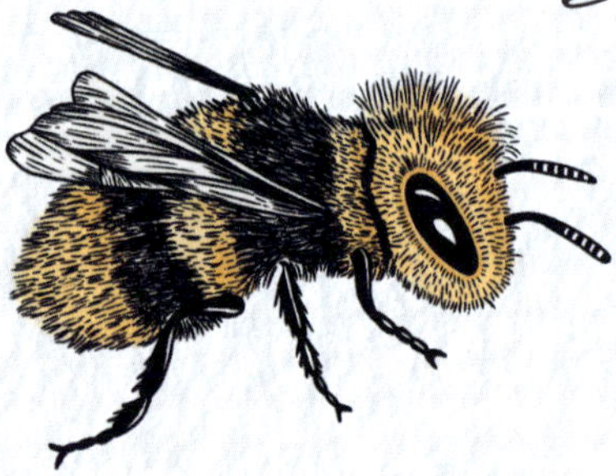

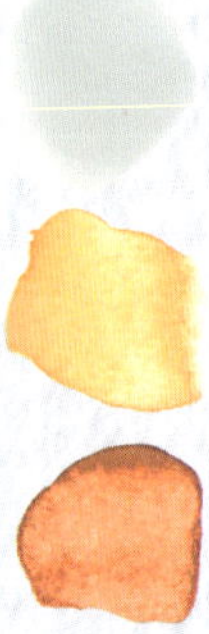

Chinese white

Cadmium yellow

Burnt sienna

HEAD

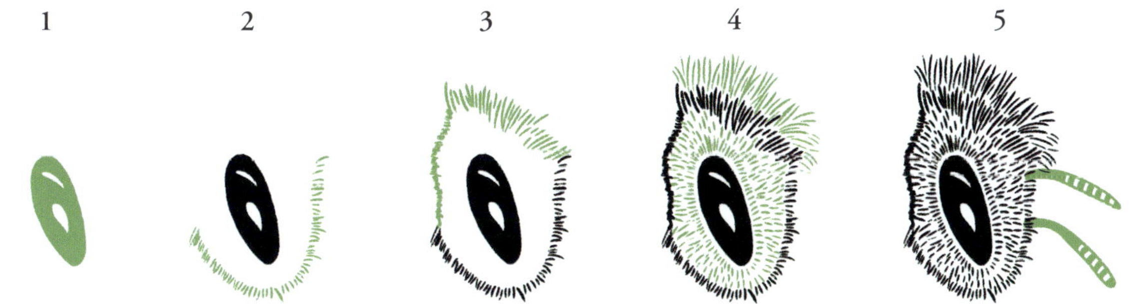

LEGS, BODY AND WINGS

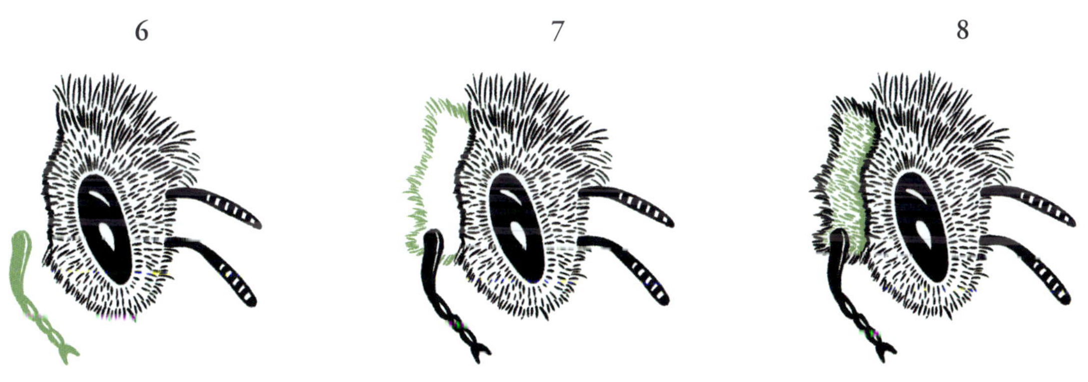

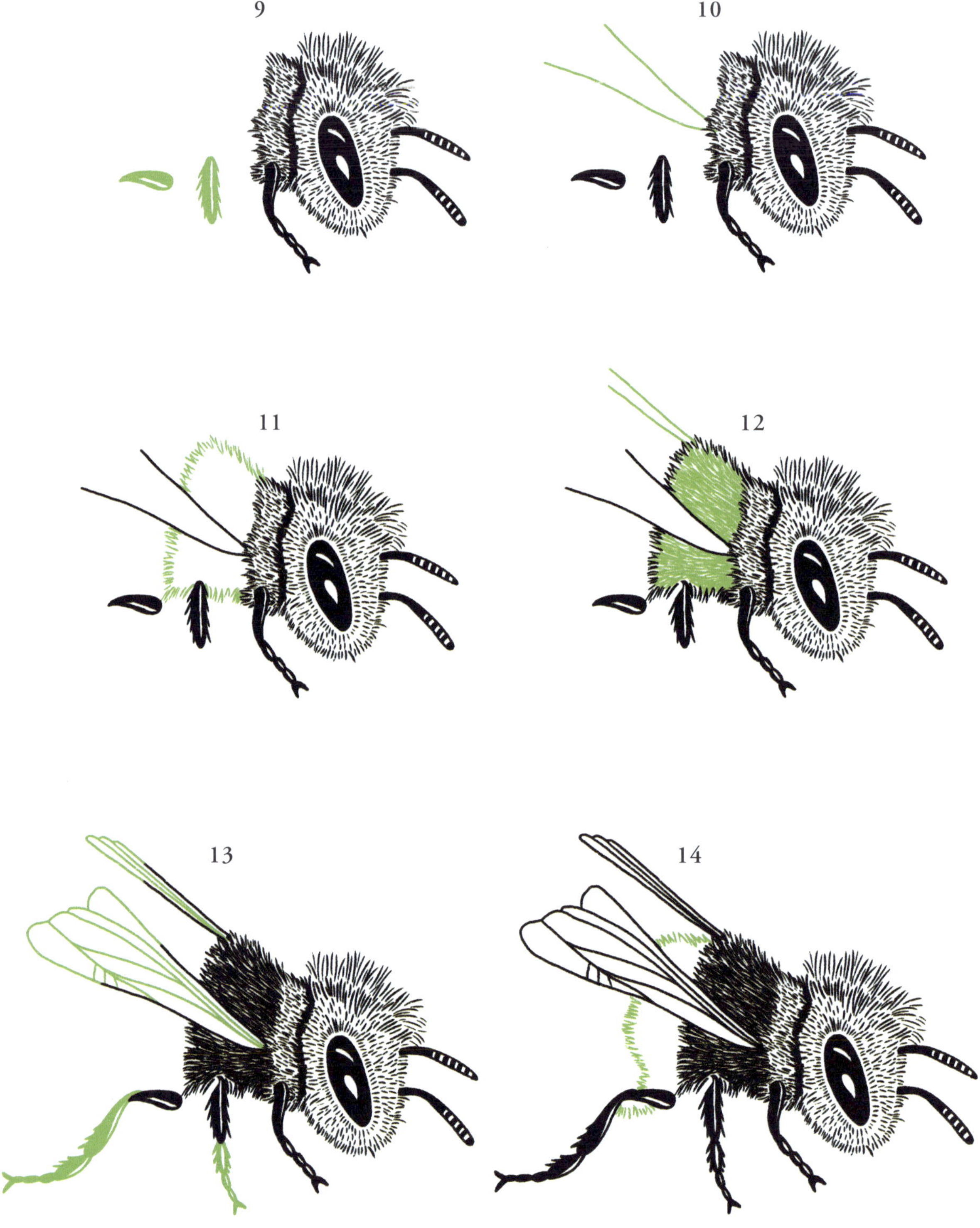

9
10
11
12
13
14

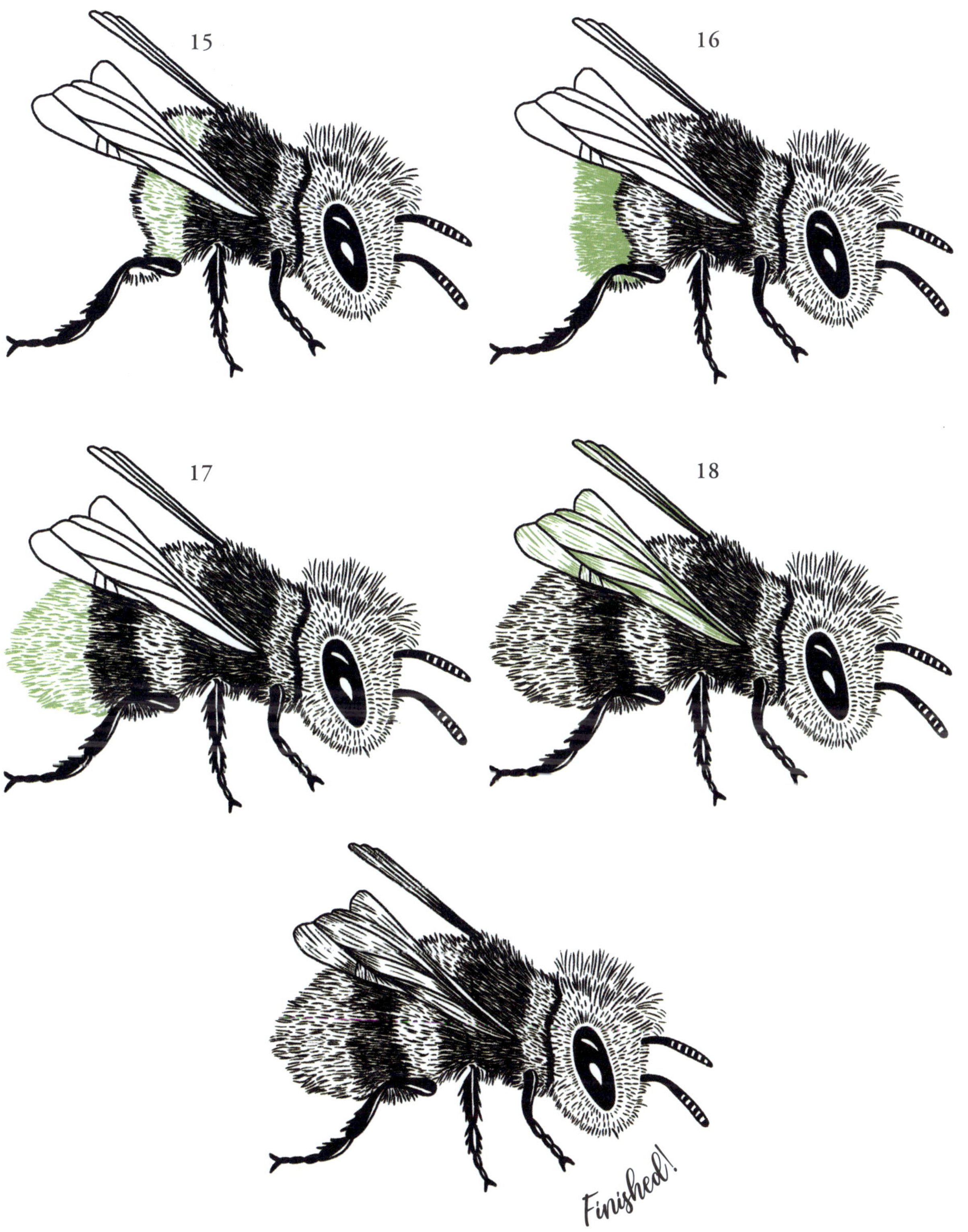

15
16
17
18
Finished!

Birds

Now you've started to learn some anatomy, textural and facial features we can begin to develop these further to draw some birds. You'll expand on texture-drawing techniques in this section and really start to mix more of them together to create even more depth and detail in your drawings.

We will also look at drawing some new feather shapes, using your shading techniques to add small scale details.

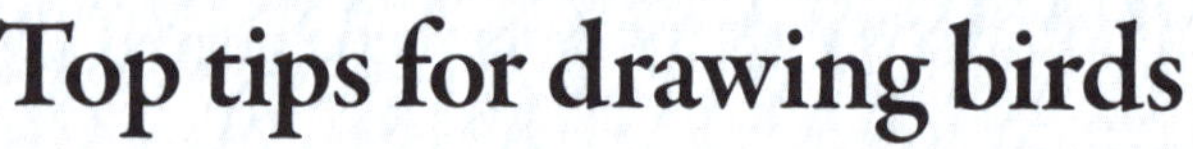

Top tips for drawing birds

◆ My approach to drawing starts to shift a little from this point onwards, and instead of breaking down these more complex subjects into outlines, shading and details, we will focus on everything combined, within each section as we go.

◆ When drawing your own birds from reference, I usually find that the eye is the best place to start.

◆ Once you have the eye in place, it is easier to map out where the beak should sit and how the shape of the head should flow into the body and wings.

◆ The wings and feathers are a great place to experiment with tweaking details, to add your own twist.

◆ Add some different line markings or patterns inside the feathers to create new and unique outcomes.

◆ Try drawing the birds perched on different shaped branches filled with leaves or flying towards their favourite flower.

◆ Add movement to your own sketches by drawing the wings and legs in different positions.

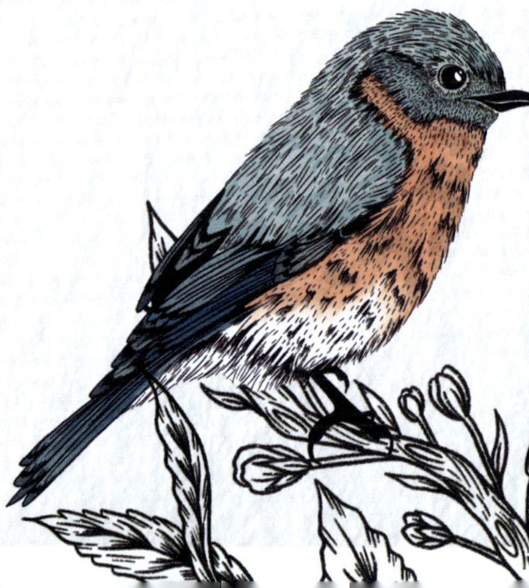

Bird drawing techniques

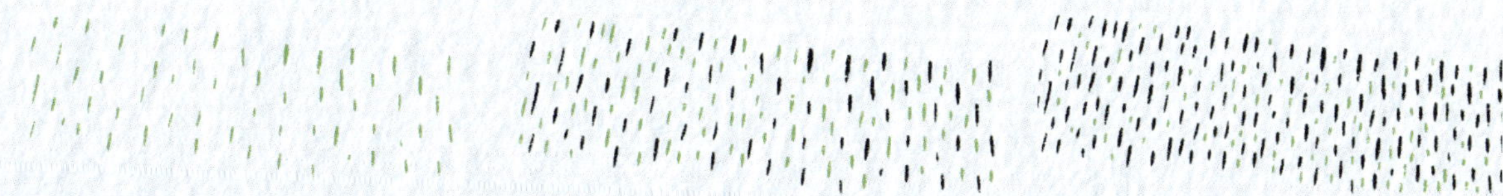

Short-length texture technique

This technique is similar to stippling, but swaps the dots for short, straight pen strokes. Start by spreading out the pen strokes within the area you'd like to fill. Using quick strokes, start to fill up the rest of the area with similar strokes that vary in height slightly.

Feathers

Start with the outlines of the feathers, making sure to create variety in the shape of each. Add a tapered line in the centre of all of them, which follows the curve of the outline. Use your shading strokes to add straight, angled lines on either side of the centre.

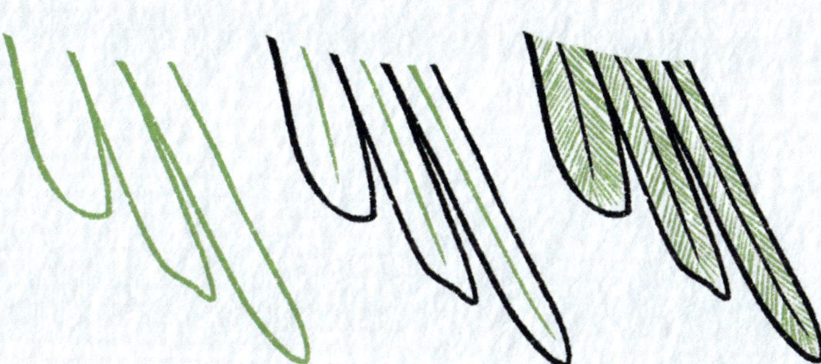

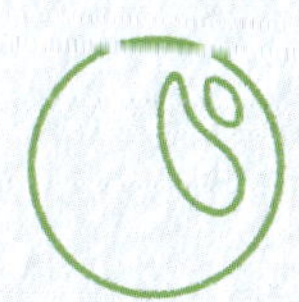 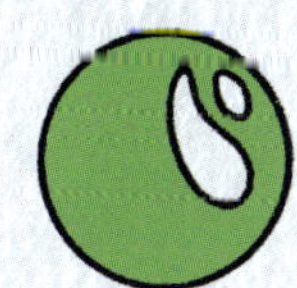 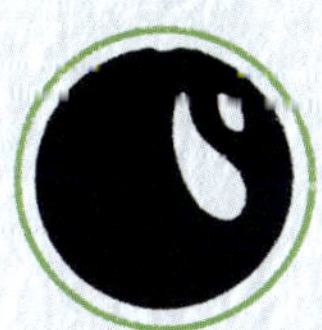 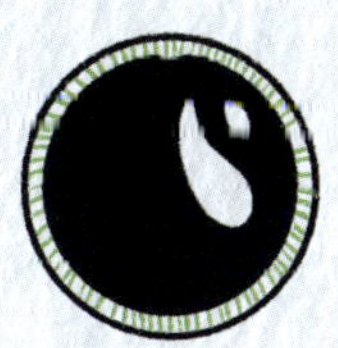 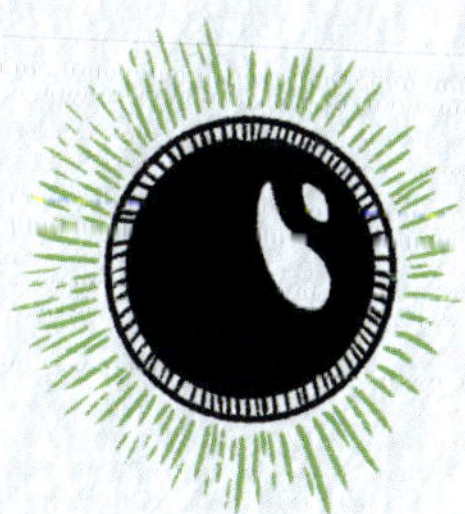

Eyes

The eyes you will need to draw in the following projects will vary slightly, but it's great to practise them from a straight-on perspective to get used to the general method. I always start with the outline of the eye and then block out spaces for the eye highlight. Then add another circle around the edge, leaving a gap for some straight edge, detail lines. From there you can start to build the strokes needed for the fur, making sure these strokes follow the curvature of the head.

Bluebird

We've tried a few insects with wings now and have even started to draw fluffy texture on the bumblebee, so let's start to tie it all together and adapt these techniques into our first bird, the bluebird.

We will draw this one from a side profile, to get the hang of some new features and techniques needed to capture all of the textures.

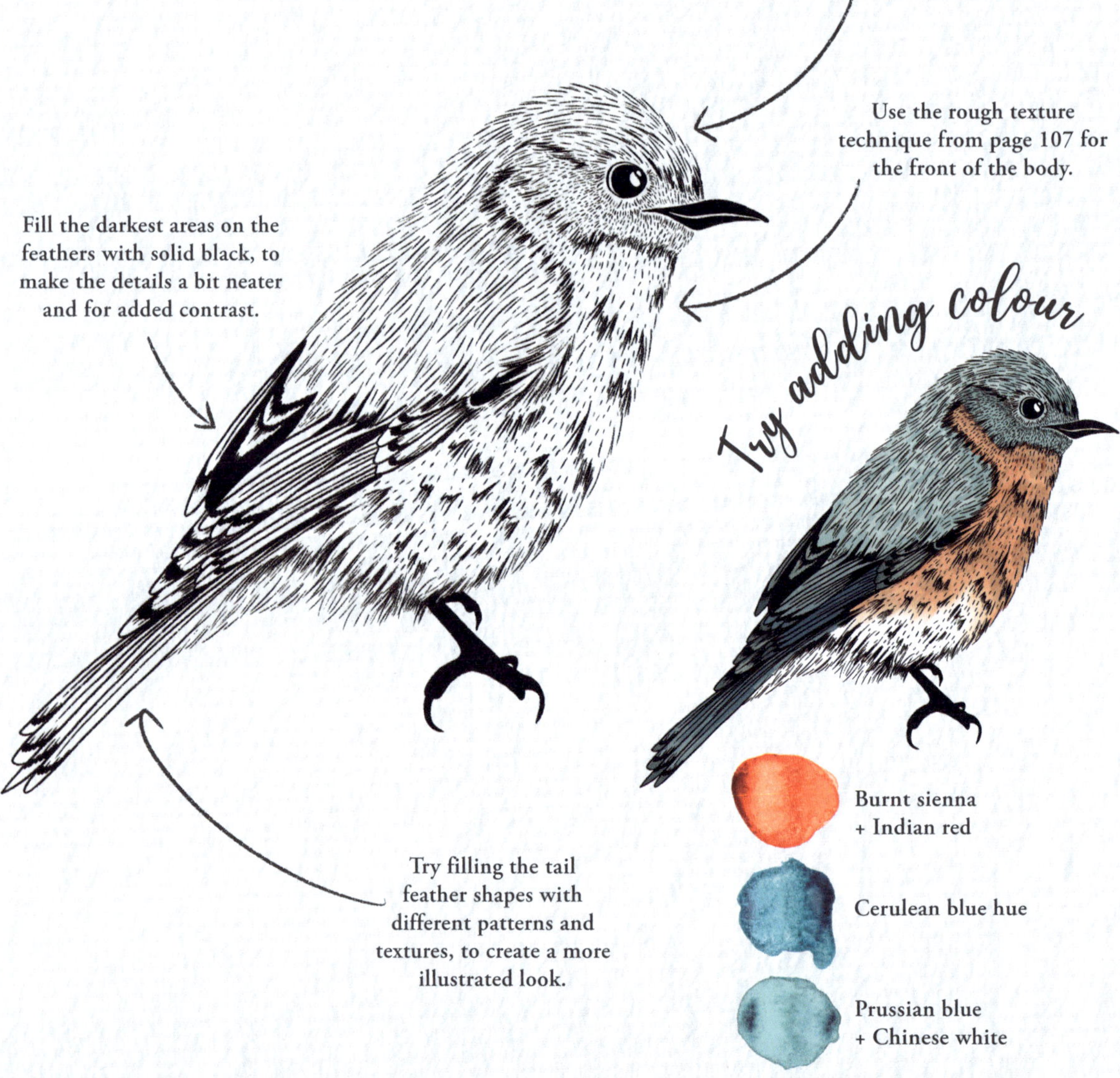

HEAD AND BODY

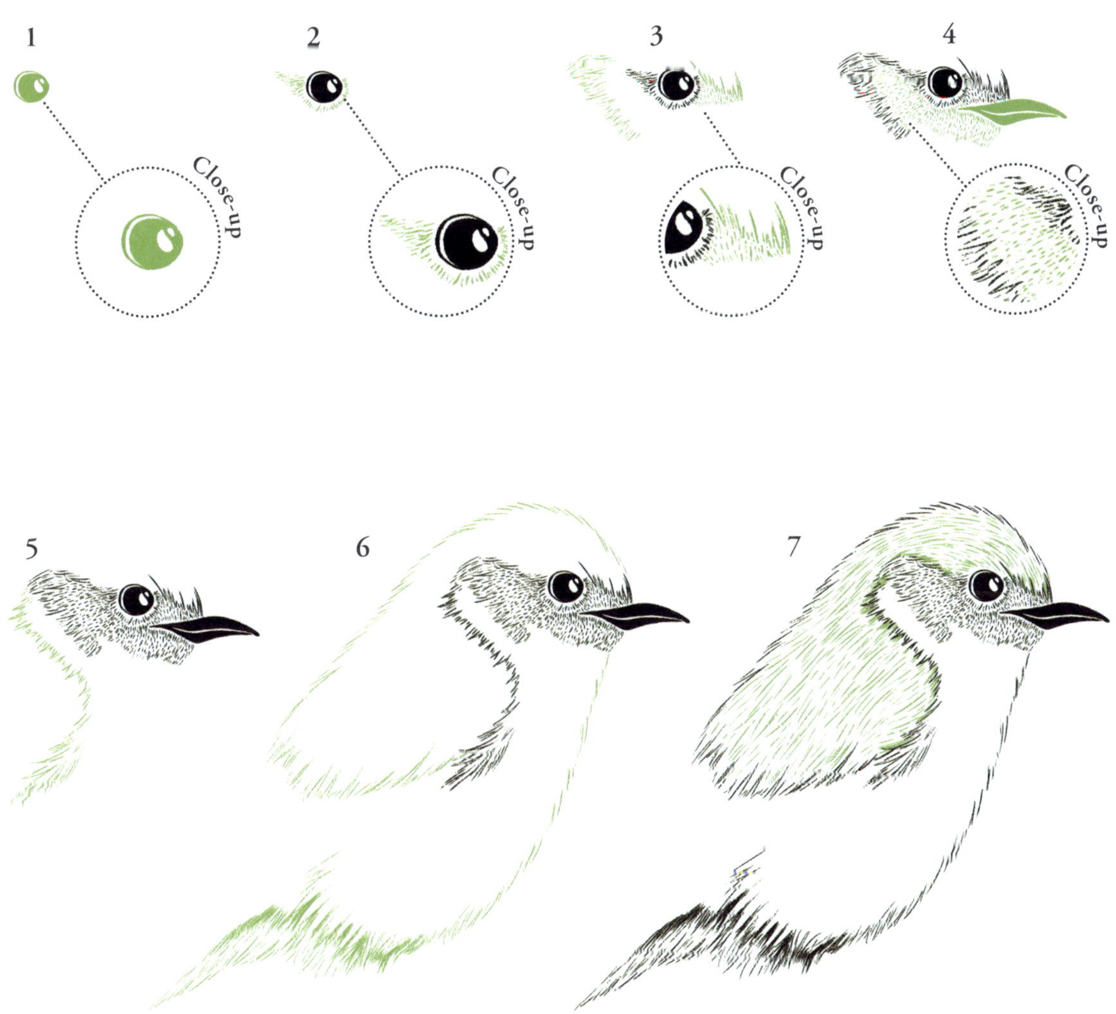

FEATHER AND LEG DETAILS

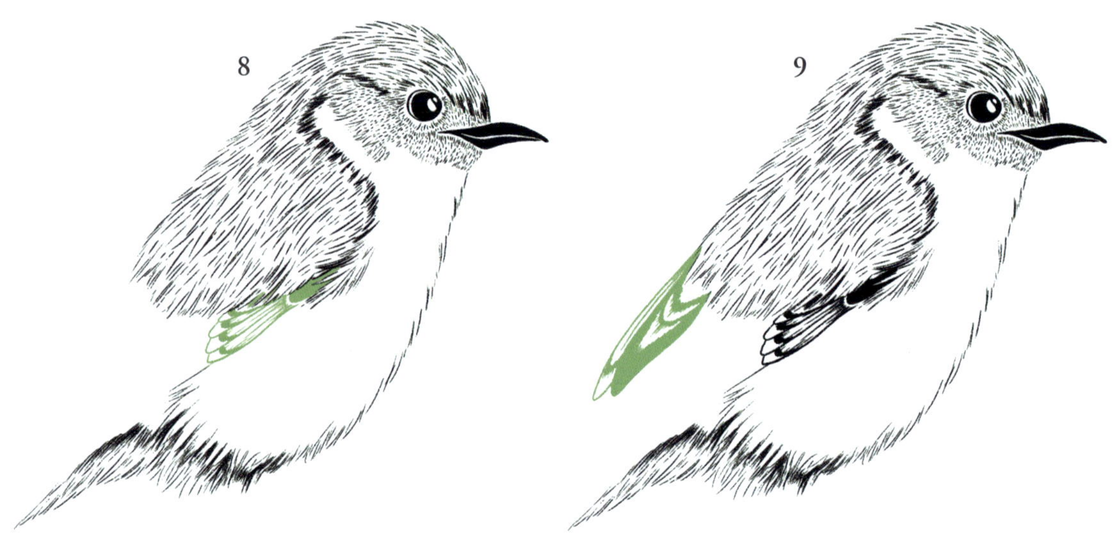

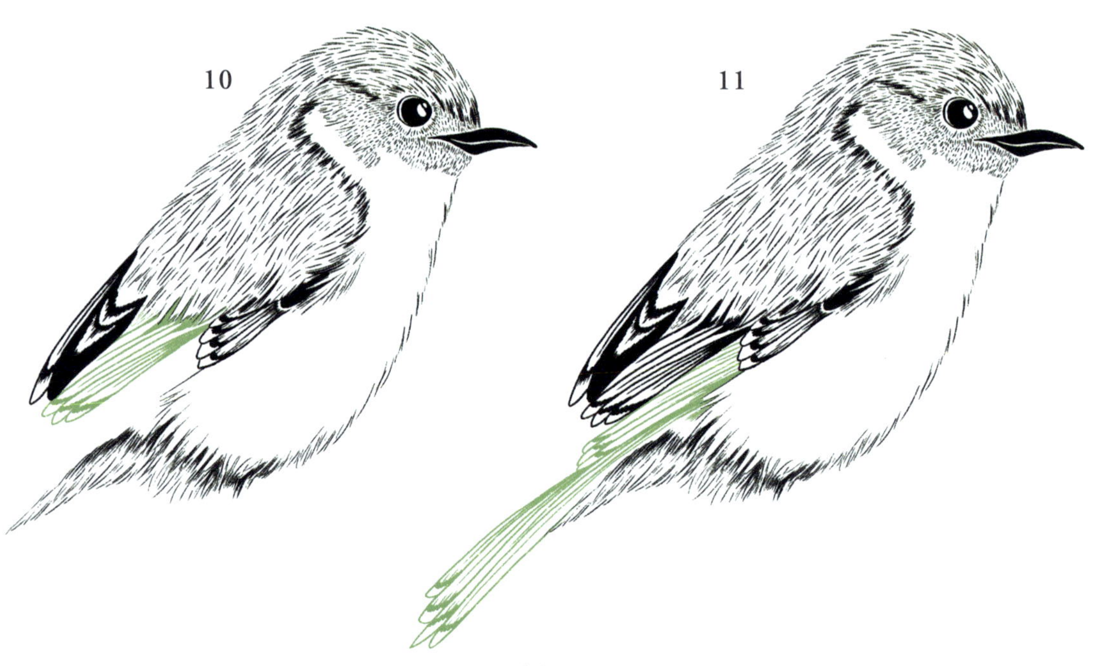

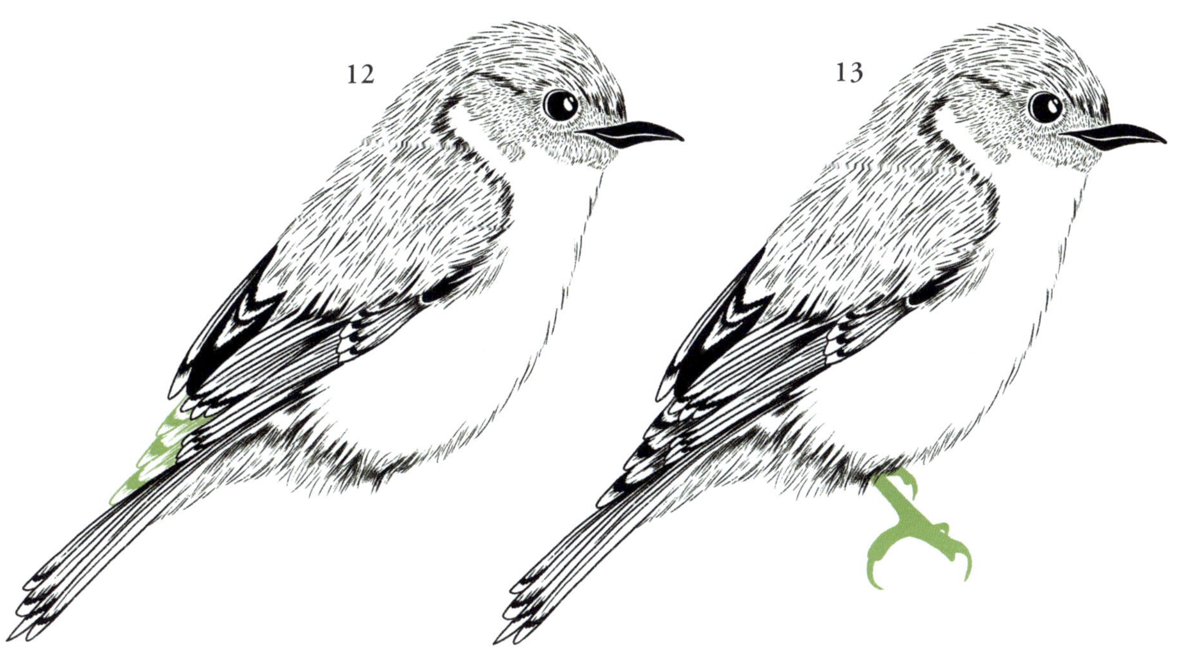

12

13

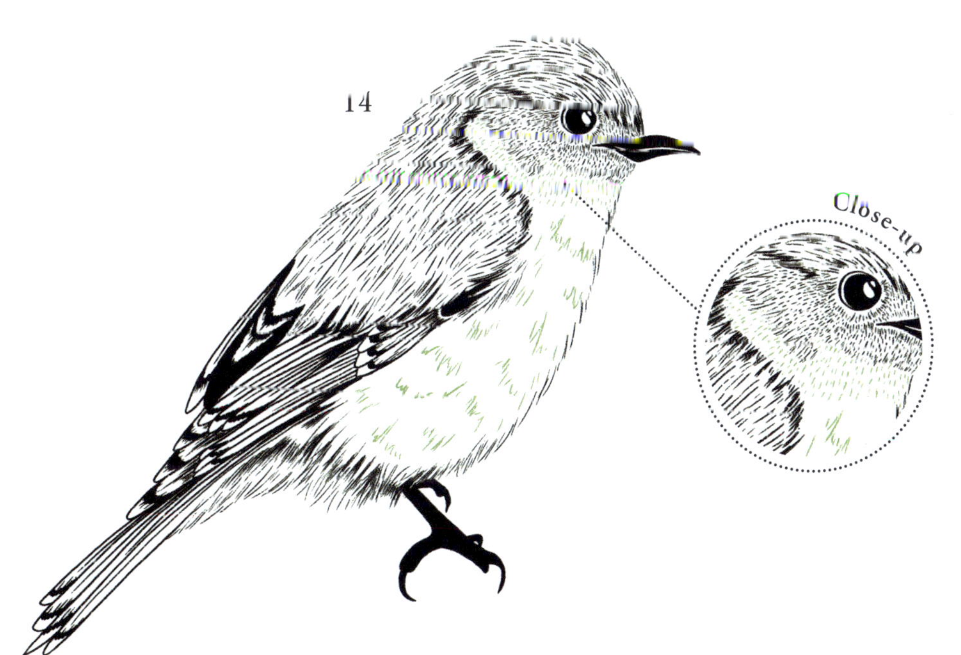

14

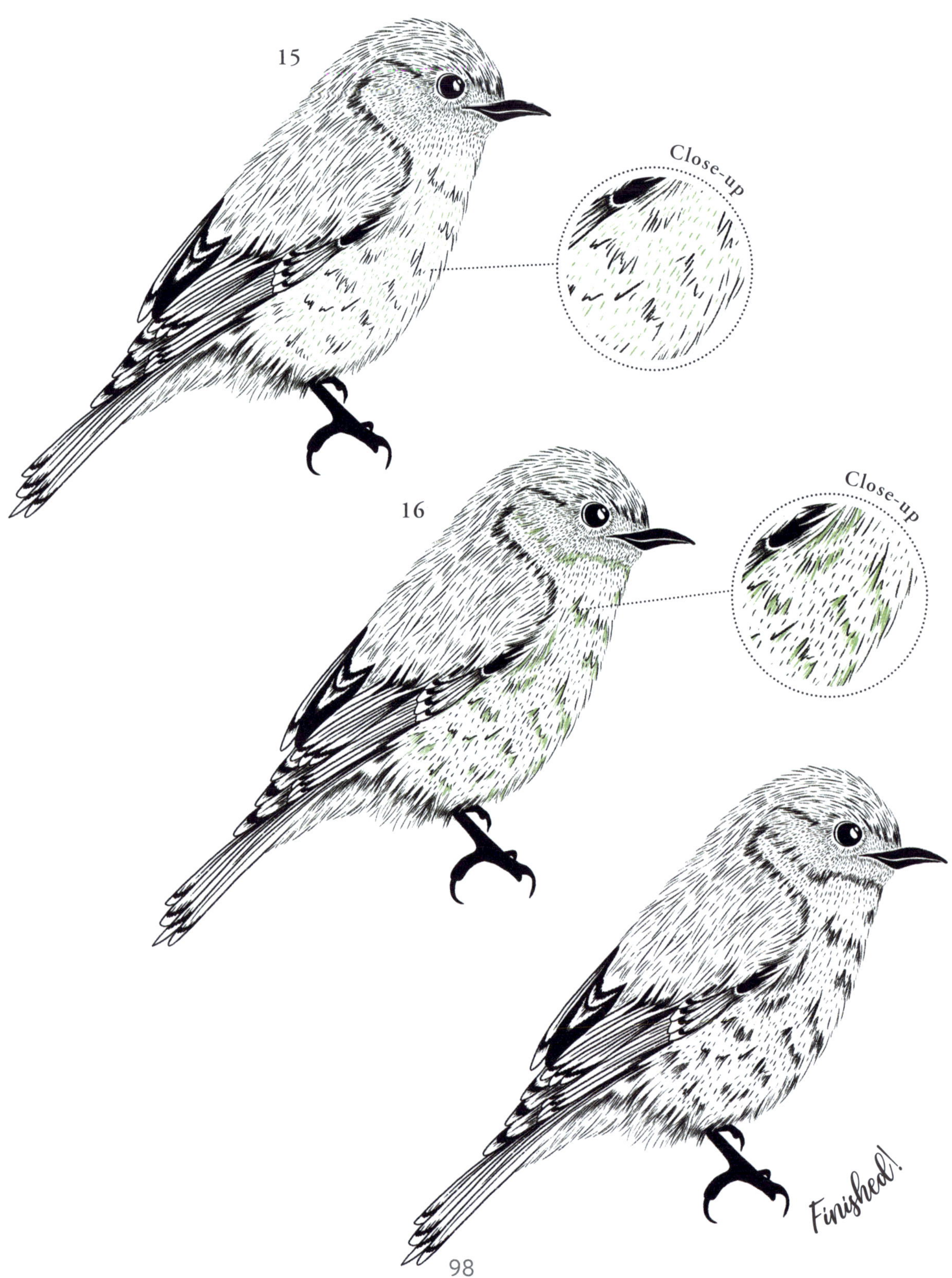

15
Close-up
16
Close-up
Finished!

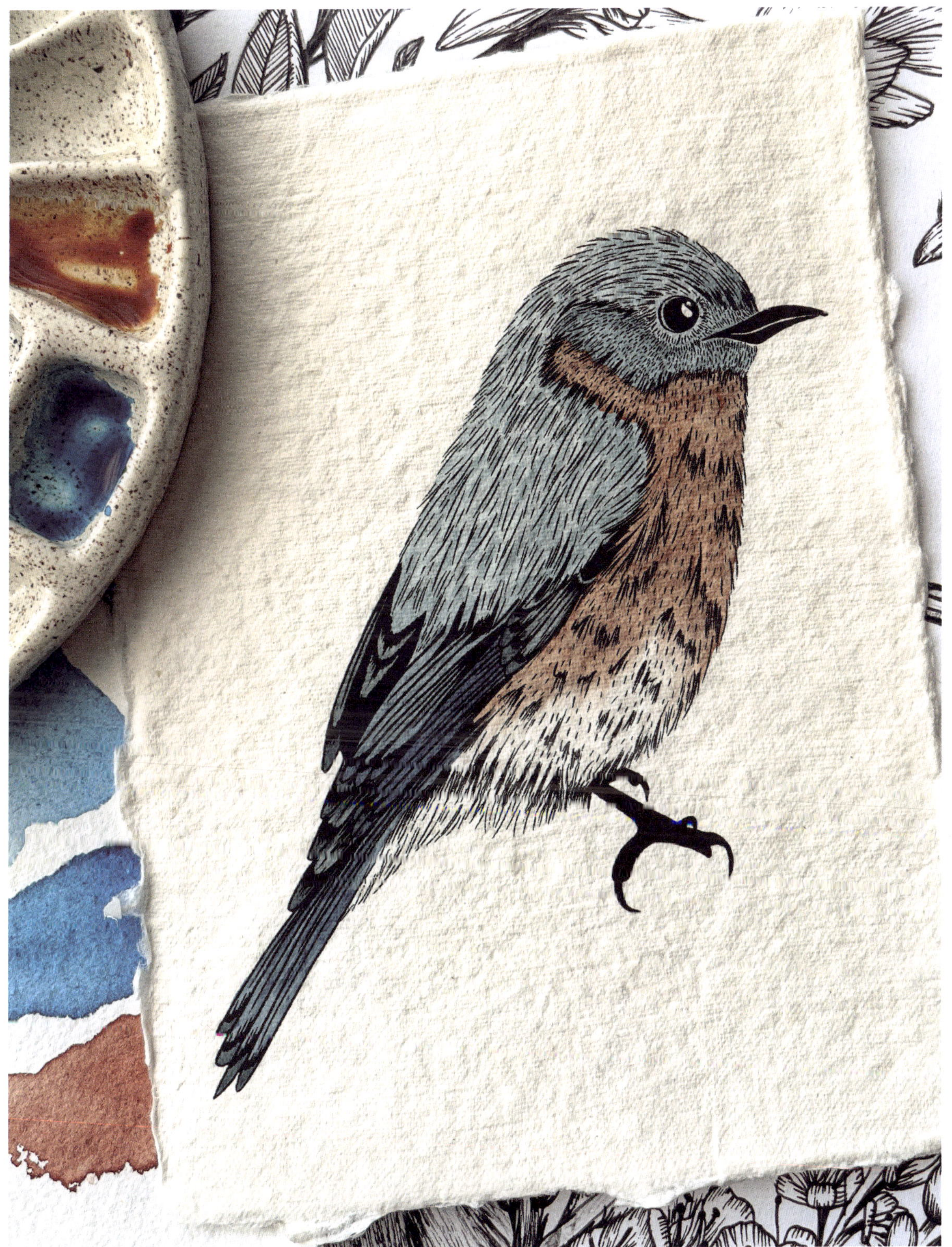

Magpie

I see a lot of magpies around my home town, which is what inspired me to include this tutorial. They have many unique features to capture, especially in the wings.

Moving on from the bluebird, we will add a bit more dimension to the side profile, with some movement in the wings, tail feathers and legs.

HEAD AND FRONT OF BODY

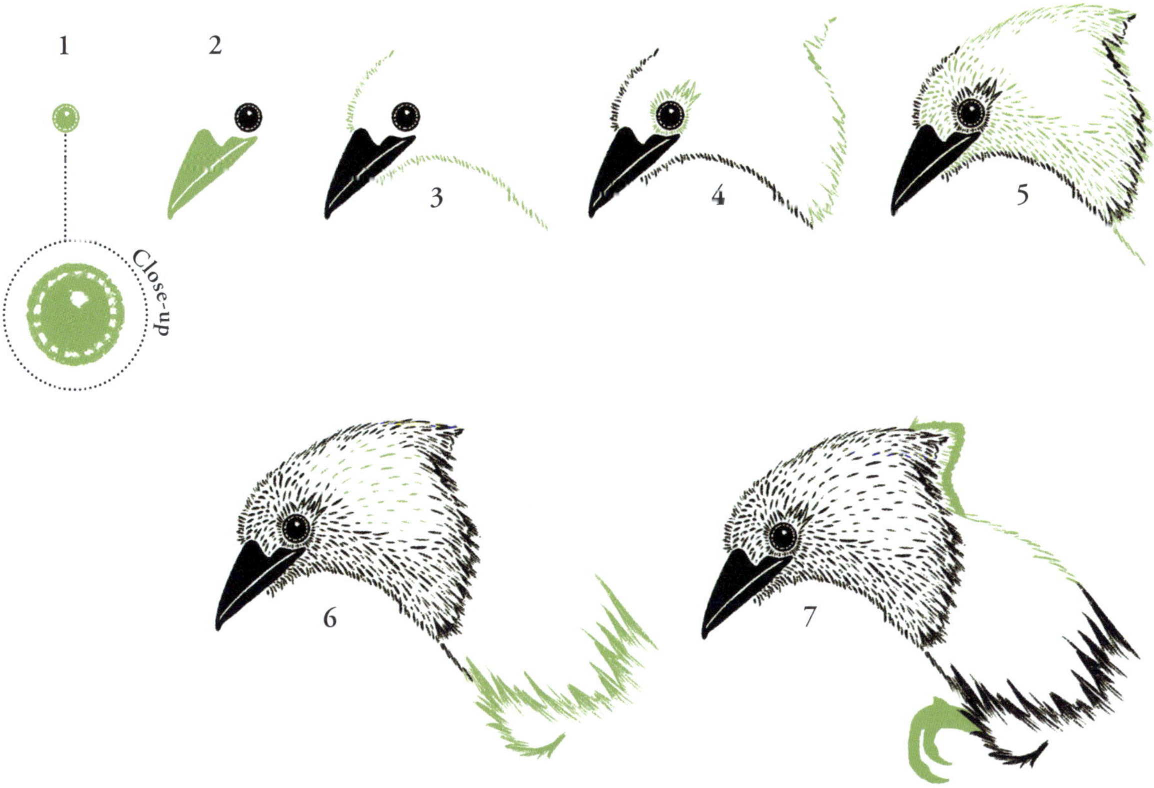

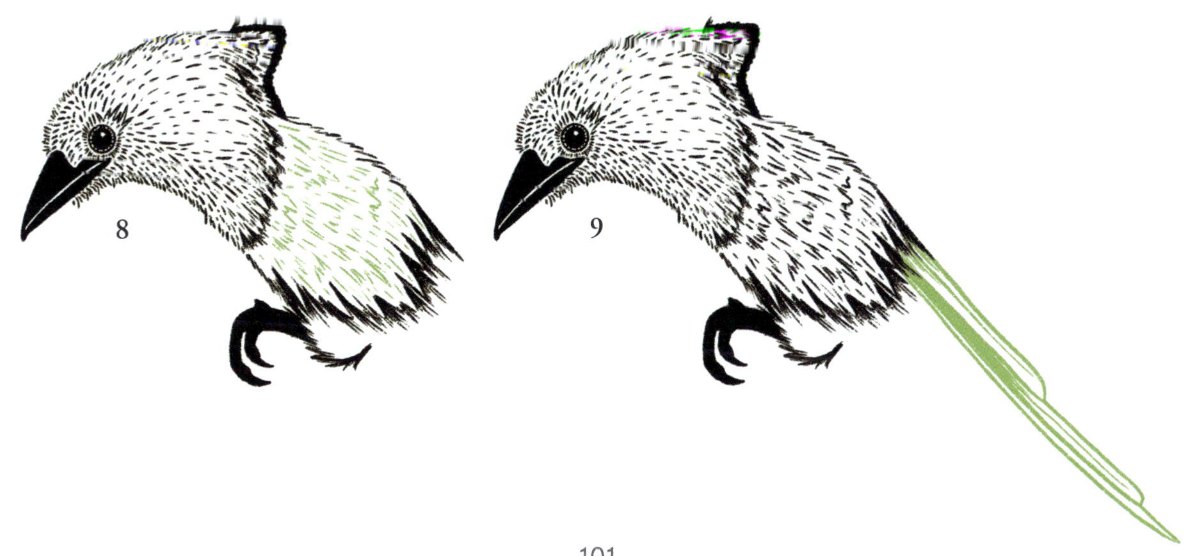

FEATHERS AND WINGS

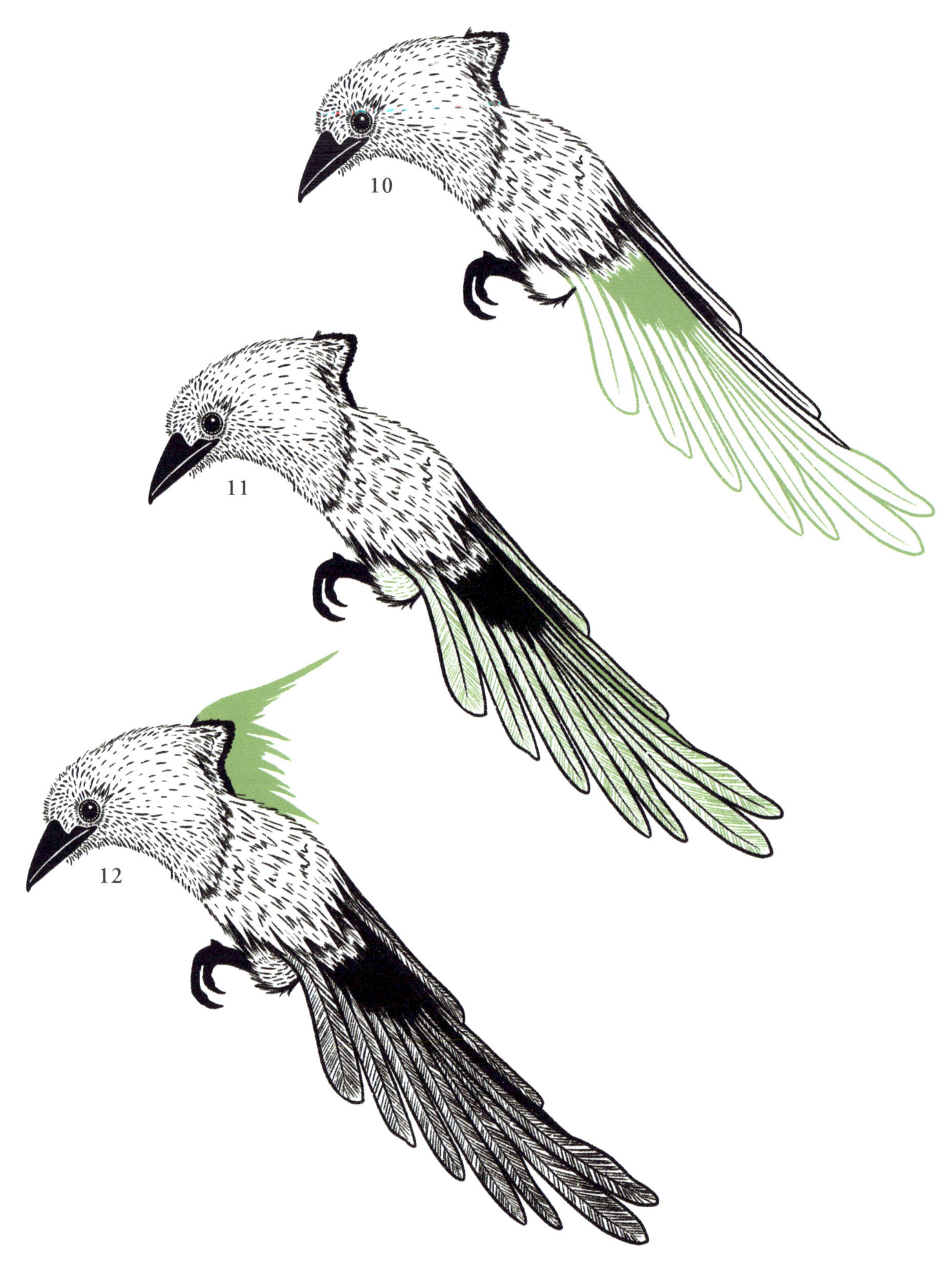

10
11
12

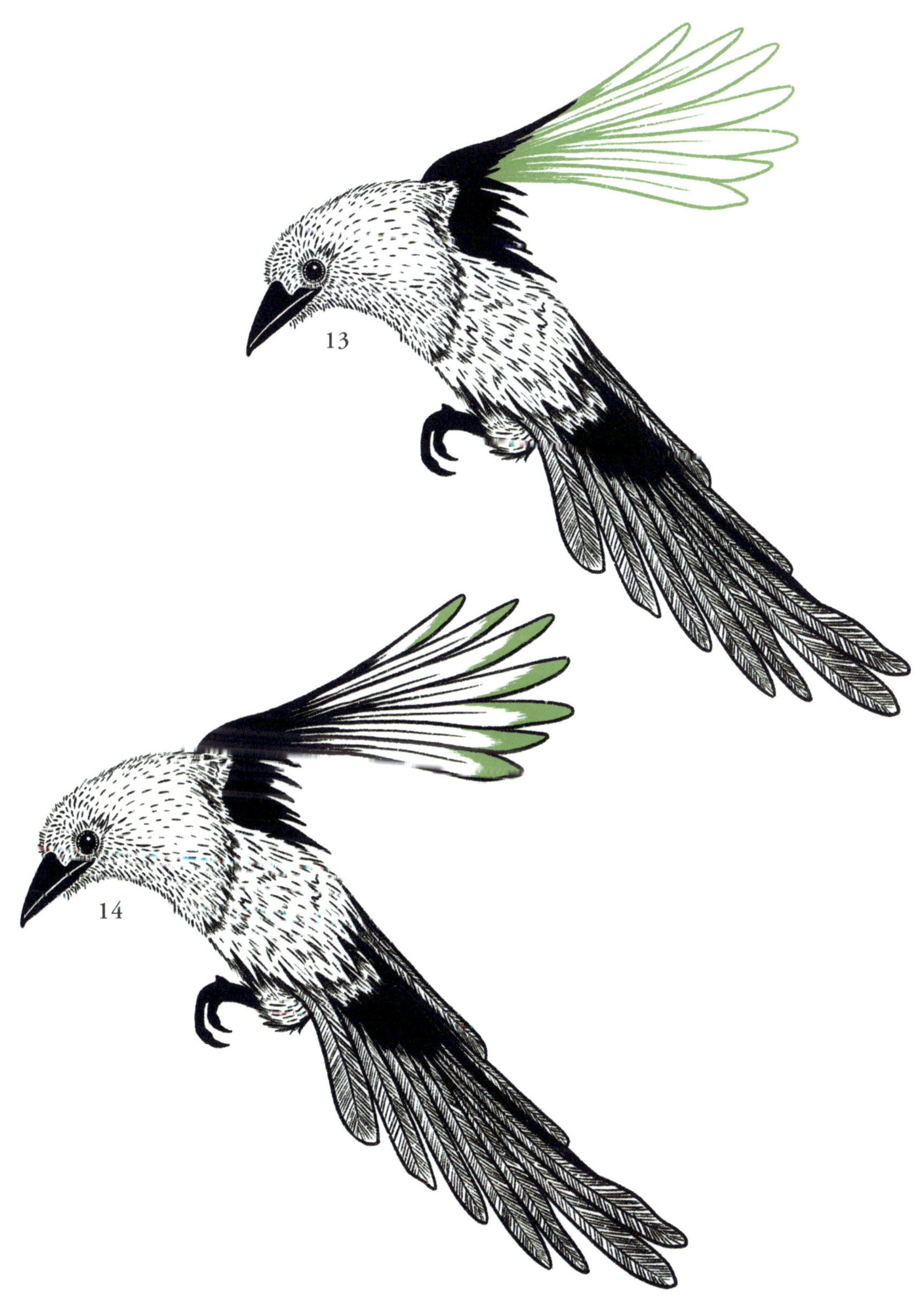

13
14

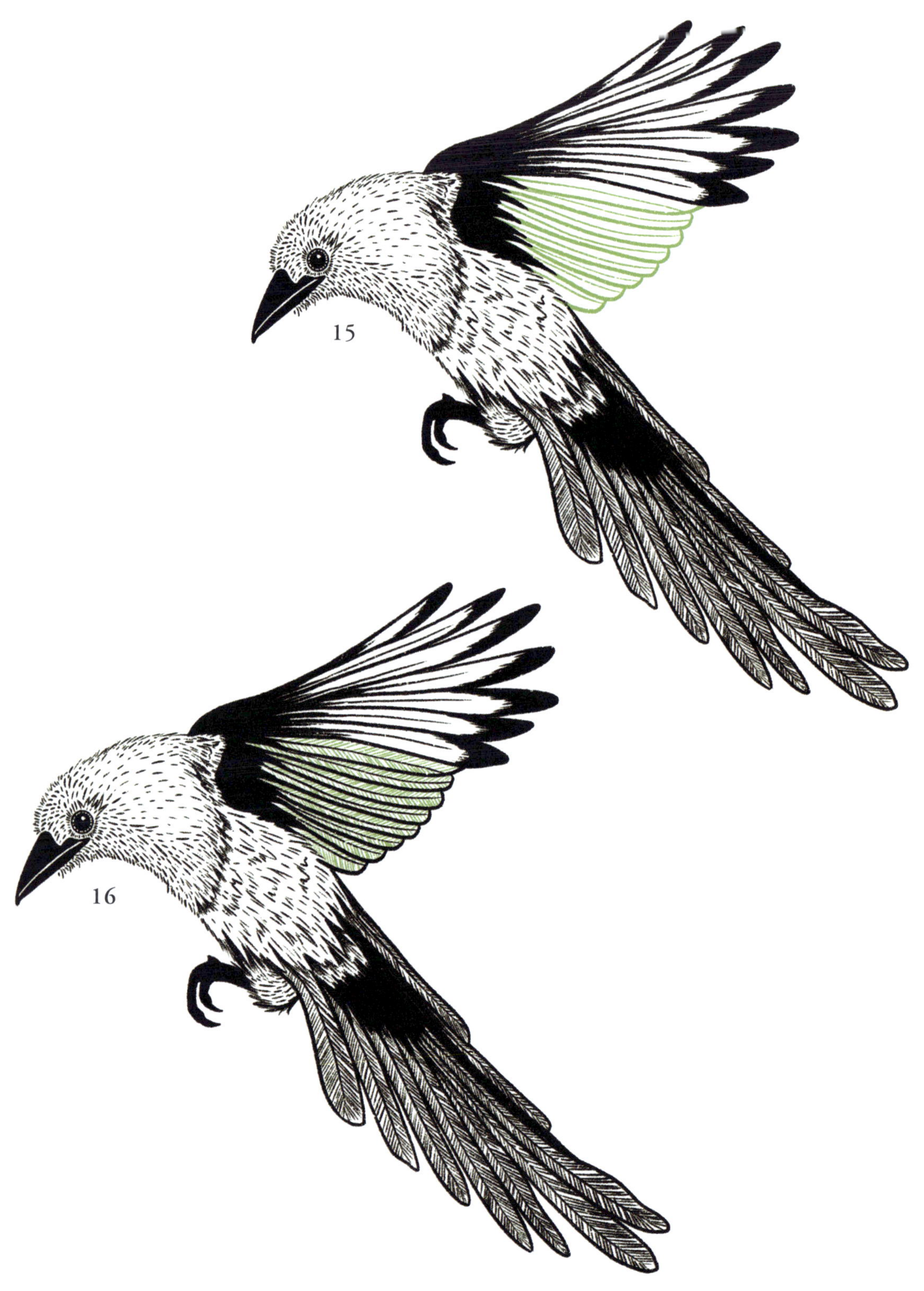

15
16

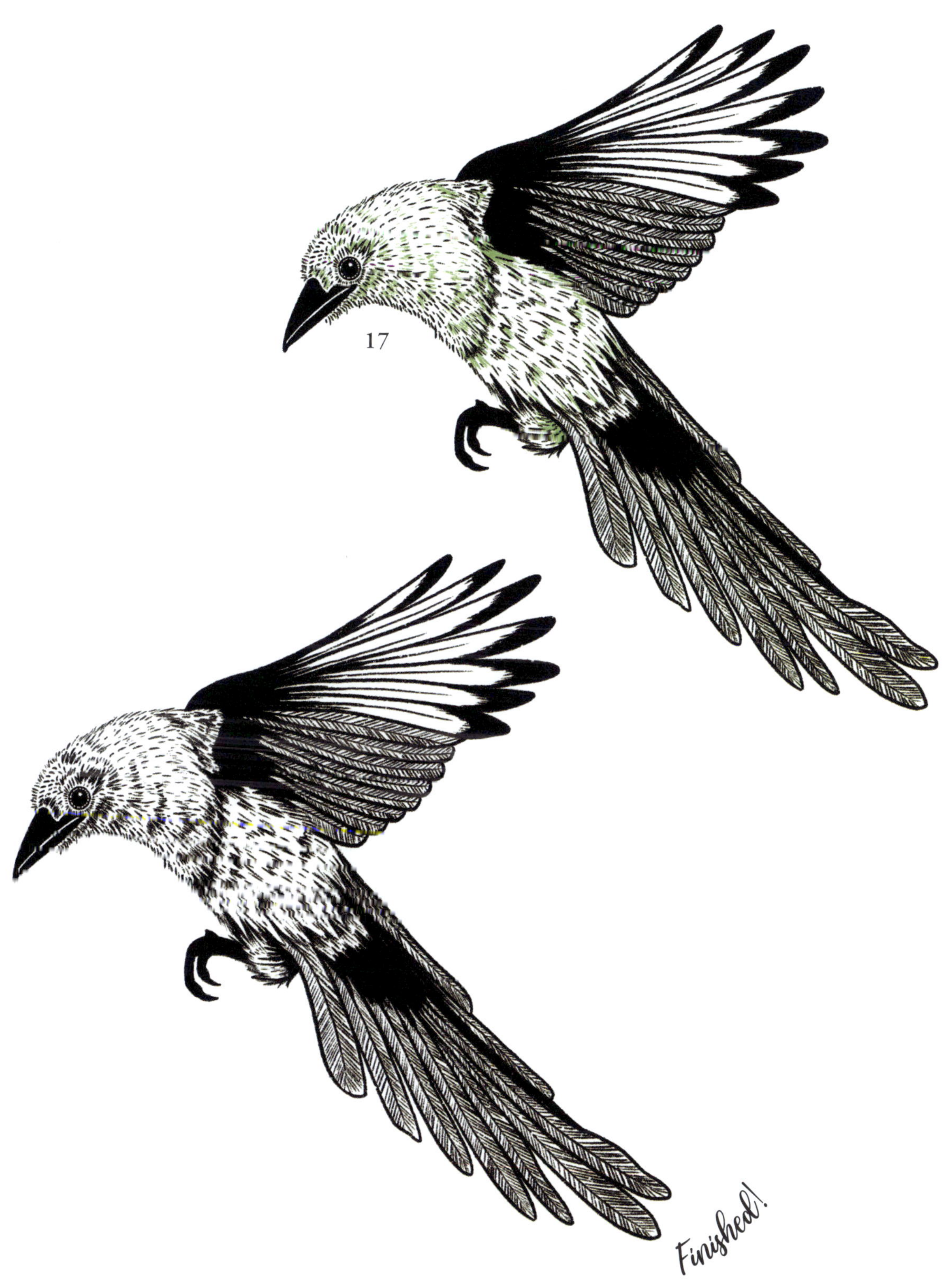

17
Finished!

Animals

Let's tie together all of the techniques you've learnt so far and combine them to draw some small animals. Using your shading and texture techniques, you will develop them further to draw a range of longer, fluffier furs.

You'll also draw more advanced anatomy and facial features in this section.

Top tips for drawing animals

◆ When drawing animals, you need to be a bit more precise to get the general anatomy and proportions looking right for the animal you're referring to.

◆ With animals I usually block out the features and sections of fur piece by piece, rather than starting with a whole outline, similar to drawing birds.

◆ You can draw a pencil outline first if you prefer. Try not to use ink for any body outlines to avoid the edges looking solid rather than furry.

◆ You can really play around with the lengths and textures of the fur by using different pen strokes and nib sizes or just by adjusting the pressure from your hand. The lighter your pen strokes, the wispier and softer you can make the fur look.

◆ For shorter, denser fur, you can apply more pressure with your pen or pencil to make these areas look thicker.

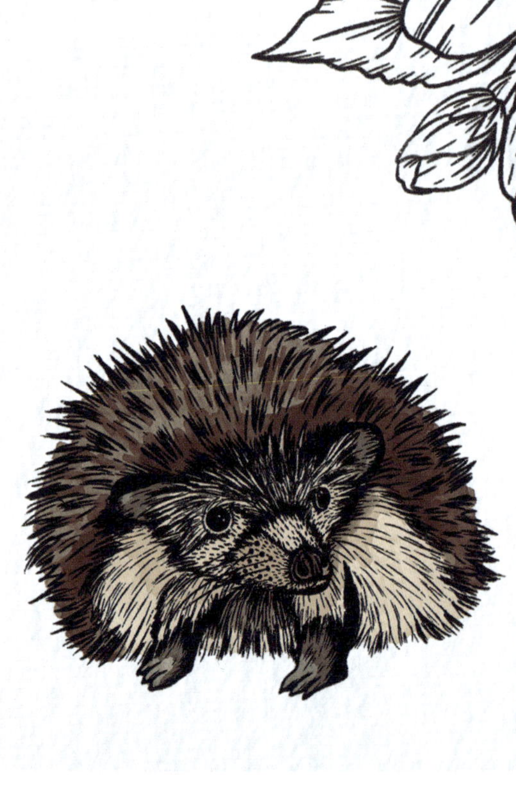

Animal drawing techniques

Mid-length texture technique

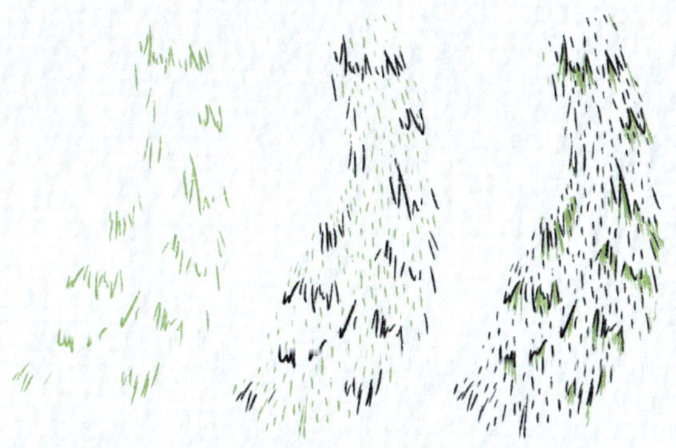

Long-length texture technique

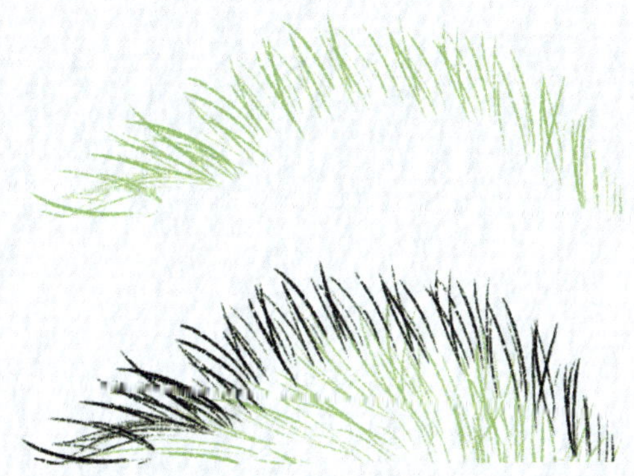

1. Start with more jagged, zigzag pen strokes, spread across the area you'd like to fill.

2. Use shorter, straighter pen strokes to fill the gaps in this area.

3. Lastly use short shading strokes, to add shadows and depth below the first jagged lines.

1. Use lighter, wispier pen strokes to block out the edge where you'd like the long fur to sit. Make sure these strokes vary in height and flow in slightly different directions.

2. Continue this technique underneath the outer edge.

Rough texture technique

This technique is quite similar to mid-length texture, there is just a slight difference to how you fill the gaps.

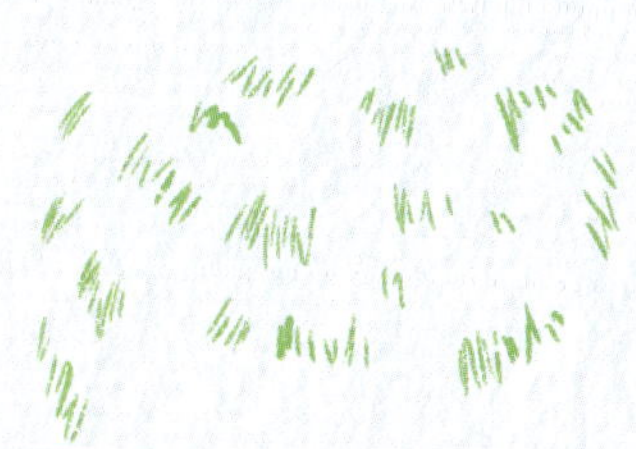

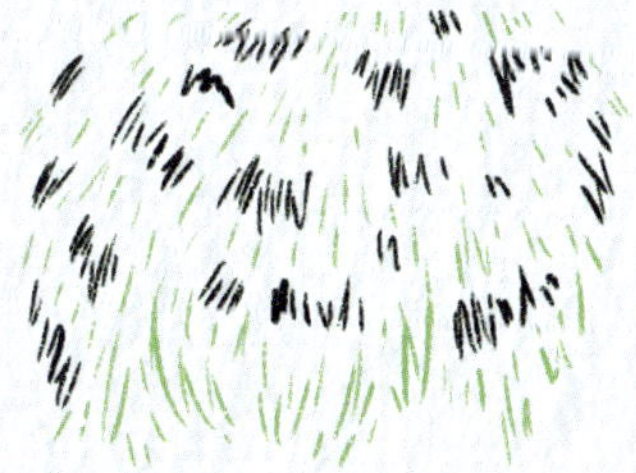

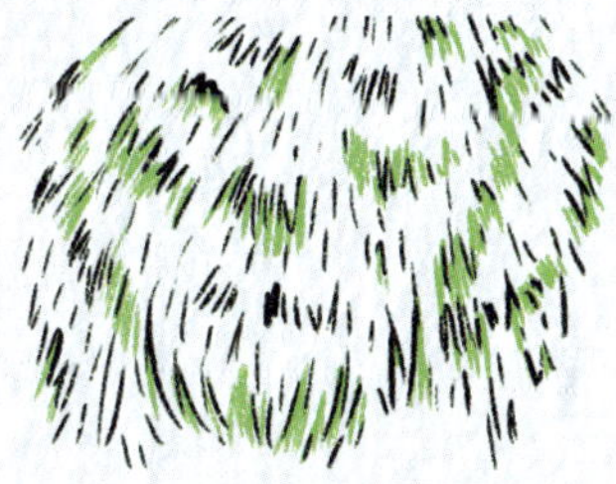

1. Use the same jagged, zigzag pen strokes from the first step in the mid-length texture technique.

2. Start to fill the gaps, using a mixture of zigzag lines, along with shorter, straighter pen strokes.

3. Add some shading below the jagged, zigzag strokes as well as in random spots dotted around.

Hedgehog

The first animal we are going to try is this cute hedgehog! Now you've tried some techniques for drawing feathered texture in the birds, we can adapt those into animals, starting with hedgehog quills.

You'll draw this one head-on and start to add some character to the facial features and stance.

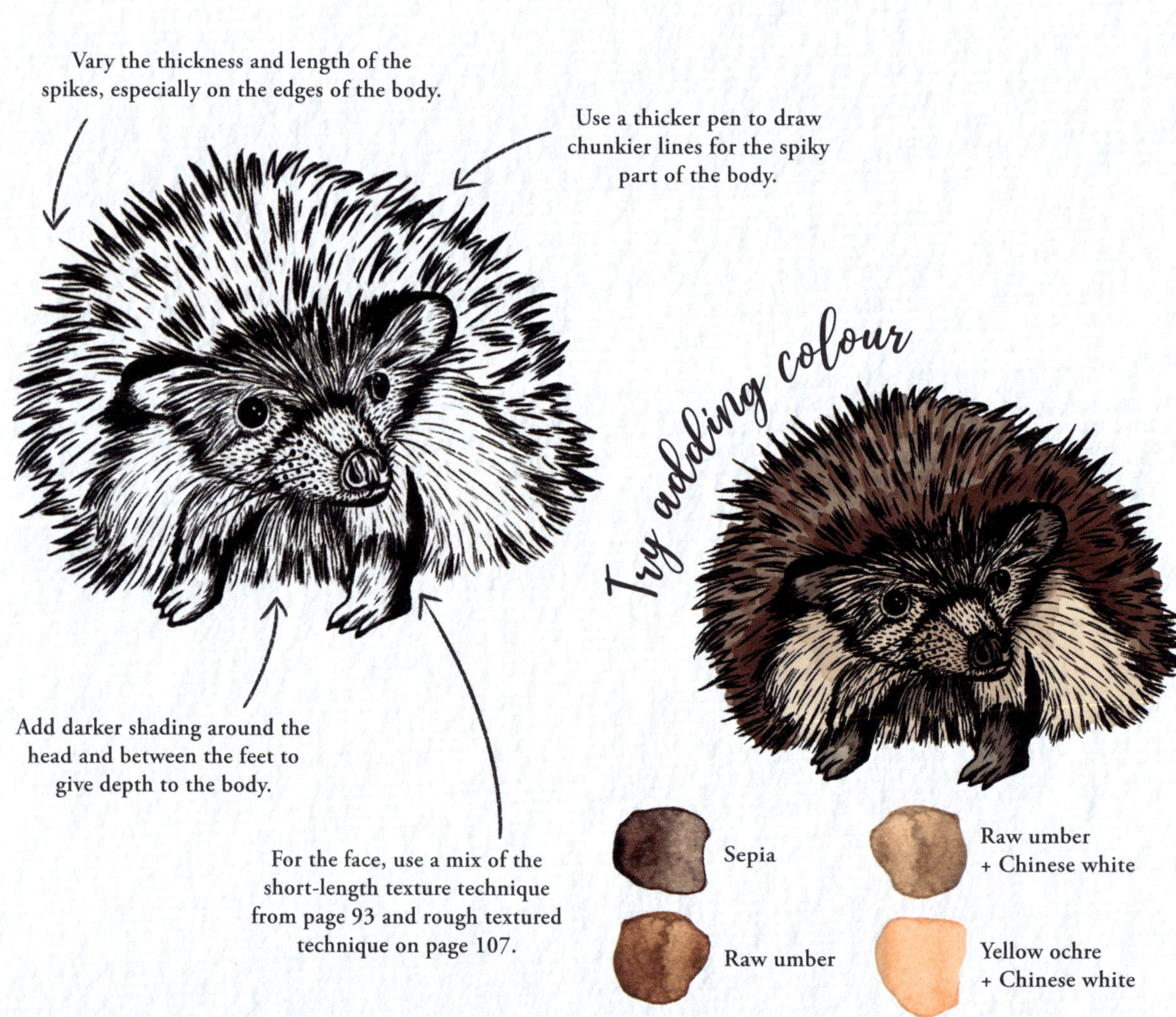

HEAD

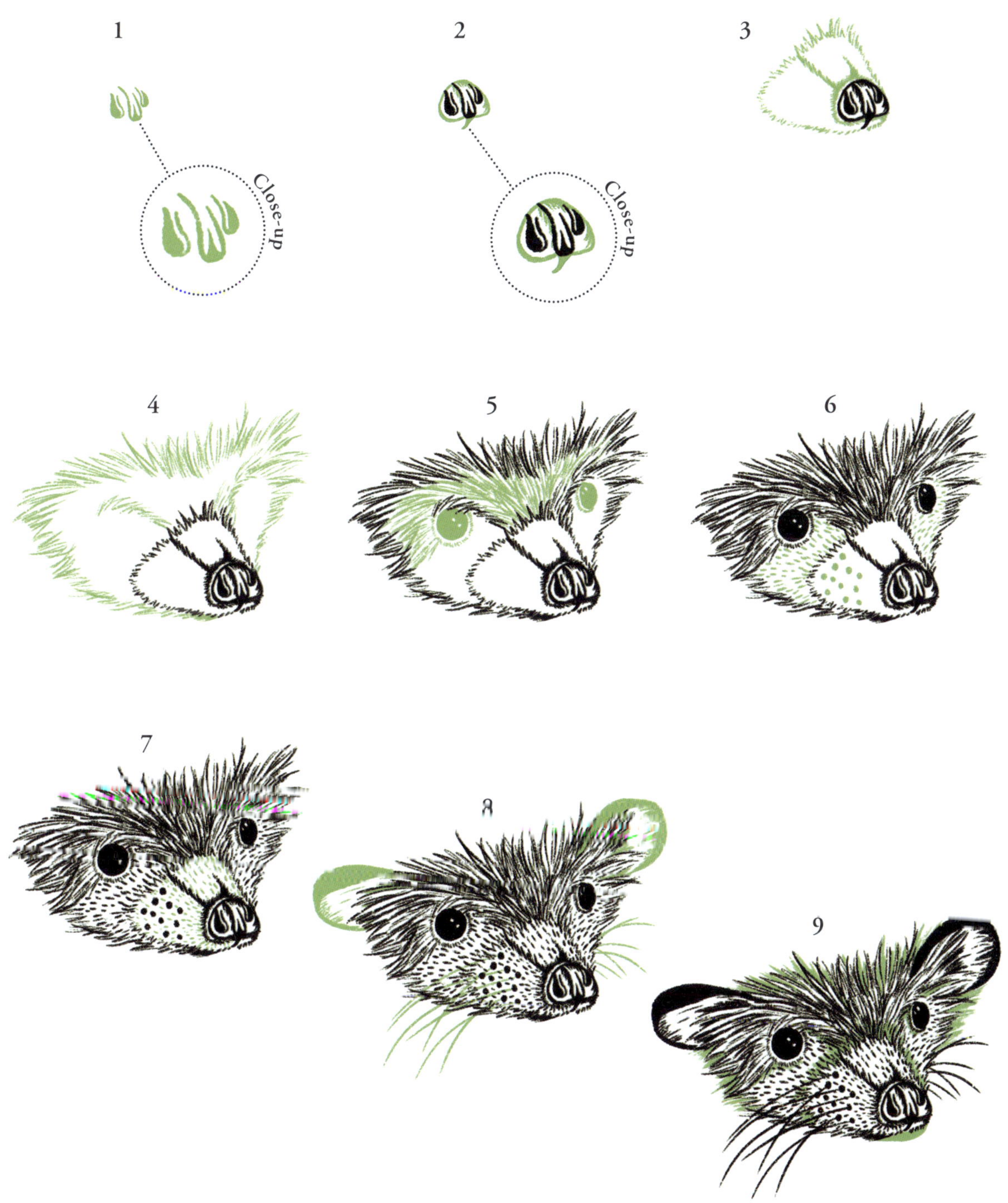

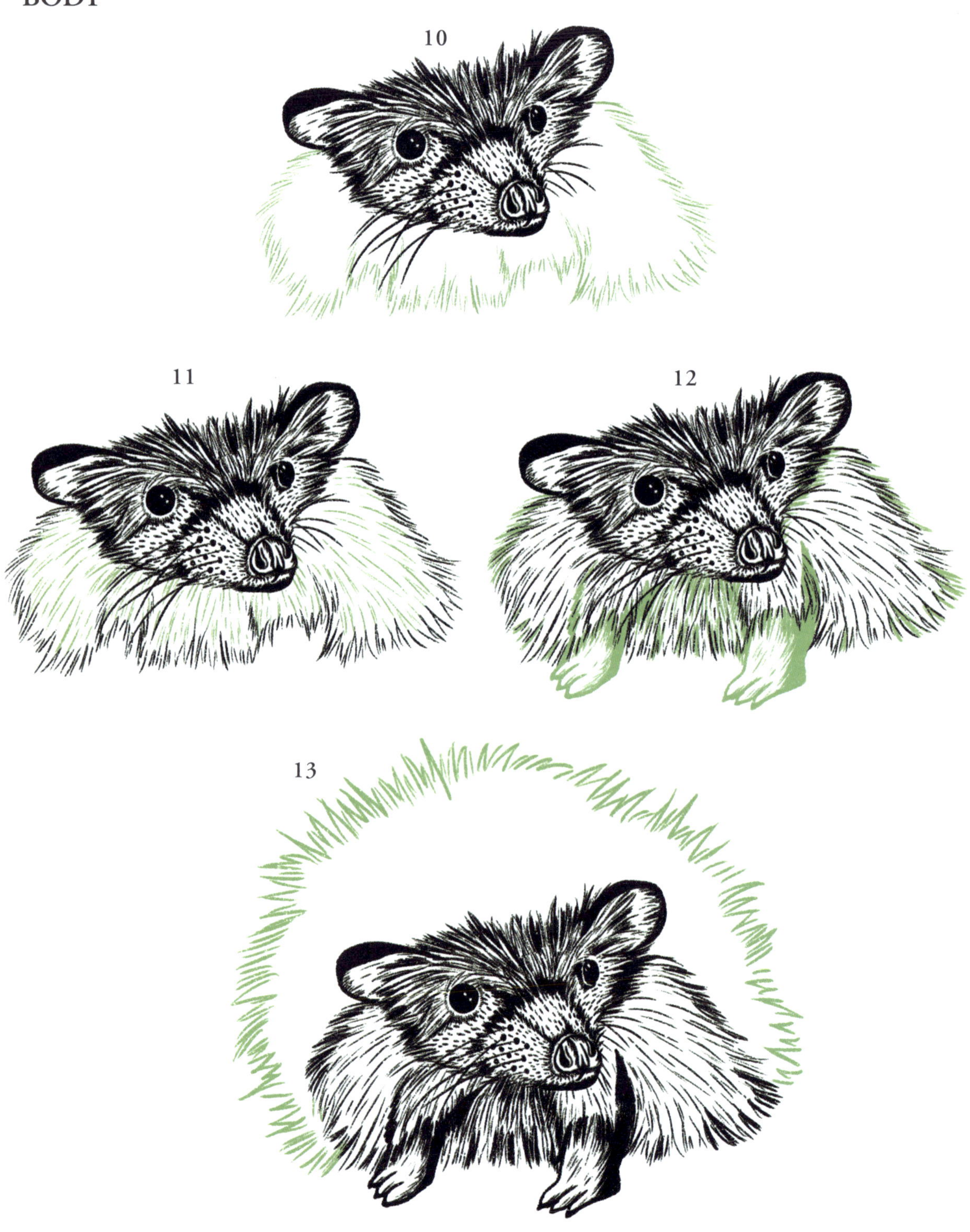
10
11
12
13

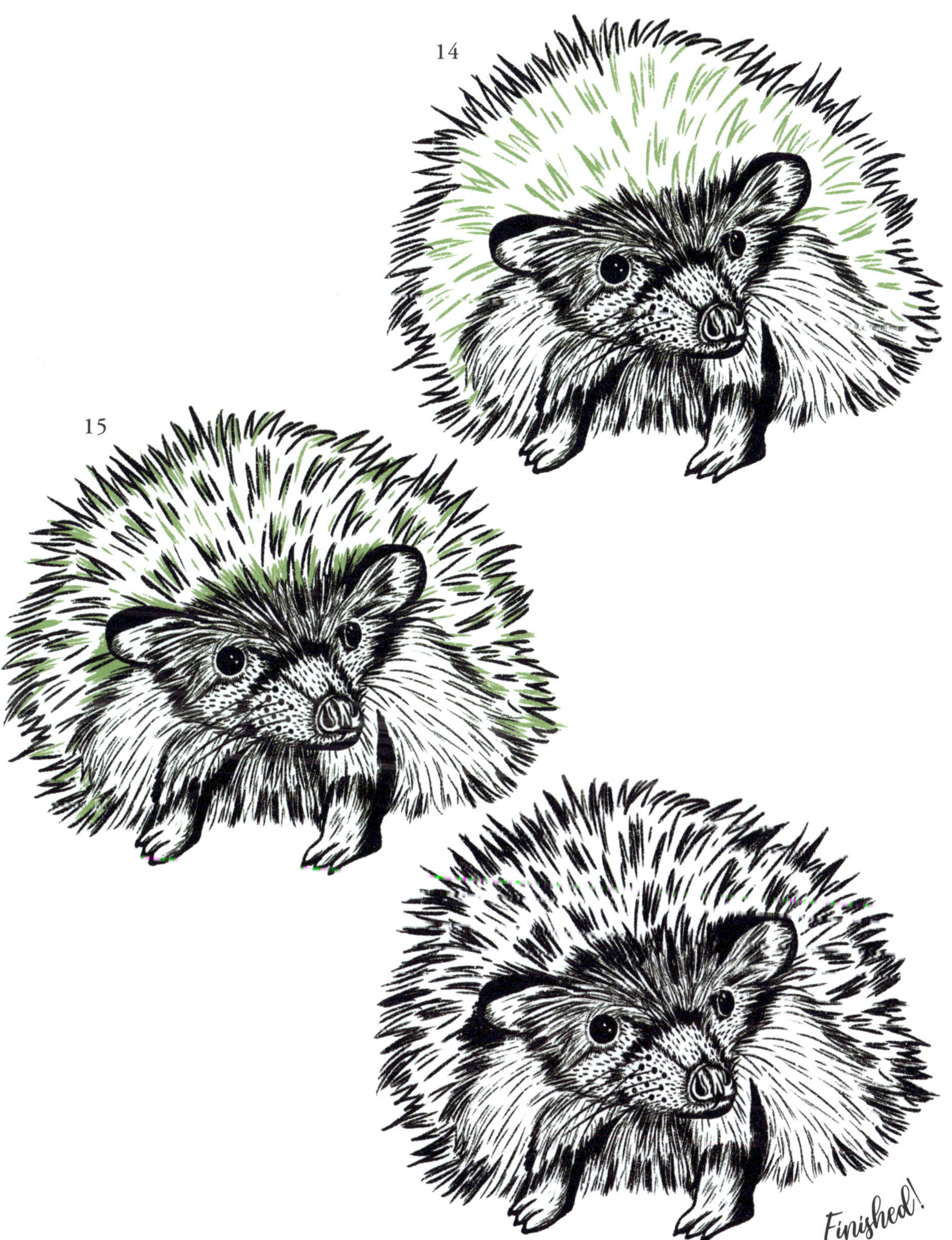

14

15

Rabbit

Now that you've tried a wider range of fur and texture techniques, let's tie them together with a larger animal and draw a rabbit.

Combining these techniques with some shading overlaid helps add dimension to your animal drawings and bring them to life.

Start with the mouth, then draw the full head, before adding the body.

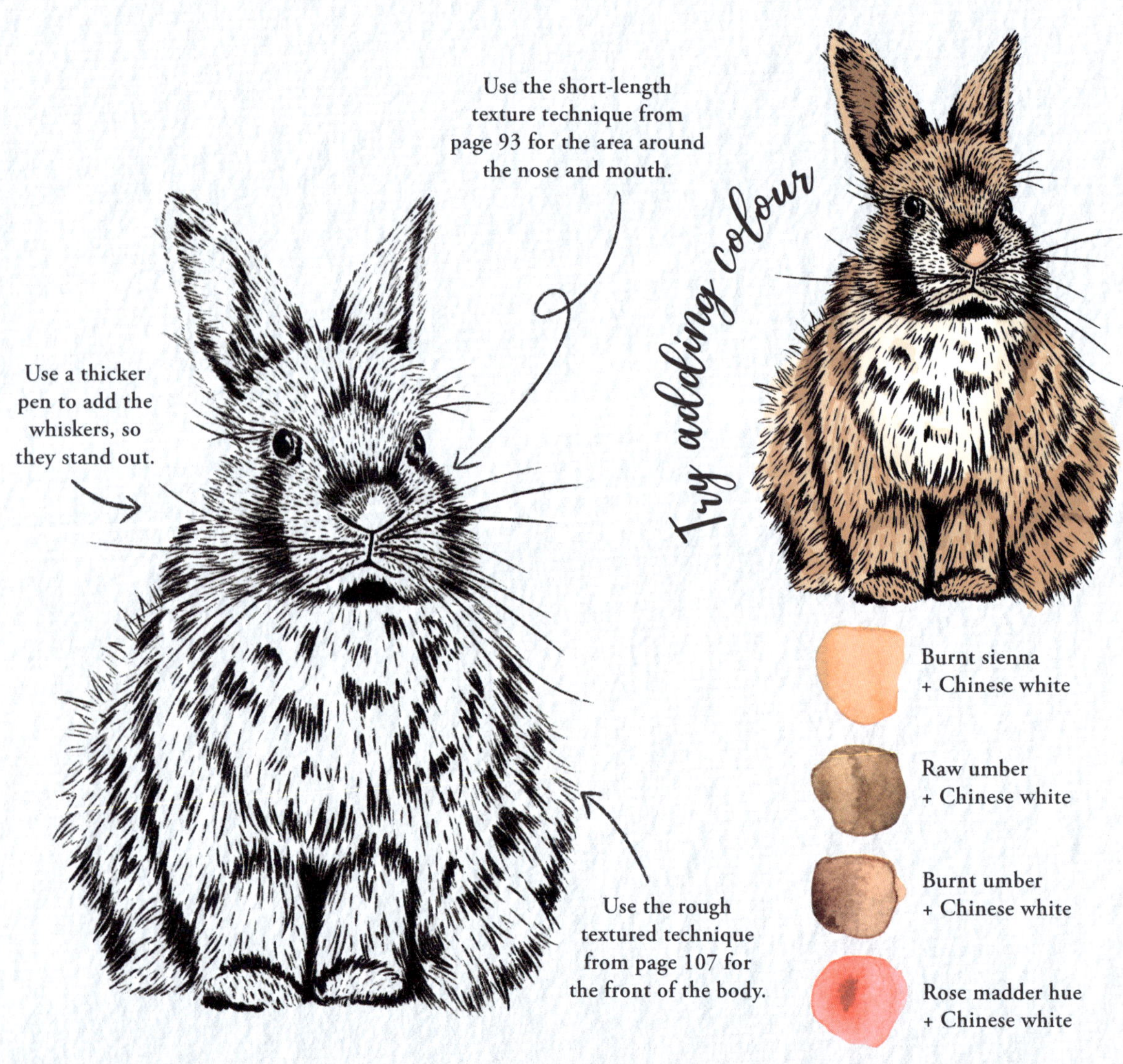

HEAD

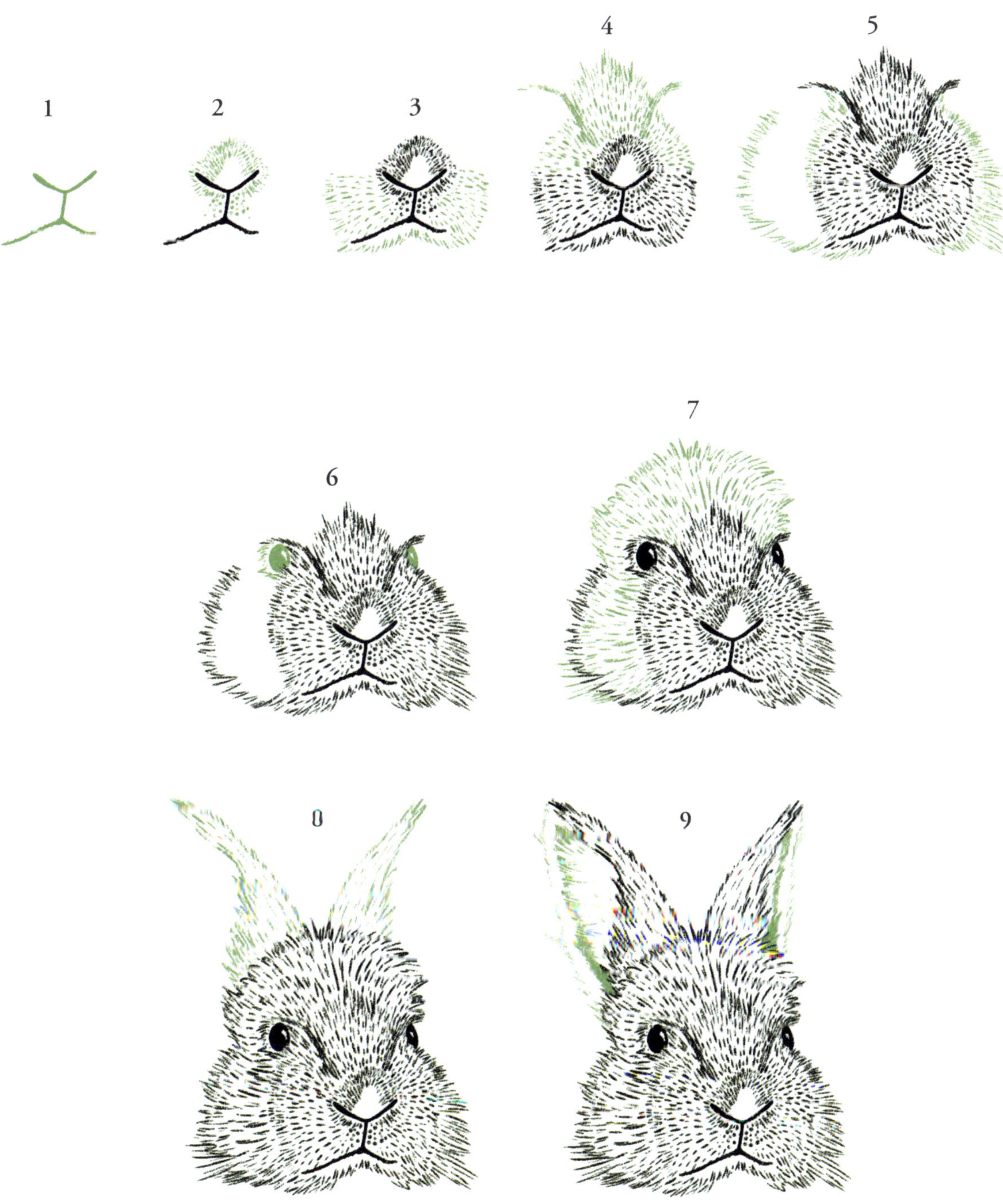

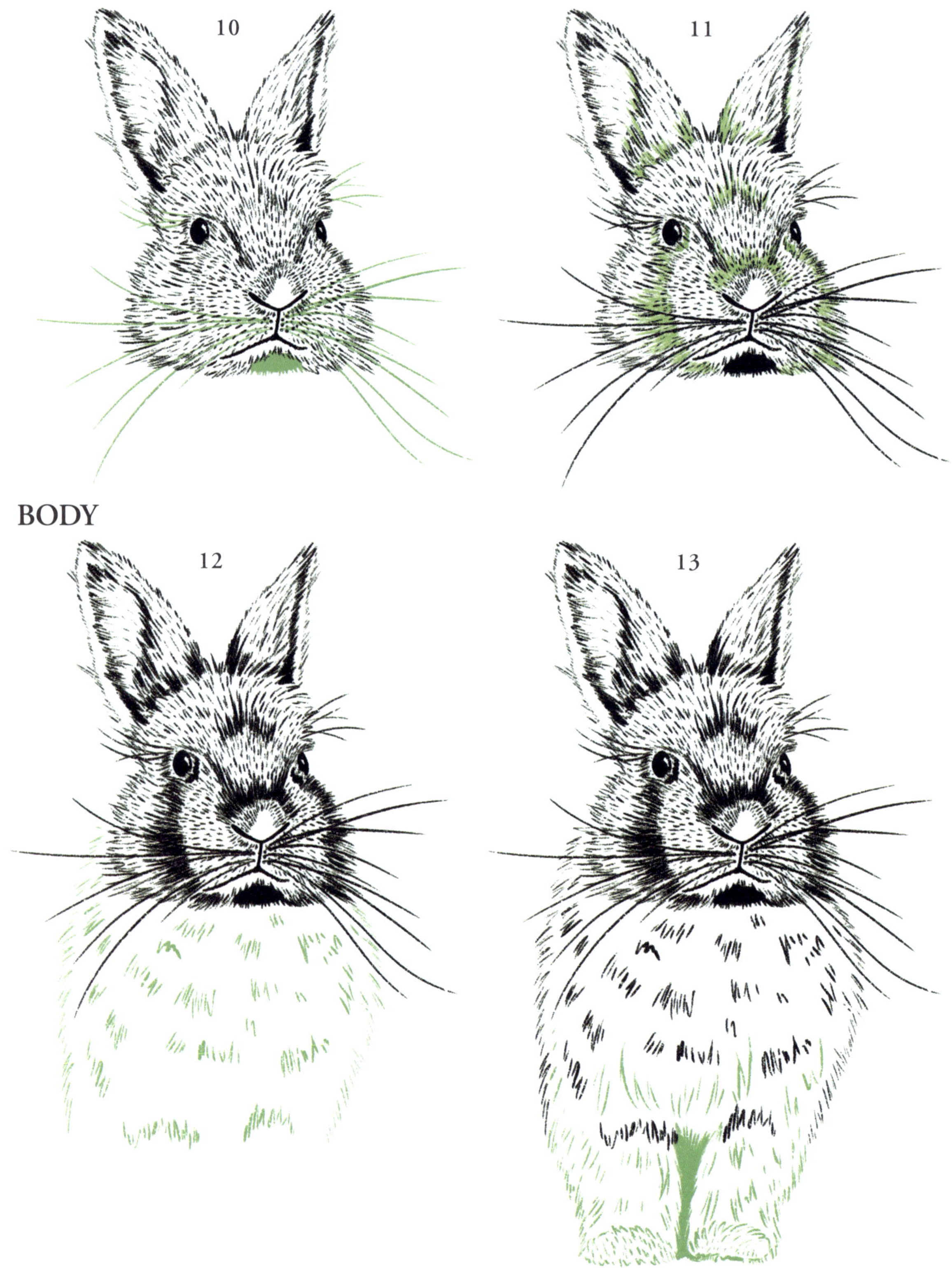

10
11
BODY
12
13

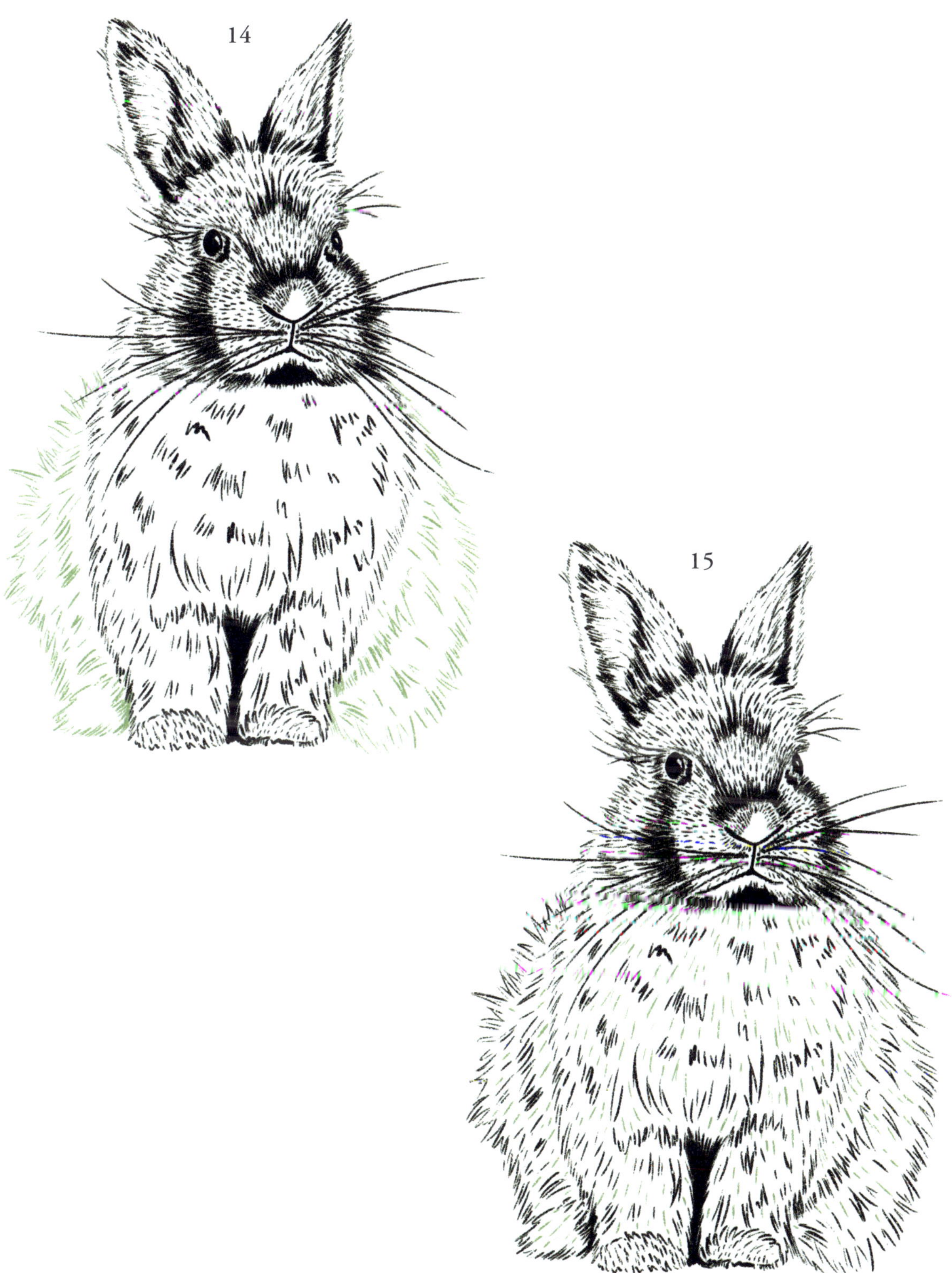
14
15

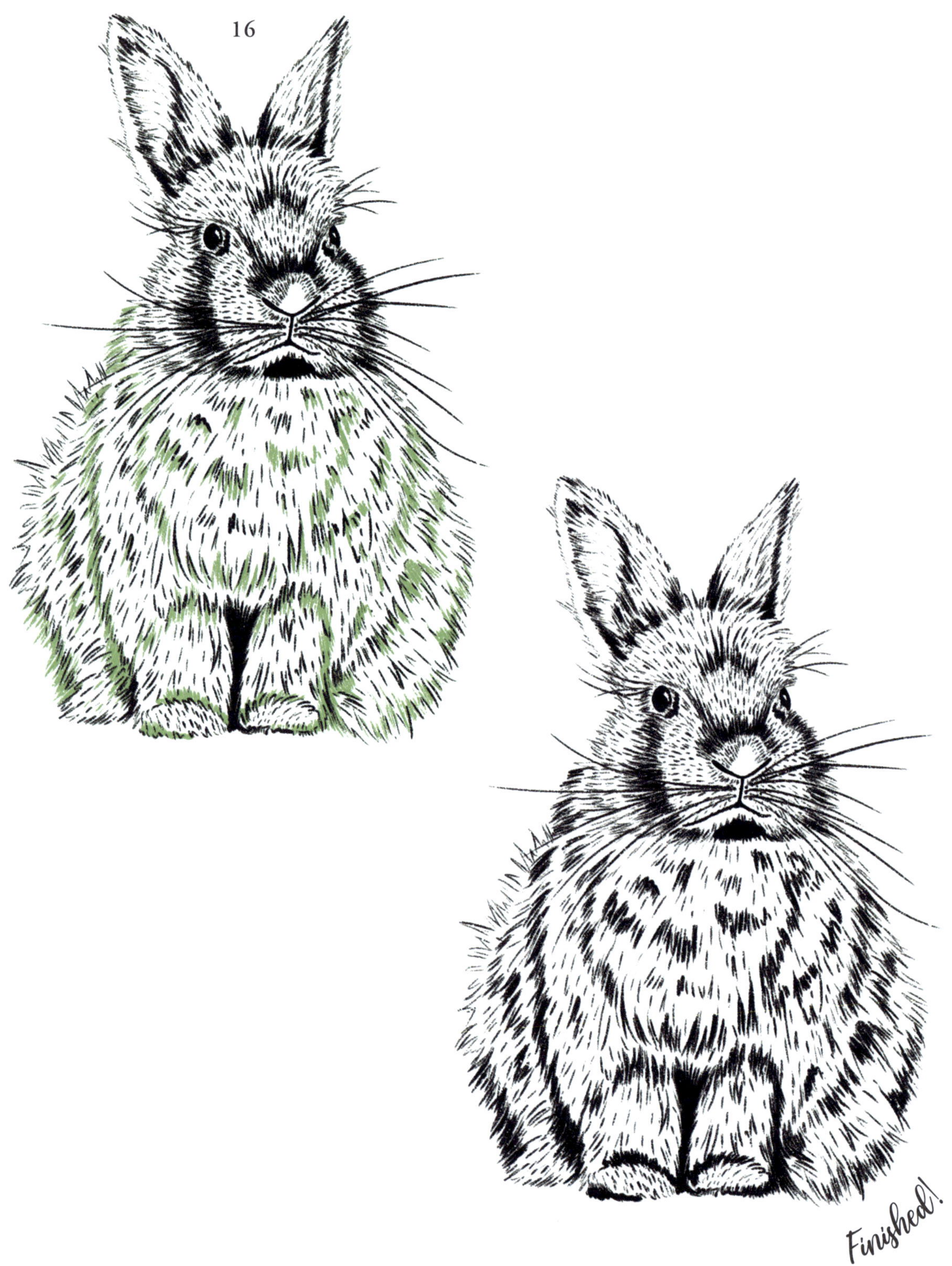
16
Finished!

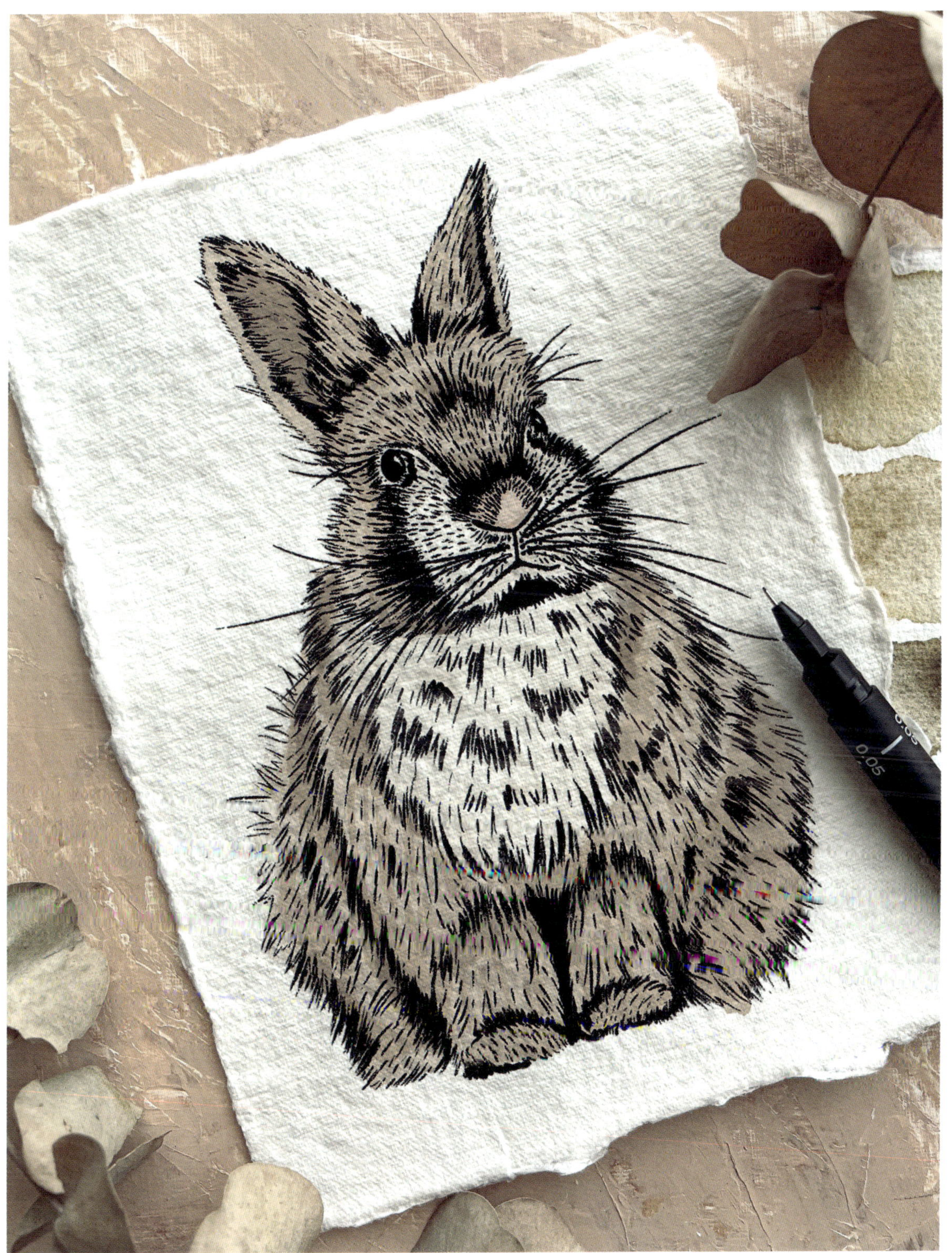

Squirrel

Lastly, let's draw a squirrel to really bring together all of the techniques learnt into one project. You'll need to use the shortest texture techniques for the head, with more texture and mid-length texture in the body, finished off with long fur for the bushy tail.

Why not try adding this squirrel into a composition, sitting on a branch or holding something in its paws?

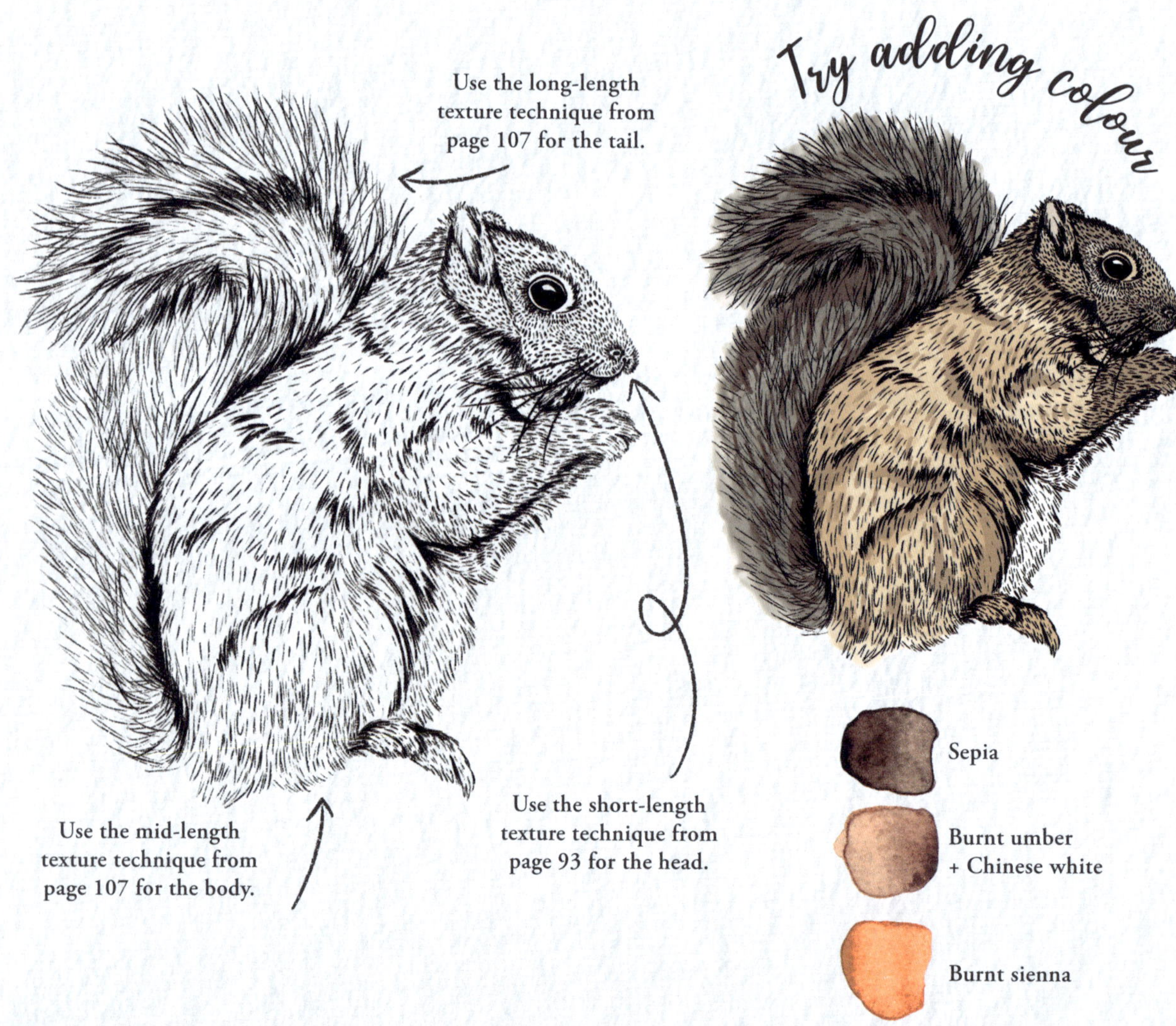

HEAD

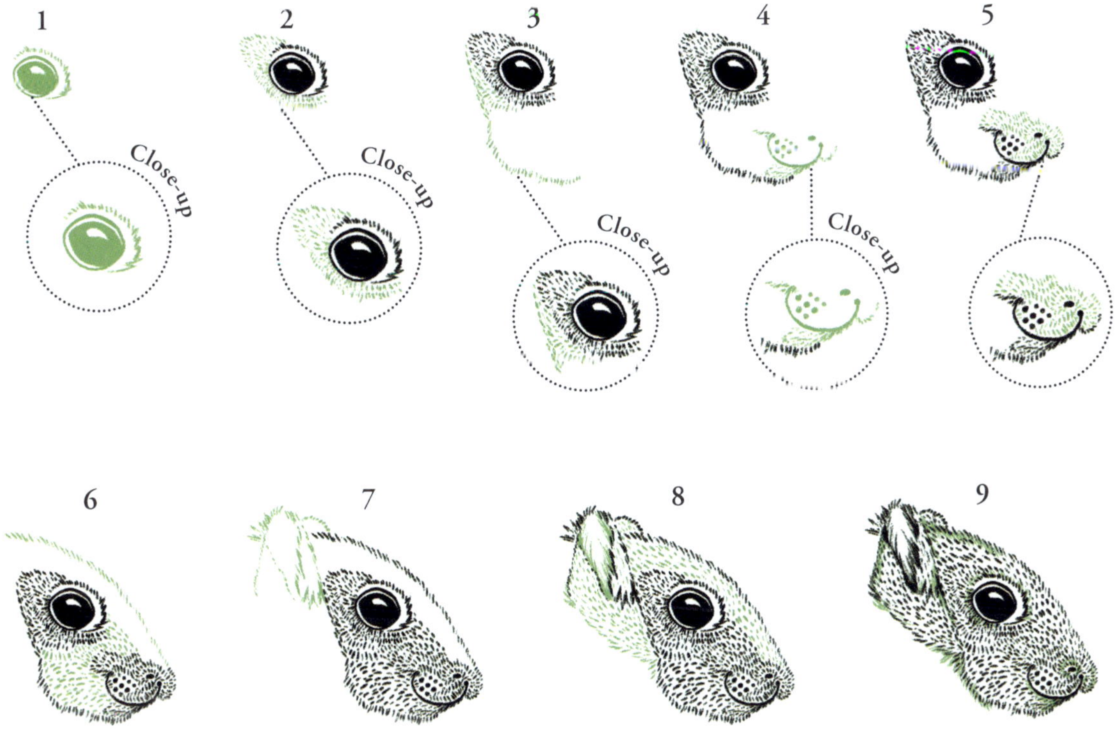

1

Close-up

2

Close-up

3

Close-up

4

Close-up

5

6

7

8

9

BODY AND TAIL

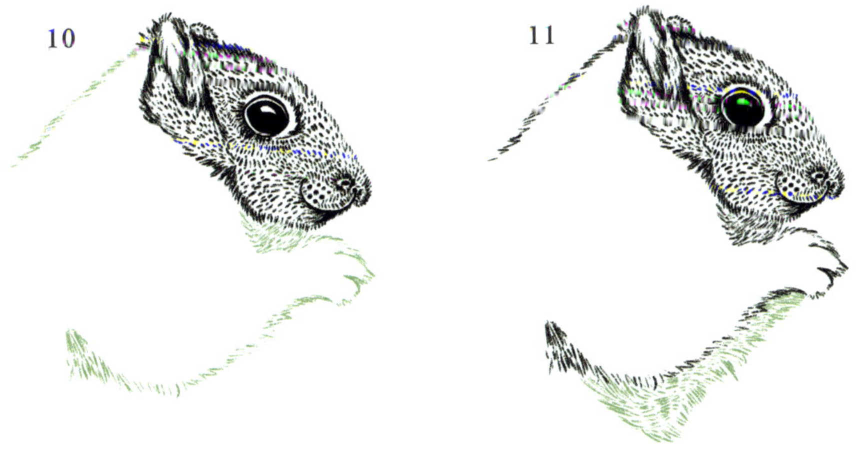

10

11

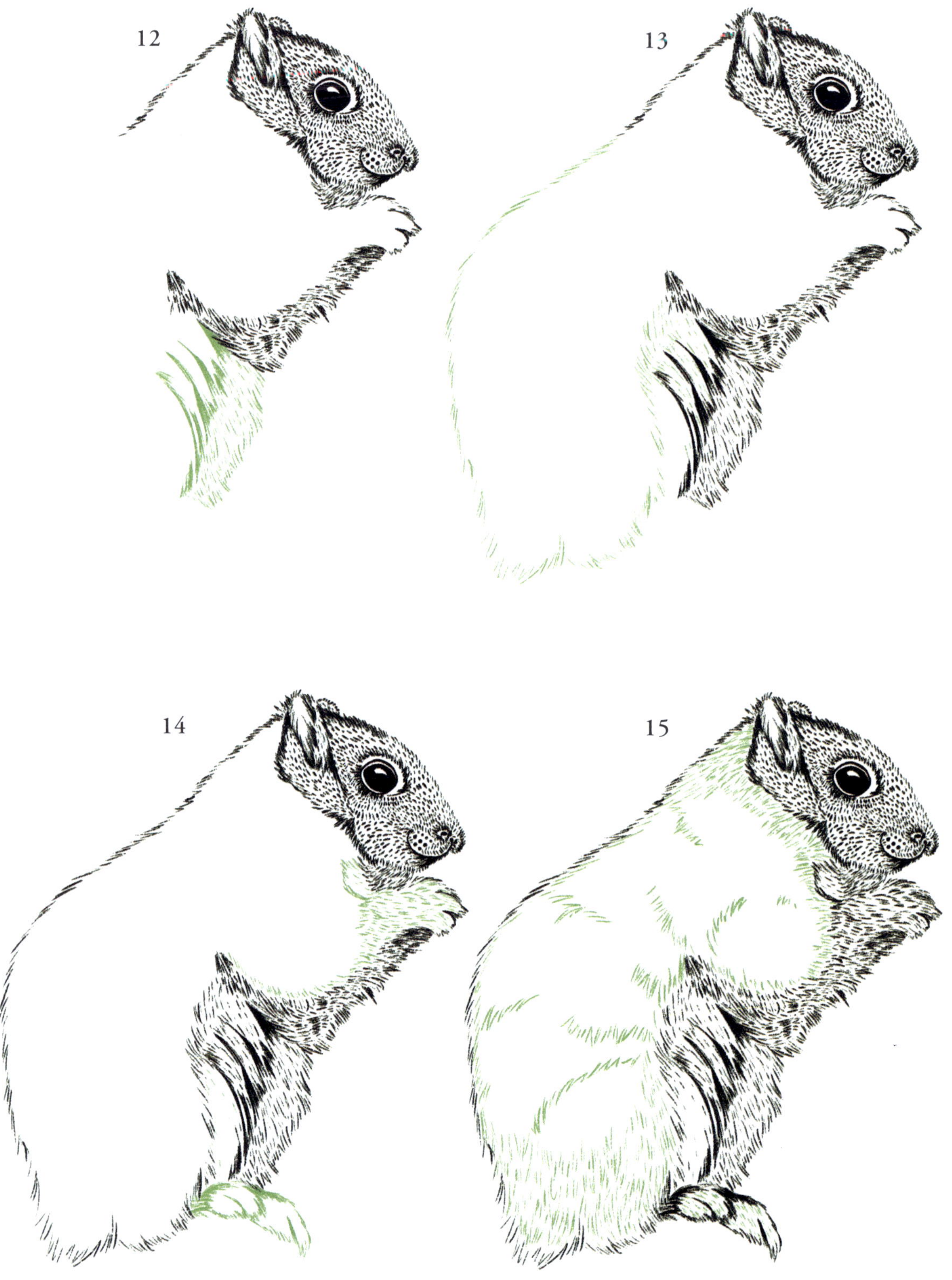

12
13
14
15

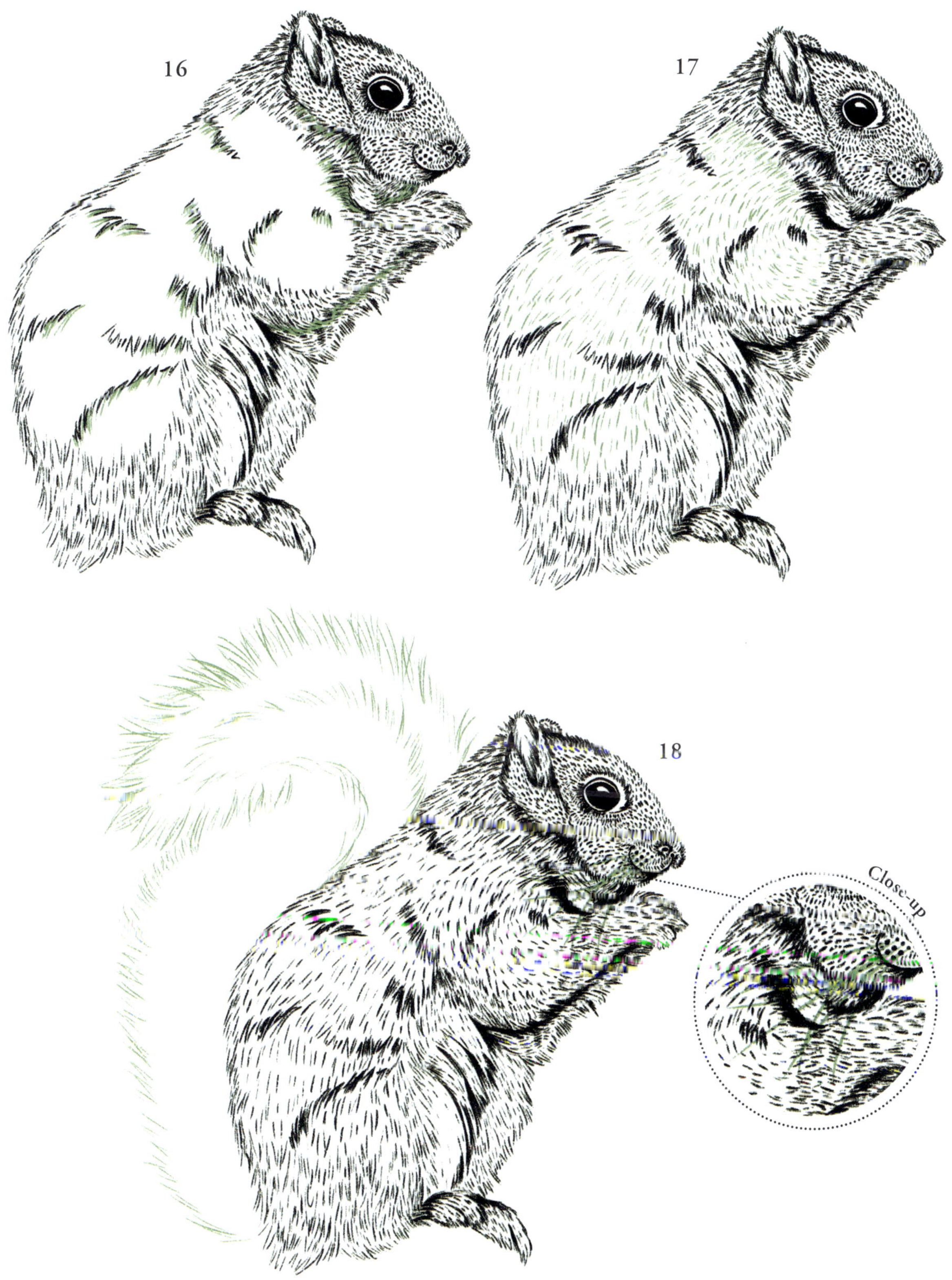
16
17
18
Close-up

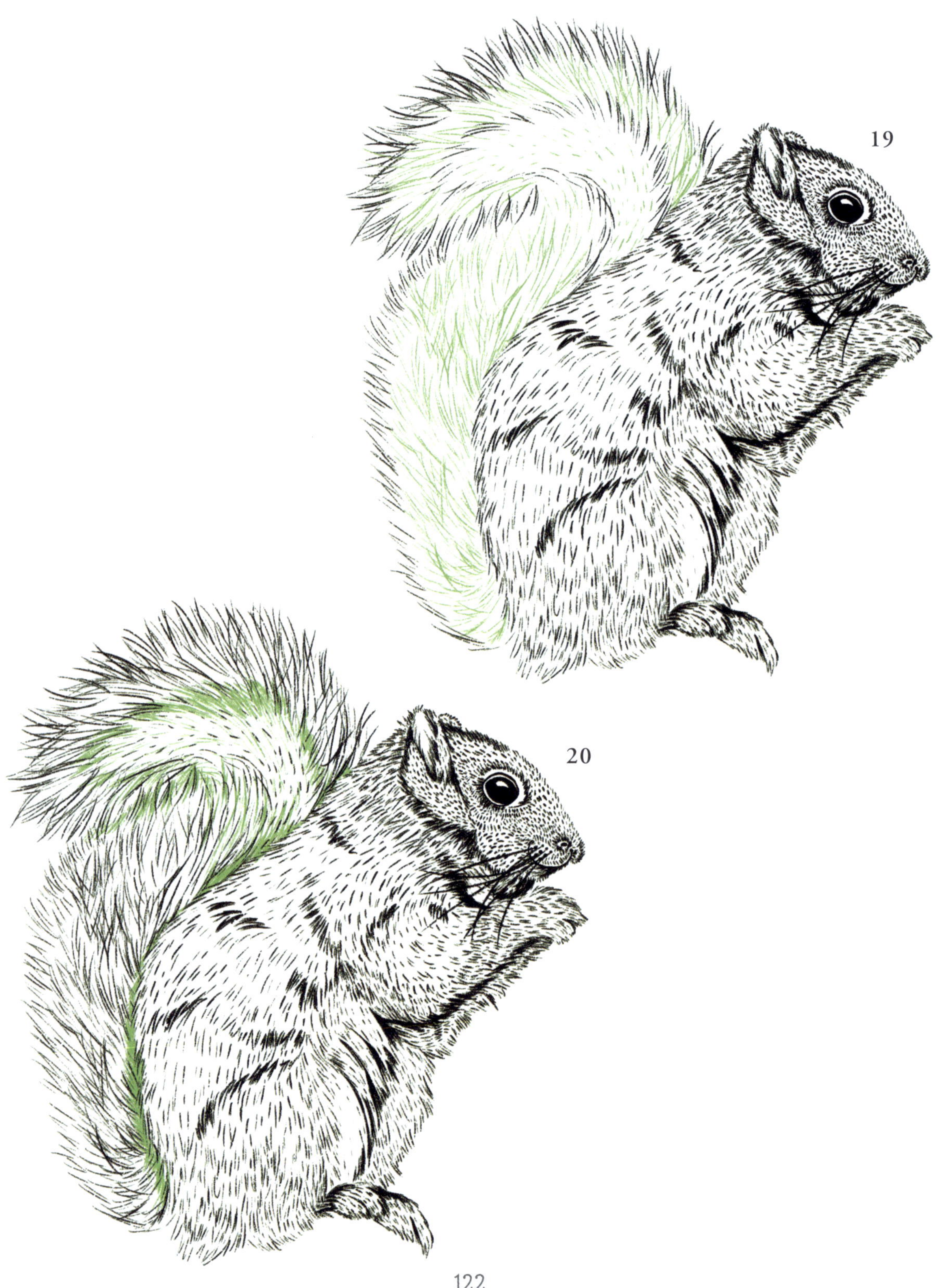

19
20

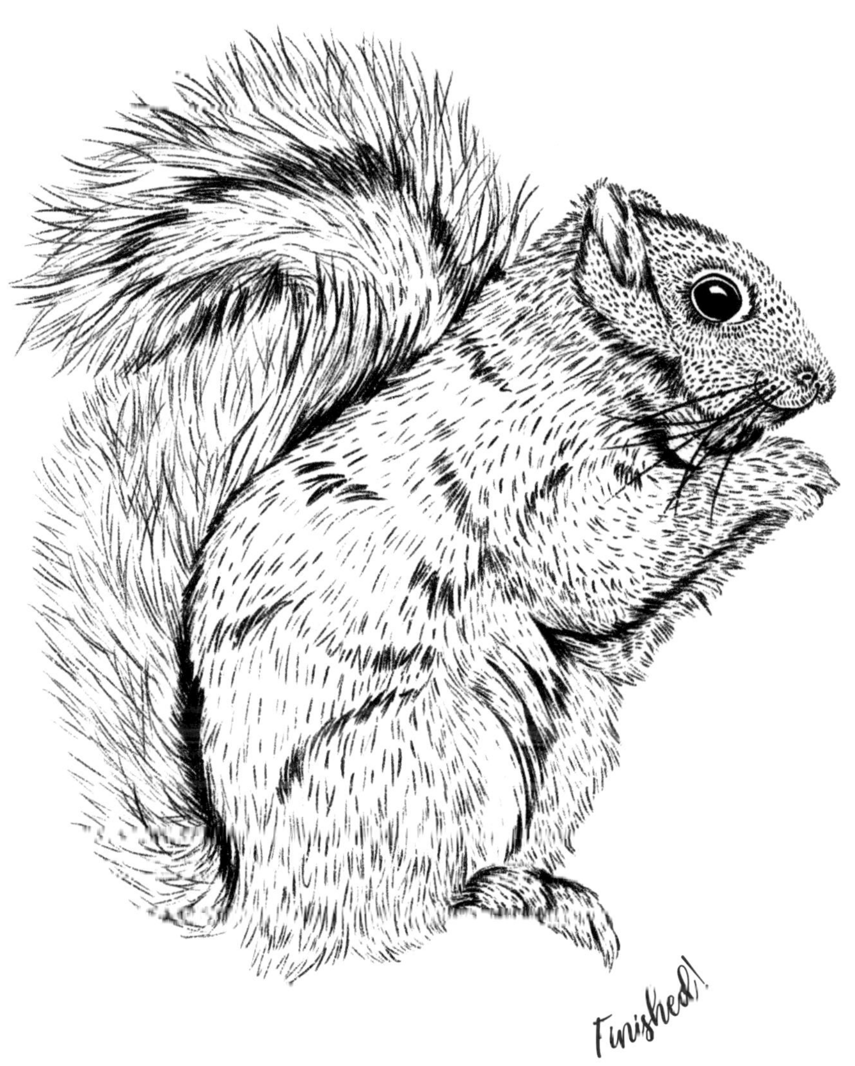

Finished!

Going further

I hope you've enjoyed the drawing projects and you've picked up some new skills along the way! Now you're hopefully feeling more confident drawing the featured subjects, try following my tips below to continue developing your skills and learn some ways you can repurpose your drawings.

Referencing

It's important while you're learning to draw, that, as well as following tutorials, you're also observing the world around you and learning how to use elements of it as your own references. Drawing from references is a wonderful way to build your drawing skills. Practice and patience are key.

This is the method I used when learning how to draw and still follow this when trying to figure out how to draw new types of subjects:

1. Break down the subject bit by bit and try not to get overwhelmed by the whole piece. Just concentrate on one area at a time.

2. Imagine the subject as individual shapes that have been pieced together, almost like building blocks.

3. When looking at the subject, where is your eye drawn to first? This is usually the best place to start.

4. Start by drawing in pencil the outline of the part that your eye was drawn to first. Expand this by drawing the shapes that are connected to it and start to piece together the whole subject in this way.

5. Remember to keep checking between your reference and your drawing, and don't worry if you're not happy with any part of your pencil outline – simply use an eraser to remove it and try again.

6. Once you have drawn the pencil outline, continue using your pencil to add some shading to the areas you can see are darker on your reference subject. If you'd rather draw in pen, go over your pencil outlines first before shading with your pen.

7. Keep a record of all of the drawings you create – it's a great way to measure progress. This is why I love sketchbooks!

Ideas to develop your drawing skills

- Take pictures of anything that sparks inspiration. It's handy to have a bank of references ready for when you want to draw. Plus, it's always easier to draw subjects that you've also seen in real life.

- Set up and draw your own still-life scene. Start with just one object to draw, add one more item at a time to the scene when you're ready to advance. Try drawing the same scene from different angles.

- Challenge yourself by setting a timer to draw one item. Notice which areas you've focused on to capture the essence of the subject in a short amount of time.

- Experiment with different mediums and drawing styles to figure out which you find the most fun.

- Use your sketchbook like a journal, to collect all of your pictures, pressed flowers, colour swatches and notes.

- Browsing books that contain lots of pictures is a great way to spark some inspiration. As well as creating moodboards on Pinterest.

- Fill the space you spend most of your time in with the colours, objects and art you're most drawn to.

- Watch tutorials and studio vlogs online. It's always inspiring to see how other artists work.

- Travel to new places when possible, read new books, listen to different genres of music or even try a new cuisine. All of which help broaden your mindset, in turn helping your creativity grow.

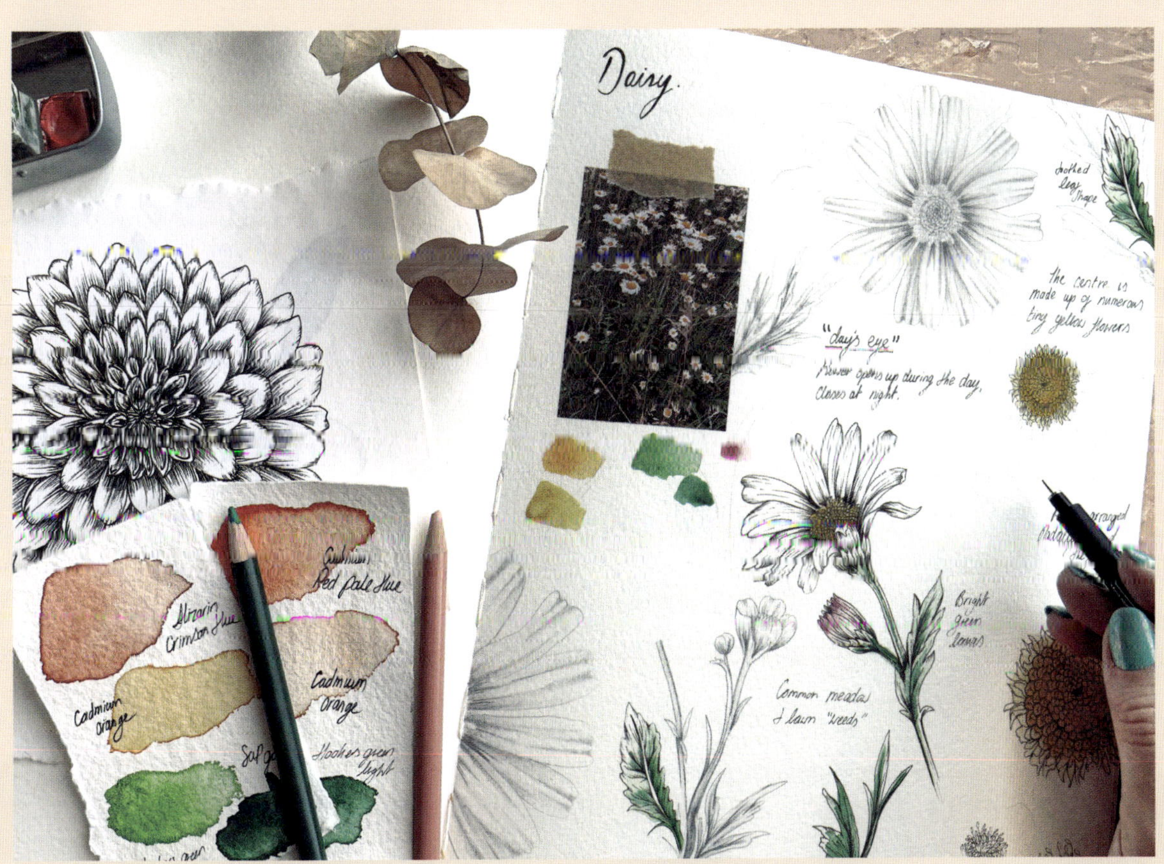

Digitizing your drawings

I've been keeping a digital library of my drawings for years.
I'd definitely recommend you do the same if you'd like to maximize
the ways you can use your own drawings in new ways and incorporate
them into any future projects.

How I digitize my drawings

When I've drawn something in my sketchbook, I scan the page at a high
resolution of at least 600dpi (dots per inch). I then use Adobe Photoshop
to edit the scan to make sure the black ink is solid black, by removing any
saturation, and to remove the sketchbook paper in the background.

If I have multiple drawings on one page I slice these apart and save them as
individual files. I find PNG files with transparent backgrounds best to work
with – this way you can layer them more easily in the future.

I keep a library of all of my PNG artwork files, organized by subject, both
on my computer hard drive as well as in an electronic cloud-based library.
That way I can easily access the drawing pieces when working on either my
computer or my tablet.

Creating patterns

Once digitized, you can use your drawings to create new compositions
and even turn them into repeat patterns. Opposite is an example of a
composition I've made using all of the tutorials we've learnt in this book.
I use Adobe Photoshop or the Procreate app to put together this kind
of composition.

If you'd like to learn more about the digital methods shown in this section,
I have step-by-step tutorials on my YouTube channel: @felicityandink and
on the Bookmarked Hub: www.bookmarked.com

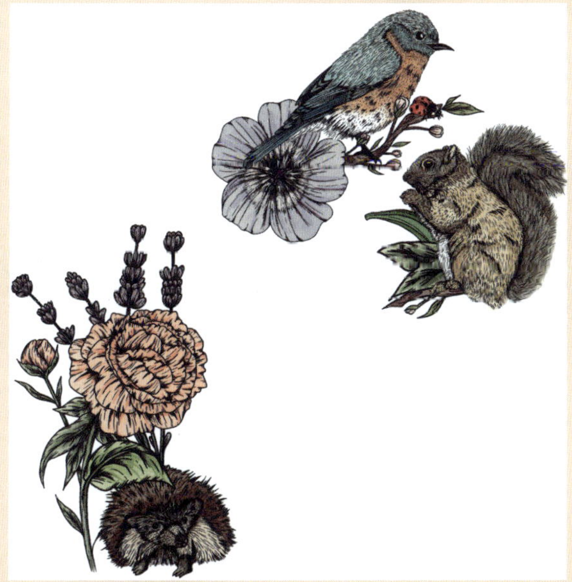

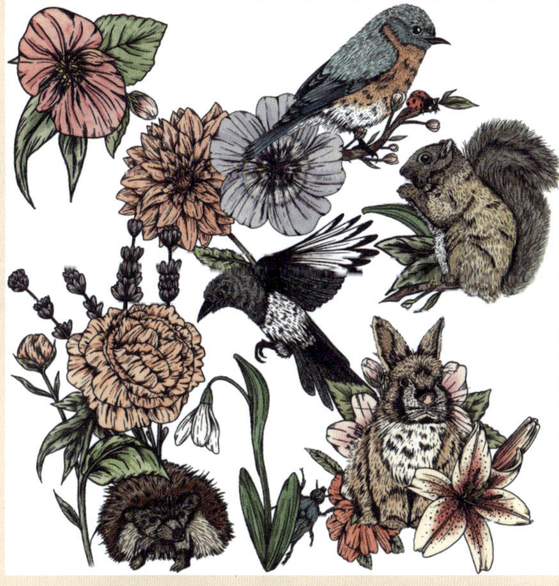

1. Create your canvas and start to add your pieces to it. I like to start by creating mini cluster compositions that combine a few pieces, varying the ways in which they overlap.

2. Fill in the rest of the space with some more mini compositions. I like to leave gaps between some of these so it doesn't feel too overcrowded, and so that each drawing has some room to stand out.

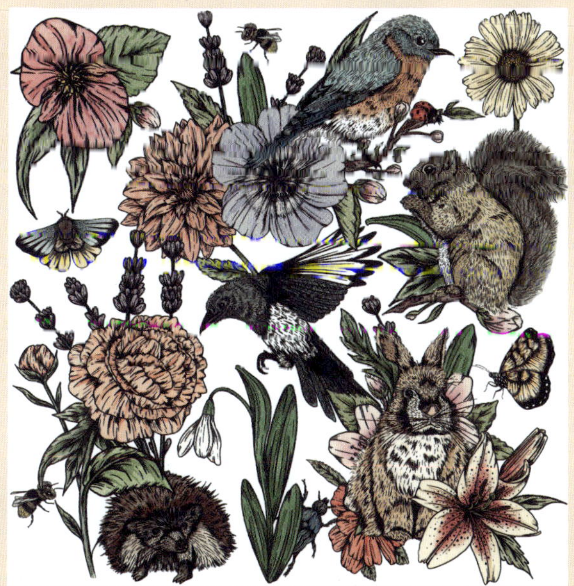

3. Use foliage, insects and smaller flowers to fill in the spaces that are left. Be careful not to overcrowd the space. Move the pieces around until you're happy with it. Use this same method to create a composition for a repeat pattern tile; the key thing is to make sure none of your drawings to touch the edges of the canvas. Turn the page to see how I've turned this composition into a pattern!

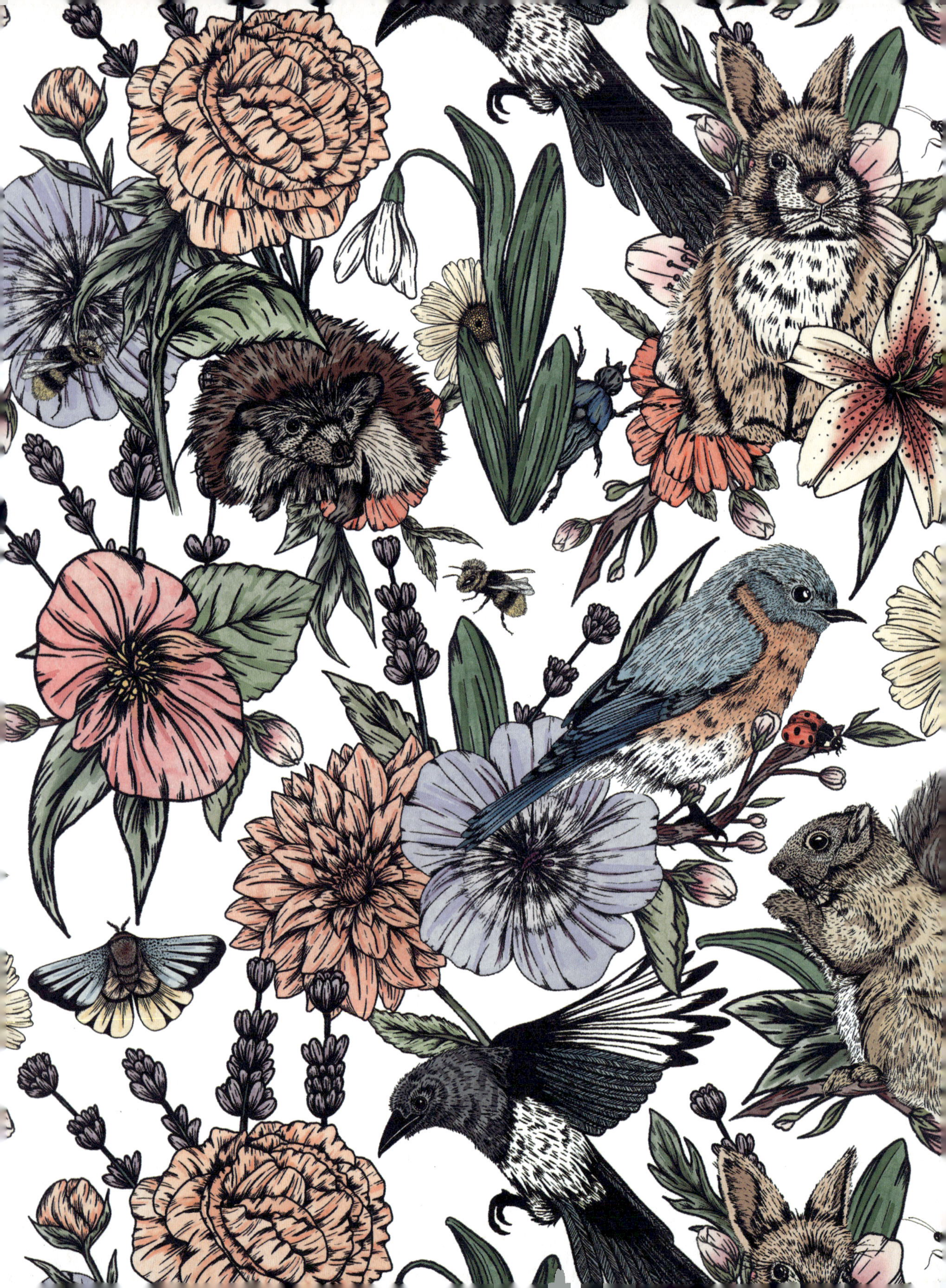